A Trustworthy Gospel

A Trustworthy Gospel

Arguments for an Early Date for Matthew's Gospel

DANIEL B. MOORE
Foreword by Phil Fernandes

WIPF & STOCK · Eugene, Oregon

A TRUSTWORTHY GOSPEL
Arguments for an Early Date for Matthew's Gospel

Copyright © 2024 Daniel B. Moore. All rights reserved. Except for brief quotations in critical publications or reviews, no part of this book may be reproduced in any manner without prior written permission from the publisher. Write: Permissions, Wipf and Stock Publishers, 199 W. 8th Ave., Suite 3, Eugene, OR 97401.

Wipf & Stock
An Imprint of Wipf and Stock Publishers
199 W. 8th Ave., Suite 3
Eugene, OR 97401

www.wipfandstock.com

PAPERBACK ISBN: 979-8-3852-1288-0
HARDCOVER ISBN: 979-8-3852-1289-7
EBOOK ISBN: 979-8-3852-1290-3

VERSION NUMBER 031924

Unless otherwise indicated, Scripture quotations are from the ESV® Bible (*The Holy Bible, English Standard Version®*), copyright © 2001 by Crossway Bibles, a publishing ministry of Good News Publishers. Used by permission. All rights reserved

Scripture quotations marked (NIV) are taken from the Holy Bible, New International Version®, NIV®. Copyright © 1973, 1978, 1984, 2011 by Biblica, Inc.™ Used by permission of Zondervan. All rights reserved worldwide. www.zondervan.com. The "NIV" and "New International Version" are trademarks registered in the United States Patent and Trademark Office by Biblica, Inc.™

Contents

Foreword by Phil Fernandes | vii
Preface | xi
Abbreviations | xiii

1. Introduction: An Early Date for Matthew's Gospel | 1
2. Is an Early Gospel Reasonable? | 6
3. Arguments from the Early Church Fathers | 19
4. Arguments from Galatians | 40
5. Arguments from Post-Reformation Era Scholars | 62
6. Arguments from the Ancients on Memory and Orators: Rejecting Bauckham's Eyewitness Memory Theory | 83
7. Arguments from the Ancients on Written Materials: Rejecting the Modern Preference for Oral Traditions | 111
8. The Impacts of an Early Matthew on NT Exegesis | 127
9. Matthew as the Messiah's Royal Chronicler | 138
10. Conclusion: A Trustworthy Gospel | 146

Bibliography | 153
Ancient Documents Index | 167

Foreword

EVANGELICAL PASTORS AND TEACHERS often accept dates for the original composition of the four Gospels which are significantly later than the dates accepted by the early church fathers. This is due to the great influence higher criticism has had on evangelical Bible colleges and seminaries. Higher critics usually promote the latest possible dates for Gospel composition, and evangelicals often accept the earliest dates allowed by these liberal New Testament critics. But evangelicals should not blindly adopt the views of these liberal critics. A growing number of evangelical scholars, though still in the minority, are now questioning the conclusions of these liberal critics and are taking a second look at what the early church fathers had to say about the origin of the four canonical Gospels (i.e., Matthew, Mark, Luke, and John). One of these evangelical scholars willing to question the status quo is Daniel Moore, the author of this book. In the pages that follow Daniel brings fresh insight into this debate and argues for an early date for Matthew's Gospel.

A question most evangelical pastors and teachers are not asking is this: "What are the earliest possible dates for the four Gospels?" In fact, in the 1930s, C. C. Torrey challenged his New Testament colleagues to present just one passage from any of the four Gospels which gave clear evidence of a date of composition later than AD 50.[1] His challenge was never met.[2] We need the courage to go against the academic tide; we need to call into question the liberal presuppositions and conclusions of contemporary New Testament scholarship. We need to take a fresh look at the evidence and draw our own conclusions. Evangelical scholars do not need to receive permission from higher critics before addressing the issues of authorship and date of composition of the four Gospels.

---

1. Torrey, *Four Gospels*, xiii.
2. Wenham, *Redating Matthew, Mark and Luke*, 299.

Foreword

Scholars who have had the courage to question the status quo of the New Testament critical "establishment" regarding the dates of origin of the four Gospels include: C. C. Torrey, John A. T. Robertson,[3] William F. Albright,[4] John Wenham,[5] Claude Tresmontant, Jean Carmignac,[6] and Jonathan Bernier.[7] Over ten years ago, I joined these scholars to uncover evidence for earlier Gospel dates.[8] But now Daniel Moore is offering the conclusions of his own research in reference to the dating of the Gospel of Matthew. Whereas most of the scholars above have produced books arguing for re-dating the Synoptic Gospels (i.e., Matthew, Mark, and Luke), all four Gospels, or the entire New Testament, Daniel Moore has been willing to devote years of research and an entire book to re-dating just one Gospel—the Gospel of Matthew. Moore has had the courage to present papers on this subject for peer-review, arguing his case at academic conferences. Now, he has authored this very important book. His research is scholarly and very meticulous. He builds a strong case for an early date for Matthew. His work is original and unique—no New Testament scholar should ignore or dismiss his case.

In the pages that follow, the author argues that there is nothing unreasonable about the view that Matthew wrote his Gospel very early—possibly within a few years after Jesus's ascension. Moore argues that Matthew was probably Jesus the Messiah's official scribe and that he probably took notes when Jesus preached his sermons. (I know if I were God, and I became a man, I would require somebody to take notes whenever I spoke.) Moore develops and defends his thesis that Matthew was Jesus the Messiah's Royal Chronicler to great detail. This is a great contribution to New Testament studies.

---

3. Robinson, *Redating the New Testament*. Robinson dated all twenty-seven New Testament books to before AD 70.

4. McDowell, *Evidence That Demands a Verdict*, 1:62–63. Albright dated every New Testament book between AD 40 and 80.

5. Wenham, *Redating Matthew, Mark, and Luke*. Wenham dated the synoptic Gospels to the AD 40s and 50s.

6. Keating, *What Catholics Really Believe*, 40–44. Tresmontant and Carmignac dated the Synoptic Gospels to the AD 40s and 50s.

7. Bernier, *Rethinking the Dates of the New Testament*, 227. Bernier dates Matthew and Mark to the AD 40s, Luke to 59, and John to the 60s.

8. Fernandes and Larson, *Hijacking the Historical Jesus*, 108–36. See also my article: Fernandes, "Redating the Gospels." I date Matthew to the AD 30s, Mark and Luke to the 40s, and John to the 50s.

Foreword

Moore turns to the early church fathers and shows that they believed Matthew wrote the first Gospel and that he composed it very early in the history of the church, probably within a few years of the ascension. The early church fathers were much closer to the origin of the Gospels. I agree with Daniel Moore that we should hold their views on the matter in higher regard than the views of liberal New Testament scholars who have arrived on the scene two thousand years later.

Moore has researched the work of post-Reformation era scholars, and he shows that they dated Matthew's Gospel extremely early. His research shows that the ancient Jews and Gentiles did not rely solely on oral teachings and memorization (a common assumption held today by many evangelical scholars and liberal critics alike). The ancients encouraged writing and did not depend merely on memorized teachings. In fact, the ancients preferred written documents over data that was memorized. In a very interesting move, Moore shows that, if we accept a very early date for Matthew's Gospel, it will greatly enhance our understanding of Paul's letters since, at times, he might be discussing teachings of Jesus found in Matthew's Gospel.

I challenge evangelical pastors and professors to read this work. If you disagree with the author's conclusions, then bring forth your case. But please do not ignore this scholarly work. Do not dismiss it merely because it goes against the current trend in New Testament criticism. We take our marching orders from Jesus, not from the consensus of New Testament critics. And, in case this well-researched book is ignored by evangelical scholars and pastors, lay Christians need to read this work and decide for themselves when Matthew wrote his Gospel.

Phil Fernandes, PhD, DMin
Pastor of Trinity Bible Fellowship
Professor of apologetics and religion, Veritas International University

Preface

I BELIEVE THAT THROUGHOUT the ages God's primary means for speaking to his people has been his written Word. Yes, the creation declares his handiwork, but it is his law which is perfect, his testimony which is sure, his precepts which cause the heart to rejoice, and his commandments which are pure and provide enlightenment.

The prophets spoke and then they wrote, as they were directed by the Spirit. And then the Son spoke, and his words and his life story were preserved for us, that we might recognize him as the promised Messiah, as God's suffering servant, and as the one who came to save a lost humanity. And ultimately, that we might believe and have life in his Name. And then the followers of Jesus continued writing as the Spirit led them, until the New Testament was complete.

Indeed, even as Jesus was publicly confronting the blind scribes and Pharisees in Jerusalem, in the final days leading up to his crucifixion, he promised that he would send his own prophets and scribes. They would both proclaim and record his teachings. And at the last supper, Jesus promised that the Spirit would help the disciples remember all that he had taught them. Thus, the divine plan anticipated the publication of a new set of Scriptures, which would chronicle the events leading up to the crucifixion and resurrection, and then beyond.

And yet, I've heard it said by many a scholar that the books in my Bible which tell the story of Jesus, the Gospels, were not written until decades or even half a century or more after his death and resurrection. How could this be? These are the books which speak of my Savior, the Scriptures which offer life. Would this not be out of character for our God? Would this reticence to write not also be out of character for the era in which the apostles lived? For, I have on my shelves the writings of Philo, Josephus, Plutarch, and other contemporaries—their tomes far outweigh the modest writings of Matthew, Mark, and the others.

But further, wouldn't late publications reduce confidence in the accuracy of the Gospel accounts, in their trustworthiness, and therefore in their authority? Yes, I have faith that his Word is truth. And yet, we live in an era where skeptical challenges are constantly being raised against all manner of biblical claims, from the creation and flood accounts in Gen 1 to the claim of ultimate judgment. Must we accept the popular paradigm that the apostles were unwilling or unable to put the narrative of Jesus into written form at an early date?

In the pages that follow, I aspire to demonstrate that it is not only reasonable to envision that the first Gospel was published even as the apostles were beginning their missionary journeys outside of Palestine, but that it is also likely. This is a viewpoint which is rarely acknowledged within modern academia, nor is this proposition typically recognized in three-view and four-view monographs which purport to look at the most credible theories concerning the origin of the Gospels. Nevertheless, I believe that this is a viewpoint which is both more historically realistic and apologetically convincing, than the paradigm that the early church had little interest or ability toward promptly publishing a written account of Jesus. To make this case, I will present the testimony of the church fathers, along with exegetical, apologetic, and historical arguments. I am eager to have this dialogue with you.

But before moving on, I want to acknowledge those who have offered encouragement and support over the past several years, as this project was germinating. To Patrick Schreiner and Adam Christian, both formerly of Western Seminary in Portland, you have my eternal gratitude for equipping and encouraging me that I might pursue this topic in the academic arena. To David Austin, my thanks for the many collaborative sessions hammering on this topic, and also to those who reviewed the various iterations. Particular recognition goes to Ed Moore, Kyle Holbrook, and Paul Ralph in northern Kentucky who incorporated the draft book into their weekly Bible study and provided many insightful comments. Likewise, my thanks to Phil Fernandes and several participants at a recent International Society of Christian Apologetics conference, who were so enthusiastic to hear my paper on post-Reformation era scholars. And finally, to my wife, Vicky, whose support, steadfast encouragement, and prayer has made this endeavor possible. Her greatest desire is that all those near her might embrace the faith and hope which we enjoy in our God and Savior, Jesus Christ.

Abbreviations

BIBLIOGRAPHIC AND GENERAL

ANF	The Ante-Nicene Fathers
BDAG	Walter Bauer, Frederick W. Danker, William Arndt, and F. Wilbur Gingrich, *A Greek-English Lexicon of the New Testament and Other Early Christian Literature*
BDF	Friedrich Blass and Albert DeBrunner, *A Greek Grammar of the New Testament and Other Early Christian Literature*, translated and revised by Robert W. Funk
EDNT	Horst Balz and Gerhard Schneider, eds., *Exegetical Dictionary of the New Testament*
ESV	English Standard Version, 2016
LSJ	Henry George Liddell, Robert Scott, Henry Stuart Jones, and Roderick McKenzie, *A Greek-English Lexicon: With a Revised Supplement*
LCL	Loeb Classical Library
LXX	Septuagint, the Greek translation of the Hebrew Bible
NIV	New International Version, 2011
NPNF²	The Nicene and Post-Nicene Fathers, series 2
NT	New Testament
OT	Old Testament
pR	Post-Reformation
SBLGNT	Michael W. Holmes, ed., *The Greek New Testament: SBL Edition*
VUL	Vulgate

ABBREVIATIONS

SELECT ANCIENT SOURCES

Ab urbe cond.	Livy, *Ab urbe condita* (*From the Founding of the City*)
Amic.	Cicero, *De Amicitia* (*On Friendship*)
Ant.	Josephus, *Jewish Antiquities*
Att.	Cicero, *Epistulae ad Atticum* (*Letters to Atticus*)
Bell. Jug.	Sallust, *Bellum jugurthinum* (*The Jugurthine War*)
Carm.	Horace, *Carmina* (*Odes*)
Dem.	Plutarch, *Demosthenes*
De or.	Cicero, *De oratore* (*On the Orator*)
Haer.	Irenaeus, *Adversus haereses* (*Against Heresies*)
Hist. eccl.	Eusebius, *Historia ecclesiastica* (*Ecclesiastical History*)
Inst.	Quintilian, *Institutio oratoria* (*Institutes of Oratory*)
Sen.	Cicero, *De senectute* (*On Old Age*)

1

Introduction
An Early Date for Matthew's Gospel

WHY SHOULD YOU CARE when the first Gospel was published? Because the earlier the first Gospel was published, the greater will be your innate confidence in the accuracy of all of the Gospels and therefore, the greater will be your trust in the message of the Gospels. And to be honest, your instinctive preference for an early text may well exist despite the confident assertions from biblical scholars who contend that publication delays don't matter, and that the early church could have faithfully preserved the events of Jesus's life and teachings for decades before the first Gospel was published. Besides, the theologians often contend, could not the Holy Spirit have ensured the accuracy of the Gospels, regardless of when they were written or even by whom? Of course. But would these bold claims reduce the skepticism of your unsaved friends and neighbors, once they discover that the disciples allegedly preserved and disseminated the life and teachings of Jesus almost exclusively by word of mouth for thirty or more years? Perhaps the experts are right, but should we not at least consider whether there is justification for endorsing an early publication of a Gospel such as Matthew, possibly within a few years or even a decade of the resurrection?

Why should you care if Matthew was published early? Because if it is true, then this suggests a completely different paradigm for how the early church took the gospel message to their world than what is commonly taught by the academic community, and it offers an apologetic paradigm which you should perhaps follow. What would it look like, if we were to accept that Paul took the Gospel of Matthew with him on his first missionary journey, as he proclaimed the word of God in the Jewish synagogues and before Roman proconsuls? Where should we therefore start, when sharing the gospel with our unsaved friends, family, and strangers? With Paul's writings? Or with Jesus, as presented in and based on the testimony of the Gospels? Conversely, when we read and study Paul's epistles, should we envision the original church audiences as having heard of the life and teachings of Jesus merely by word-of-mouth, or did the audiences perhaps have a Gospel available which was regularly read to them? Would this context not change how we understand and teach Paul's epistles today?

I believe that Matthew was published within roughly a decade of the resurrection, and I invite you to pass judgment on whether this belief is reasonable, defensible, and even preferable, over the popular belief that the church instead waited for decades before publishing the life and teachings of Jesus in written form. The following chapters make the case for an early Gospel, not by performing detailed comparative analysis between the Synoptic Gospels (Matthew, Mark, and Luke) and then assessing whether the earliest church could have possessed the theological maturity to produce these documents, but by considering whether the premise of an early Gospel is reasonable, consistent with the practices and needs of the early church, and congruent with the expectations of contemporary authors and audiences. I contend that contemporary needs and expectations would have motivated the apostles to favor an early Gospel publication, in order to maximize the trustworthiness of the gospel message even in their own day. And clearly, if we defer to the testimony of the church fathers, then that early Gospel was Matthew's Gospel. Ultimately, my proposition will be tested against its ability to provide reasonable insights into other portions of the New Testament.

Yet before moving on, I should clearly articulate what this book is not. It is not my intent to provide an impartial survey of the various theories which aspire to explain the similarities and differences between the Gospels, nor a methodical history lesson surveying the scholars who have contributed to this debate over the centuries, although we will certainly refer to various theories and their advocates. Nor will I provide an annotated listing of the perceived deficiencies of each theory. This ground is well traveled by texts which address Gospel origins, the Synoptic problem, or which introduce the NT; and these texts are generously footnoted below. Rather, this book is unashamedly polemic in nature, seeking to challenge modern

Introduction

speculations concerning the apostolic age, which do not reflect either Christian or Greco-Roman realities. More properly, this book is apologetic in nature, seeking to increase our trust in the apostolic testimonies found within the Gospels.

We will begin with a simple question: *Is an early Gospel reasonable?* I will contend, in the first chapter below, that there was indeed the means, motive, and opportunity for the early church to promptly publish Gospels. Correspondingly, various deficiencies in modern Gospel origin theories will be identified. The second chapter will consider *arguments from the early church fathers*, who consistently declared that Matthew wrote the first Gospel. However, as there are apparent conflicts in their testimonies concerning how and when Matthew was written, particularly with regard to the writings of Irenaeus, I will offer several simple interpretive approaches for reconciling their testimonies.

The subsequent chapter is exegetical in nature, as two *arguments from Galatians* are presented for an early Gospel. The initial argument observes that Paul found it essential for his early ministry to write an account of his biography and of his core teachings in his earliest letter, shortly after his visit to the Galatians. And, therefore, this suggests that Paul would have found it equally essential for someone to quickly publish an account of Jesus's biography and core teachings. Next is an argument contending that in Gal 3:1, Paul is referring to what was "previously written" concerning Jesus's crucifixion, rather than to what was "publicly portrayed."

This is followed by a chapter which is apologetic in nature, as a series of *arguments from post-Reformation era scholars*, spanning AD 1650 to 1900, are presented. These authors identified a number of motivational reasons which would have driven the apostolic church to publish Matthew within a decade of the resurrection. In truth, these motivational arguments remain compelling, even in our current era. And, as with our present concern, these polemicists were themselves motivated to uphold an early publication date as a means of defending the Gospels against contemporary attacks on their authenticity, accuracy, and authority.

Next are two chapters which turn to the writings of ancient authors who were roughly contemporary with the apostles. One chapter reviews *perspectives from the ancients on memory and on orators* in order to argue against Richard Bauckham's eyewitness memory theory. Bauckham has published a substantive treatise theorizing that the eyewitnesses played a significant role throughout the early decades in accurately preserving the life and teachings of Jesus, within an oral tradition framework, until the Gospels were eventually published.[1] It is an important proposition which many contemporary apologists leverage in defense of Gospel integrity, against the skeptics who challenge the accuracy both of long-term memory and of the story and teachings of Jesus, if primarily preserved via oral tradition methods. However, I demonstrate that even ancient authors and orators were concerned about long-term memory loss, and that they also asserted that orators should be active writers. Ultimately, I will argue, contra Bauckham, that the original audiences themselves, those to whom the apostles were preaching, would have expected that the events of Jesus's life and of his teachings would be distributed in a written form at an early date. This is followed by a chapter which reviews *perspectives from the ancients on written materials*, including both biographical writings and written testimony, in order to argue against modern writers who theorize that oral traditions were substantially prioritized over the use of written materials.

Then we will briefly consider *the impacts of an early Matthew on New Testament exegesis*. If one approaches the NT with the premise that Paul carried Matthew's Gospel with him on his first missionary journey, then how does this impact our understanding of his missionary approach and of his epistles? Several passages are assessed from this perspective. But further, I show that the methods commonly used in NT studies, for identifying potential allusions and broad references to OT passages, may now be used for identifying NT allusions and broad references to the Gospels. For example, there are several passages within 1 Timothy which are better understood because of their broad reference links to Matthew.

Lastly, there is a chapter which simply presents *Matthew as the Messiah's royal chronicler*. If the various arguments in this book have found traction, then I want to encourage the reader to step with me into a new paradigm. Let us envision Matthew as being intent on publishing the words and deeds of the Messiah from his earliest days as a disciple of Jesus. Indeed, let us picture Matthew as being in the crowd at the Sermon on the Mount, carefully taking the first notes of what would ultimately become his Gospel. Let us remember that Jesus had declared his intent to send his own scribes, who would be trained for the kingdom of heaven, and who would provide Scriptures to the people of God. Let this be how we picture Matthew.

In summary, it is my hope that this work will encourage both scholars and students of the Bible alike to stand firm in the belief that the early

---

1. Bauckham, *Jesus and the Eyewitnesses*.

Introduction

church was not hesitant in broadly publishing the life and teachings of Jesus. As will be argued, the apostles were well aware that their testimony would be found most trustworthy if published early. But above all, let this work increase our confidence in the authenticity, accuracy, and authority of the Gospels.[2] May we also have a renewed appreciation for how God has consistently favored the use of written Scriptures for conveying his message to his people, including those within the early church. And let us emulate the apostolic example when proclaiming the good news of Jesus Christ, both orally and in written form.

---

2. By authenticity, I am referring to the conviction that the Gospels were written by the traditionally accepted authors, who were either disciples of Jesus or who had direct access to the disciples. By accuracy, I am referring to the conviction that the Gospels carefully present the life and teachings of Jesus, without corruption, such as that due to memory loss. In contrast, I am persuaded that presently popular Gospel origin theories, which presume that decades passed before the earliest Gospel accounts were published, do not engender confidence in either the authenticity or accuracy of the Gospels and thereby serve to undermine, whether intentionally or not, the authority which modern Christians attribute to these Gospels.

2

Is an Early Gospel Reasonable?

CAN WE PROVE THAT any of the New Testament Gospels were published within a handful of years after the resurrection and ascension of Jesus? Or within a decade or so? We cannot. However, neither can it be proved that several decades passed before Gospels began to be written and widely distributed to an expanding church. The New Testament itself does not make any explicit claims regarding Gospel publication dates, one way or the other, and so we are left to speculate concerning the situation of the early church, to theorize concerning the textual relationships between the Gospels, to assess the contemporary writings, to interpret the testimony of the church fathers, etc.[1]

Over the past century, the academic community has largely aligned with the view that the first Gospel to be published, Mark, was written in the AD 60s, and that perhaps another decade or two passed before subsequent Gospels were published. Of course, there are scholars and theologians who argue either for slightly earlier dates or for slightly later dates. Many also hypothesize over the potential existence of earlier documents, which may have offered source material for our canonical Gospels, supplementing the

---

1. Hagner echoes this challenge of "making guesses on the basis of . . . indirect indications." Hagner, "Determining the Date of Matthew," 78, 92.

oral traditions preserved by the church.² These competing theories are well known to those who have investigated the topic of Gospel origins.³

In contrast, this book will advance arguments that the first Gospel, Matthew, was actually published within a decade of the ascension. And then, the reader will be left to draw their own conclusions. However, before wading into my arguments, we must at least open up the possibility that the apostles could have published early, and that this is indeed a reasonable proposition.

MEANS, MOTIVE, AND OPPORTUNITY

And the word of God continued to increase, and the number of the disciples multiplied greatly in Jerusalem, and a great many of the priests became obedient to the faith. . . . And there arose on that day a great persecution against the church in Jerusalem, and they were all scattered throughout the regions of Judea and Samaria, except the apostles. (Acts 6:7; 8:1)

Did the means, motive, and opportunity exist for the production of written Gospels by the apostles during the earliest years following the death and resurrection of Jesus, in support of an expanding church?

Apostolic Means for Publishing Early Gospels

The New Testament repeatedly attests to the use of written materials during the apostolic age. The NT reflects the use of written Hebrew Scriptures within the synagogues (Luke 4:16–21; Acts 15:21) and quotes extensively from the law, prophets, and writings. Further, Acts records the sending of letters by Jewish leaders (Acts 9:2), by the Jerusalem church (15:23), and by military officers (23:25). Indeed, while the general Greco-Roman population possessed at most only limited or functional literacy, higher

---

2. For example, many scholars conceive of an early Q document which collected many of the sayings of Jesus, despite there being no extent manuscripts, with some specialists going so far as to extrapolate and publish critical editions of the document. Kloppenborg et al., *Critical Edition of Q*; Powelson and Riegert, *Lost Gospel Q*.

3. Adam Christian has recently published a useful monograph which surveys the various theories of literary dependence and oral transmission, before assessing differences in how Gospel authors cite OT texts versus how they interact with material which is common between the Synoptic Gospels. Christian, *Synoptic Composition*.

levels of literacy among the upper and bureaucratic classes is well attested, supported by professional educators and scribes who attended to the production of letters, reproduction of literary documents, etc.[4] Papyrus was readily available to those who could afford it, and especially to those of "the upper classes and the imperial civil service of Rome."[5] Accordingly, both letters and literature were typically penned by a scribe, then replicated before release, and then potentially copied by both the recipient(s) and by third-party copyists.[6] This process is generally understood by students of the New Testament.[7]

Perhaps less familiar is the magnitude of contemporary literature which was produced during and around the first century within the Greco-Roman world, and the capacity of the Roman trade network to facilitate the movement of people and materials throughout the empire. Thus, it is not unusual for modern commentators to characterize early Christian publications (e.g., Paul's letters) as major endeavors, almost beyond the ability of early Christians to undertake.[8] Now certainly, Paul's letters were larger than the average letter.[9] However, in comparison to publications by famous authors of other types of literature, Paul's letters were modest in size, as were the Gospels.

During and around the first century, there were many authors who wrote substantive works in Greek. These include authors such as Appian of Alexandria, Arrian of Nicomedia, Dio Chrysostom, Epictetus, Josephus, Philo, Plutarch, and Strabo. By my count, the extant works of these specific authors comprise over 2.5 million words of Greek text, with Plutarch himself contributing over a million words in the writings comprising his

---

4. Winsbury and Eve report that while some of the population likely had a limited or functional level of literacy, sufficient for reading inscriptions or short texts, there was perhaps a full literacy rate of 5 percent to 10 percent overall. Winsbury, *Roman Book*, 115; Eve, *Behind the Gospels*, 10, 11. Cribiore elaborates on the literary education which the upper classes received and on their access to skilled scribes to serve their needs. Cribiore, *Gymnastics of the Mind*, 6, 163, 247.

5. Winsbury, *Roman Book*, 19–20, 25.

6. Richards, *Letter Writing*, 89–90, 156; Winsbury, *Roman Book*, 129.

7. For example, Carson and Moo, *Introduction to the New Testament*, 334–35.

8. Richards, *Letter Writing*, 169. Likewise, Botha emphasizes the "fairly serious investment of resources . . . the many hands involved . . . [and that] producing literary texts was in many ways labor intensive." And yet, using his calculations, a text such as Matthew could still be produced with a month, with "patrons [probably] providing writing materials and scribes." Botha, *Orality and Literacy*, 80–81.

9. Richards, *Letter Writing*, 163–70.

Morals and *Parallel Lives*.¹⁰ In addition, there were many notable authors who produced works in Latin, such as Livy, Ovid, Pliny the Elder, and Quintilian. These four Latin authors account for the equivalent of almost 1.5 million words of Greek text.¹¹ In comparison, the Gospels of Matthew and Mark are comprised of less than 20,000 words each—hardly a significant undertaking, by comparison.

During this period, with the population of Rome approaching a million people, a constant flow of goods moved towards the city.¹² Thousands of ships made the one- to two-month journey from Alexandria to the Italian coast, and Palestine contributed its own exports.¹³ In addition, trade carts brought in more goods, while individuals traveling by foot could cover fifteen to twenty miles per day.¹⁴ This infrastructure provided sufficient opportunity for the distribution of NT writings throughout the empire, arriving within just a few months of when they were produced, weather permitting.

Thus, not only was it feasible for the earliest Christians to produce the modestly sized literary works which were incorporated into the New Testament, but it was also reasonable for the authors to expect for these works to be broadly available to both remote churches and other New Testament authors within a relatively short period.

Apostolic Motive for Publishing Early Gospels

Many of those who heard the gospel at Pentecost eventually returned home to Rome, Libya, Egypt, the Persian Gulf (Elam), northern Asia Minor (Pontus), etc. Thus, it is plausible that there was an immediate demand by remote Jewish believers for an account of the life and teachings of Jesus, from the earliest days of the church.¹⁵ Craig Evans's survey of near first-century AD

---

10. Other prolific writers include Josephus, who wrote around 450,000 Greek words, between his *Jewish Antiquities*, *Jewish War*, and *Against Apion*; Philo with 425,000 words; Strabo with around 285,000 words. Logos Bible Study software was used for these counts.

11. This total reflects the literature which I had readily available in Logos in 2021. The actual total is presumably higher.

12. Kessler and Temin, "Organization of the Grain Trade," 315.

13. Thompson provides a useful chart portraying travel times to Rome from key cities across the eastern Mediterranean. Thompson, "Holy Internet," 61.

14. Rickman, "Grain Trade," 263–70; Richards, *Letter Writing*, 190–91, 199. Richards also notes foot travel adjustments due to weather, Sabbath restrictions, etc.

15. Wenham affirms that "it would be felt necessary to secure accuracy in the

Jewish texts, such as those which are identified as Old Testament Pseudepigrapha or which are part of the Dead Sea Scrolls, plus those identified as early targumim writings, convincingly demonstrate a Jewish interest in written materials during this period.[16]

James's epistle to the dispersed Jewish church, presumably sent prior to the conversion and inclusion of the gentiles, also suggests an early need for a copy of Jesus's teachings, as the letter assumed that the recipients were as familiar with Jesus's teachings from the Sermon on the Mount as they were with Solomon's Proverbs.[17] And yet, while the Jewish synagogues provided access to Solomon's teachings in written form, it is asserted by some scholars that James's readers would only have had access to memorized oral versions of Jesus's teachings.[18] However, these historians offer no convincing basis for this dichotomy, especially since Matthew's version of the Sermon on the Mount is only slightly larger than the size of James's letter itself, making it no more difficult to put at least portions of Jesus's teaching into written form than James's letter.[19] More broadly, Michael Kruger has persuasively argued against those who categorically assert that early Christians were predisposed against written documents.[20]

Even more pressing would be the need of early gentile converts for a written copy of Jesus's teachings, along with the interpretive framework provided by the Gospels, as gentile believers lacked ready access to the synagogues.[21] Moreover, since the Roman oratory practice involved the use of a written "text as a mnemonic aid" for oral performances, whether of poetry, histories, or whatever, the believers would surely have appealed for written materials to support their gatherings.[22] Hence, the apostles had

---

substance of what was being taught in the scattered Christian communities." Wenham, *Redating Matthew, Mark and Luke*, 200.

16. Evans, *Ancient Texts*, 26–154, 186.

17. Burdick, "James," 164.

18. Davids, "James," 1354. Also, Carson and Moo, *Introduction to the New Testament*, 630.

19. Other biblical commentators note the close affinity between James and Matthew and therefore postulate a late first-century or early second-century publication for James's letter, given a presumed late first-century date for Matthew's Gospel. This, of course, runs counter to James's introductory address to the exclusively Jewish church. Shepherd Jr., "James and Matthew," 47–49.

20. Kruger, *Question of Canon*, 79–118.

21. Birks, *Horae Evangelicae*, 231–32.

22. Winsbury, *Roman Book*, 105, 122.

Is an Early Gospel Reasonable?

motive to produce written Gospel materials for both Jewish and gentile believers.

Apostolic Opportunity for Publishing Early Gospels

The book of Acts reports that the apostles remained in Jerusalem, even during the period of persecution following Stephen's death (Acts 8:1). Then later, after Saul's conversion, the church "throughout all Judea and Galilee and Samaria had peace and was being built up" (9:31). These years in Jerusalem would have provided an excellent opportunity for the apostles to collaborate on collecting, editing, and translating the Jesus narrative. During this period, they enjoyed the resource benefits of being in a major city and they had "favor with all the people" (Acts 2:47), which surely included some wealthy and influential benefactors. Zacchaeus of Jericho is described as "a chief tax collector and wealthy" (Luke 19:2), Matthew himself was wealthy enough to entertain a large company in his home (Matt 5:29), and John Mark's home was large enough to host "many," even having a servant girl and a secluded outer gate (Acts 12:12–13).

While in Jerusalem, the disciples also had access to the services of a great number of priests who had "become obedient to the faith" (Acts 6:7). These priests would have included at least some with scribal skills (Matt 23:34). Plus, bureaucrats such as Matthew, Zacchaeus, and Cornelius would have had some level of literacy and access to scribal resources.[23] Consequently, the apostles' period of residency in Jerusalem would have been an ideal time for the development and publication of Gospels for both Jewish and gentile Christian constituencies.[24]

The Potential for Early Gospel Publication

Modern biblical scholars commonly assert that the initial written Gospels were the product of decades of oral transmission, leading up to the gradual authoring of proto-Gospels, Q, Mark, and the other Gospels, or

---

23. Hendriksen, *Matthew*, 95–96; Howard, "Introduction," 14; Winsbury, *Roman Book*, 162. Miller elaborates on other early believers who likely offered literary skills. Miller, "'Write' Stuff," 91.

24. With the Gospel of Matthew targeting the predominately Jewish constituency of the early church and Mark targeting the gentile (Roman) constituency, after the conversion of Cornelius and friends.

some variation of such.[25] However, these theories typically do not adequately consider the volume of literary production and trade during the first century, the demand which existed within the distributed Christian communities for written materials to support oral recitation of the gospel accounts, or the capability of the apostolic church to produce gospel materials.[26] This has led many modern Christians to too easily accept synoptic theories which assert that Gospels were composed without full access to prior publications, supposing that the authors of Mark and Luke published without being aware of the Gospel of Matthew (or vice versa).[27]

In contrast, what this chapter suggests is that Gospels were likely in circulation early in the life of the church, in response to the demands of the dispersed Jewish and gentile constituencies, and that it is reasonable to assume that these materials were available to be referenced as each subsequent Gospel was composed. The virtues of this proposition will be elaborated on later. However, it is worth noting that this proposition does provide a simple explanation for Paul's failure to supply any substantive details about the life, miracles, and verbatim teachings of Jesus.[28] It likewise resolves the apparent difficulties in interpreting the apostle's teachings which refer to "Scripture" within Christian contexts (e.g., 1 Tim 4:13; 2 Tim 3:15–17).[29]

In summary, this chapter has thus far argued that there were means, motive, and opportunity for the early publication of Gospels for the benefit of the apostolic church, within the earliest years after the resurrection of Christ. It has been shown that there was a substantive amount of literature being published during this era, such that the Gospels were only modest accomplishments, and that the Roman trade network provided ample opportunity for the circulation of these documents. Further, the scattering of the Jewish and gentile church would have provided a sufficient motivation for the effort. A collaborative effort, especially while the apostles were yet in Jerusalem, would have been supported by local resources and a literate

---

25. France, "Reading the Gospels," 897–98, 900; deSilva, *Introduction to the New Testament*, 149–50, 154.

26. Hurtado, *Destroyer of the Gods*, 108–11, 117.

27. For example, Bock, "Questions about Q," 47–48.

28. In this I concur with Bird, "The death of Jesus made no sense apart from his life, his teaching, and his deliberate effort to follow a prophetic script for his work." Bird, *Gospel of the Lord*, 24.

29. Commentaries often try, unconvincingly, to exclusively connect these "Scripture" references to OT passages. For example, Guthrie, *Pastoral Epistles*, 111; Towner, *Timothy and Titus*, 585–88.

priesthood. Thus, my contention is that it is reasonable to postulate that the Gospels might have been published at a relatively early date.

DEFICIENCIES IN MODERN GOSPEL ORIGIN THEORIES

If my means, motive, opportunity argument has merit, then several deficiencies can be claimed, relative to popular modern theories of Gospel origins. First is the futility of trying to establish the order in which the Gospels were published primarily on the basis of comparative analysis between the Gospels, given that the order of publication was arguably demand based. But further, the subjectivity evident in many modern comparative exercises also limits the reliability of any derived conclusions. A second deficiency is the refusal of certain theories to recognize that previously published Gospels were readily available to subsequent authors. These deficiencies will be elaborated below. The third perceived deficiency is the assumption that there was an extended delay before the Gospels were published, during which the primary means for preserving the stories and teachings of Jesus were via oral tradition methods. A later chapter will address this particular issue.

Comparative Analysis Deficiencies

Numerous books have been written which explore the literary relationships between the Synoptic Gospels. These studies tend to carefully compare pericope ordering, vocabulary, grammar, parenthetical material, omissions, patristic testimony, etc. to develop theories of interdependence and of Gospel development.[30] Appropriately, most introductory works on the New Testament leverage these studies to derive background material for the Gospels, as they consider issues of authorship, date, source materials, and publication sequence.[31] However, while these comparative studies are

---

30. For example, Stein, *Synoptic Gospels*, 7–9.

31. The following resources provide helpful overviews of this field of study. Carson and Moo, *Introduction to the New Testament*, 77–103; France, "Reading the Gospels," 896–903. The study of Gospel origins often also encompasses the consideration of alternative Gospels, theological development over time, and the development of the canon. These aspects are not addressed herein, given the focus on the potential for early Gospel publication.

insightful, it can also be argued that Gospel origin theories which are derived from such are of limited value.

Which comparative analysis is correct? Though not the first to advance his theory, Robert Stein provides a detailed comparative analysis between the Synoptics, and then supplements such with arguments based on Mark's shorter length, poorer writing style, more primitive theology, etc. to resolve that there must have been a Q document which informed Mark, before both Q and Mark fed into Matthew and Luke, along with some amount of independent material.[32] Recent advocates of this particular theory have also argued that Matthew followed Mark, as Matthew presumably simplified Mark's more complicated narratives.[33] Other analysts justify Q and Markan priority on the basis of affinities in genre, which is to claim that a sayings document like Q would be similar to the "dominical sayings ... found in the epistle of James and the anthology of [Jesus sayings] ... in the *Gospel of Thomas*," while also being akin to contemporary "Jewish wisdom literature."[34] In contrast, Mark Goodacre does his own comparative analysis and supplements such with observations of editorial fatigue to dismiss the need for a Q document, while still defending Markan priority, that Mark was the first Gospel.[35]

On the other hand, John Wenham argues that the Synoptics were written in the Matthew, Mark, and Luke order found in our modern Bibles by offering his own comparative assessment, and then leveraging the testimony of the church fathers, plus a supposed early trip to Rome by Peter, along with arguments from perceived originality.[36] Bernard Orchard does his own extensive comparative analysis in support of a Matthew, Luke, Mark sequence for the Synoptics, which David Barrett Peabody also supports by finding "evidence of conflation in Mark's Gospel," highlighting the "limited number of literary units unique to Mark," etc.[37] Other scholars contribute their perspectives via "Three Views" and "Four Views" style books.[38] The

---

32. Stein, *Synoptic Gospels*, 151–52.
33. Osborne and Williams, "Markan Priority," 53.
34. Bird, *Gospel of the Lord*, 165.
35. Goodacre, "Farrer Hypothesis"; Goodacre, *Case against Q*.
36. Wenham, *Redating Matthew, Mark and Luke*, 11–115, 146–49.
37. Orchard, *Matthew, Luke, and Mark*; Peabody, "Two Gospel Hypothesis," 72–81.
38. For example, Thomas, *Three Views on the Origins*; Porter and Dyer, *Synoptic Problem: Four Views*; Black and Beck, *Rethinking the Synoptic Problem*.

variety of analytical approaches and opinions can be challenging to grapple with.

My point is not that a disparity of views renders the Synoptic Problem unsolvable, but that we ought to try harder to find a solution which is not dependent on the above methodologies, which are primarily based on comparative analysis between the Gospels, paired with subjective presuppositions concerning primitive theology, originality, presumed simplifications, presumed amplifications, literary styles, etc. to arrive at a subjective conclusion. Again, I suggest that a closer look at other evidence is warranted. More specifically, I contend that more attention needs to be given to considering the situation within the early church and how this might have driven the need for an early Gospel.

Limited Circulation Deficiencies

Some Gospel origin theories preclude the possibility that Gospel authors had access to or leveraged previously published Gospels. For example, those theories which envision a Q document characteristically deny that Luke would have had access to a previously published Gospel of Matthew. This runs counter to my proposition above, that the means, motive, and opportunity existed in the earliest years of the church to widely distribute NT writings, as they were published. Therefore, the credibility of Q-dependent theories is reduced, in my opinion, given that they don't realistically reflect the situation during the first century, as expounded above.

From an altogether different perspective, the *literary independence theory*, as presented by some scholars, is unique in its assertion that "each Gospel writer worked independently of the other three, each having no need to derive information from the other three. The writers . . . authored four independent accounts of Jesus's life. The Gospels originated without direct literary interdependency."[39] Rather, accordingly to F. David Farnell, the Gospel authors are said to have obtained oral accounts from "eyewitnesses whose sharp memories, aided by the Holy Spirit, reproduced the exact wording of dialogues and sermons (John 14:26)."[40]

The literary independence theory is to be applauded for aspiring to defend the Gospels against critical challenges, which seek "to discredit

---

39. Farnell, "Independence View," 255. This view is also promoted in Thomas and Farnell, "Preface," 11; Fernandes and Larson, *Hijacking the Historical Jesus*, 71.

40. Farnell, "Independence View," 279.

the historical reliability of the New Testament."[41] However, the theory unnecessarily precludes the disciples from taking written notes during Jesus's sermons, of collaborating in how to convey the events of the life and teachings of Jesus to their various audiences, and of staying well informed of the inspired writings of the other authors, as each work was published. Further, the approach does not align with authorial practices elsewhere in the Bible, where inspired biblical authors profusely quoted from and alluded to prior biblical writings. For instance, in the NT era, 1 Tim 5:18 quotes Luke 10:7 as Scripture, on a par with Deut 25:4, and Peter refers to Paul's writings as Scripture (2 Pet 3:15–16).[42]

In addition, the leveraging of John 14:26 to support this view, as Jesus promises that the coming "Helper, the Holy Spirit" will "teach you all things and bring to your remembrance all that I have said to you," appears to go beyond what John understands this role of the Spirit to encompass, as illustrated by the instances in which John demonstrates what remembrance involves. In John's Gospel there are six passages in which remembrance is anticipated or affirmed (John 2:17; 2:22; 12:16; 13:19; 16:4; 20:9). And the implication in each of the illustrations is that these remembrances all occurred shortly after the crucifixion and resurrection, as the disciples then came to understand Jesus's teachings more fully, in the context of the OT Scriptures. The one exception is that John 16:4 is tied to a future time of persecution, presumably that which followed Stephen's martyrdom. Therefore, if we defer to John's representation of what this promised Spirit-empowered remembrance offered, then it is not that the Spirit would provide remembrance or perfect memory for decades, but rather that this Spirit-empowered remembrance would occur almost immediately after the resurrection. That said, we must affirm that the Gospel authors were certainly moved and inspired by the Spirit (2 Tim 3:16; 2 Pet 1:20–21), such that all that was ultimately written is truth (John 17:17). Nevertheless, we must be cautious to not overly conflate these disparate workings of the Spirit.

Again, my primary quarrel with the literary independence theory is that it presupposes that the Gospel authors did not have access to or did not consult previously published Gospels—Spirit inspired Scriptures—when composing their own accounts of the life and teachings of Jesus. However,

---

41. Fernandes and Larson, *Hijacking the Historical Jesus*, 66; Farnell, "How Views of Inspiration Have Impacted."

42. Swinson offers a robust discussion on the use of γραφή in the Pastoral Epistles. Swinson, *What Is Scripture?*

IS AN EARLY GOSPEL REASONABLE?

it is not my intent to argue concerning the manner in which the authors actually employed these previously published Gospels in their own compositions. The literary independence theory rejects the notion that the authors directly copied from one another, and this may or may not be valid. Correspondingly, Adam Christian has recently published an intriguing book which contrasts the "significant grammatical changes" found between parallel Gospel accounts with the more limited level of grammatical changes found when parallel passages include "overt quotations of the Old Greek text (rather than the Hebrew)," where "there is a high degree of certainty that the authors were indeed copying from a written source."[43] Ultimately, he concludes that "an oral, rather than a literary, relationship stands behind the similarities and differences found in the synoptic accounts."[44] Although Christian embraces the common theory that the earliest Gospels were published at later dates than what I will argue in this book, his study does appear to lend some credence to the approach envisioned by the literary independence theory, which contends that the Gospel authors did not directly copy from one another.

CONCLUSION

It is indeed reasonable to postulate that one or more Gospels were produced by those of the early church, within a few years after the resurrection and ascension. The means, motive, and opportunity did exist. We can thus envision the apostles and those within the Jerusalem church as endorsing and participating in the creation of authoritative literature for the Christian diaspora following Pentecost, and certainly later in support of those persecuted believers who fled to regions outside of Palestine. We can also envision the apostles as ultimately sanctioning the production of Gospels for Roman and gentile audiences, as these non-Jewish believers sought authoritative accounts of the life and teachings of Jesus.

It is also reasonable to postulate, given the Roman trade network and the collaborative dynamic of the early church, particularly while the apostles were yet in Jerusalem, that each Gospel author would be fully aware of what had been previously published and would leverage such to the extent that it suited their purposes. Accordingly, modern theories are deficient,

---

43. Christian, *Synoptic Composition*, xii–xiii, 16, 18–19.
44. Christian, *Synoptic Composition*, xiii.

which postulate that the Gospel authors wrote without full awareness of prior publications.

In this next chapter, I will survey the testimony of the church fathers who claimed that Matthew was the first Gospel to be published.

3

Arguments from the Early Church Fathers

THE CHURCH FATHERS MADE claims regarding the origin of the Gospels; however, these claims are sometimes difficult to interpret and can appear contradictory.[1] In particular, Irenaeus's *Against Heresies* 3.1.1 has long been a mixed blessing for those who want to leverage the church fathers to argue that Matthew was published early, within a decade of the resurrection. On the one hand, Irenaeus uses sequential language in this passage to convey that the Gospels were written in the order found in our modern Bibles, with Matthew being first. This aligns with the other church fathers. On the other hand, traditional translations of Irenaeus include declarations concerning the timing and original language of Matthew's Gospel which aren't easily reconciled with our understanding of history. This leads many scholars to deprecate or altogether dismiss the testimony of the church fathers, relative to the origin of the Gospels. In this chapter, my intent is to demonstrate that the difficulties in Irenaeus can be resolved through a fresh reading of the Greek text, such that Irenaeus and the other early church fathers can be understood as affirming that Matthew's Gospel was published first, in Greek, coincident with the events of Acts 10–11, as Peter and Paul began preaching to the gentiles within roughly a decade of the resurrection. This fresh reading resolves the difficulties which lead some scholars to dismiss

---

1. An extensive survey of the writings of the church fathers is found in both Wenham and Black. Wenham, *Redating Matthew, Mark and Luke*, 116–45; Black, *Why Four Gospels?*, 21–32.

Irenaeus, brings renewed credibility to Matthean priority, and affirms that the earliest Gospels were published well before the passage of time could reduce confidence in the Jesus traditions.

For those unfamiliar with the writings of Irenaeus, the five books of his *Against Heresies* were originally written in Greek but the full work has only survived in Latin. Certain Greek excerpts, however, were included in Eusebius's *Ecclesiastical History*. Therefore, the discussion below will move between the various English translations of these two documents and their underlying Greek and Latin texts. For our purposes, we will primarily be referencing the equivalent passages in *Against Heresies* 3.1.1 and *Ecclesiastical History* 5.8.1–4.

THE CHALLENGE OF IRENAEUS

How is it that Irenaeus (AD 115–200), that articulate defender of Christian orthodoxy and careful refuter of contemporary heresy, could leave us with such a confused testimony concerning the origins of Matthew's Gospel?[2] He and Clement are the first church fathers to clearly specify that Matthew wrote first; subsequent authors echo this belief. This is helpful. However, he then goes on to apparently assert that (1) Matthew published in the Hebrew dialect, or perhaps Aramaic, and that (2) Matthew published "while Peter and Paul were preaching at Rome and laying the foundations of the church."[3] Yet, (1) we have no copies of a Hebrew or Aramaic version of the canonical Matthew, nor (2) were Peter and Paul together at Rome prior to the AD 60s, to our knowledge, and by that time the Roman church had long been established. Further, if the publication was in the AD 60s, then there would have been little motivation to write in a language that only a limited number of Jews across the empire would understand, when so much of the New Testament correspondence had already been written in Greek, and when a letter would soon be written with primary focus on the Hebrews—written in Greek. In addition, if Irenaeus and the other early church fathers, those who ministered within a couple centuries of the resurrection, are indeed referring to a Hebrew or Aramaic version of Matthew as they discuss the four-fold Gospel which had come down to them, then

---

2. Reference is to Irenaeus, *Against Heresies* 3.1.1, and to Eusebius's version of such in Eusebius, *Ecclesiastical History* 5.8.1–4. Church father dates in this chapter are per Niemelä, "Two-Gospel," 142.

3. Irenaeus, *Haer.* 3.1.1 (Roberts and Donaldson, *ANF*, 1:414).

Arguments from the Early Church Fathers

none of them have explained to their readers where the Greek version of Matthew had come from.

Scholars, over the centuries, have offered various approaches for reconciling Irenaeus's claims.[4] Nonetheless, these historical discontinuities have broadly served to undermine the credibility of all of the church fathers relative to Gospel origins, and has encouraged scholars to leverage textual comparisons between the Synoptic Gospels (Matthew, Mark, and Luke), along with various speculations, to advance a variety of theories concerning the development of the Gospels, with the frequent assertion that Matthew was not first and that the first Gospel, whatever it was, was not published until decades after the resurrection.[5] Further, because of the presumption that decades transpired, those aspiring to claim that the Gospels preserved reliable testimony, concerning the life and teachings of Jesus, have had to subscribe to theories of oral tradition, in which the apostles, other eyewitnesses, and authoritative preservers of the traditions (the tradents) were supposedly imbued with memorization capabilities which substantially exceed our present experience. This, despite the skepticism expressed by contemporaries of the apostles, concerning the reliability of aging memories, which we will explore later.

This all leads to our present endeavor. Can Irenaeus be understood as affirming an early Greek version of Matthew? In this chapter, after a brief survey of the assertions by the church fathers that Matthew was published first, I will offer solutions for reconciling several perceived issues with Irenaeus's testimony. Most significantly, I will make the case that to preach "at Rome" is to preach within the Roman Empire, to preach other than "among the Hebrews." This is supported by an assessment of the contemporary usage of "Rome" to refer to the empire, and of the Greek prepositions used in Eusebius's version of Irenaeus. I also offer an interpretive approach by which Irenaeus can be understood as asserting that Matthew was first written in Greek. Other church fathers will also be assessed briefly to ensure that this approach to Irenaeus can be reconciled with their testimony.

Again, I will argue that Irenaeus can be understood as affirming that the publication of Matthew's Gospel, in Greek, was coincident with the

---

4. Some of these will be introduced below.

5. For example, Darrell Bock raises a broad challenge to the church fathers, in the context of whether Matthew was written in Greek: "This example shows the difficulty that can exist in the appeal to tradition. If we cannot be sure of its accuracy at one point or at several points, then what does that say about the other points the tradition makes?" Bock, "Questions about Q," 45. Similarly, Niemelä, "Two-Gospel," 136.

events of Acts 10–11, as Peter and Paul began preaching to the gentiles within roughly a decade of the resurrection. But further, within this framework Irenaeus and Clement can also be understood as affirming a publication of Mark shortly thereafter, presumably at the request of the converts in Caesarea Maritima.

MATTHEW WAS PUBLISHED FIRST

Not all of the church fathers speak to the publication sequence of the Gospels; however, where order is addressed, Matthew is consistently identified as the first to be published.[6] The one possible exception might be in Eusebius, in a chapter covering the writings of Papias (AD 95–110), where Eusebius concludes with two quotes which describe how Mark and Matthew compiled their narratives.[7] However, although the order of these quotes does not align with their modern canonical order, Eusebius's purpose in including these two disparate quotes does not appear to be for the purpose of establishing a particular publication order.[8]

In contrast, Irenaeus (AD 115–200), in a passage which will be examined below, uses sequential language (*prōtas, meta, epeita*) to convey that the Gospels were written in the order found in our modern Bibles.[9] Clement of Alexandria (AD 150–215) also affirms that Matthew was first, although he offers contradictory testimony concerning which Gospel was second. Clement is cited by Eusebius as saying that the Gospels with the genealogies (i.e., Matthew and Luke) were "first written" or "previously written (*progegraphthai*)" before Mark, and that John was then written

---

6. An extensive survey of the writings of the church fathers is found in both Wenham and Black. Wenham, *Redating Matthew, Mark and Luke*, 116–45; Black, *Why Four Gospels?*, 21–32.

7. The Papias quote is in Eusebius, *Hist. eccl.* 3.39.14–16.

8. Craig Evans, however, does find Papias's "Mark-then-Matthew" sequence to be significant, particularly when combined with the Gospel of Thomas's "Peter first, followed by Matthew" sequence. Evans, "Two Source Hypothesis Response," 115–16.

9. "πρώτας . . . μετὰ . . . ἔπειτα." Eusebius, *Hist. eccl.* 5.8.1–4. Farnell points out that Irenaeus elsewhere "follows a variety of sequences," but that these are "perhaps because of theological rather than historical reasons," as Irenaeus pursues various topics, such as the various epochs of salvation history. Farnell, "Synoptic Gospels in the Ancient Church," 72; Farnell, *How Reliable Are the Gospels?*, 29. For example, when Irenaeus presents the symbols for the four Gospels in Irenaeus, *Haer.* 3.11.8.

last.[10] However, elsewhere Clement appears to attest that the actual order was Matthew, Mark, Luke, and John:

> Nevertheless, of all the disciples of the Lord, only Matthew and John have left us written memorials, and they, tradition says, were led to write only under the pressure of necessity. For Matthew, who had at first preached to the Hebrews, when he was about to go to other peoples, committed his Gospel to writing in his native tongue, and thus compensated those whom he was obliged to leave for the loss of his presence. And when Mark and Luke had already published their Gospels, they say that John, who had employed all his time in proclaiming the Gospel orally, finally proceeded to write for the following reason.[11]

Origen (AD 185–253), in his commentary on Matthew, likewise affirms the modern biblical sequence:[12]

> First was written that according to Matthew, who was once a tax-collector but afterwards an apostle of Jesus Christ, who published it for those who from Judaism came to believe, composed as it was in the Hebrew language. Secondly, that according to Mark, who wrote it in accordance with Peter's instructions.... And the third by Luke.... Last of all that by John.[13]

In addition, several of the church fathers speak of the circumstances surrounding the publication of the Gospels. For example, Eusebius conveys a tradition that Mark wrote in response to a request by those who had heard Peter preaching, and that Peter had approved of what he wrote.[14] And further, that the Gospel was composed in Rome before Mark went to Egypt to preach and establish churches.[15] Several of these traditions will be discussed later. Nevertheless, my first objective here has merely been to recognize that Matthew is consistently identified as being published first.

---

10. Eusebius, *Hist. eccl.* 6.14.5–7 (Lake, LCL, 2:49).
11. Eusebius, *Hist eccl.* 3.24.5–7 (McGiffert, *NPNF*² 1:153; see also Lake, LCL, 1:251).
12. Niemelä, "Two-Gospel," 143.
13. Eusebius, *Hist. eccl.* 6.25.3–4 (Lake, LCL, 2:47–49).
14. Eusebius, *Hist. eccl.* 2.15.1–2.
15. Eusebius, *Hist. eccl.* 2.15.2—2.16.1.

RECONCILING IRENAEUS WITH HISTORY

Reasonable solutions are available for reconciling perceived conflicts between Irenaeus and what we know from history. In this section, solutions will be offered for resolving three apparent historical issues with Irenaeus: (1) Irenaeus's statement that Matthew wrote while Peter and Paul were preaching in Rome; (2) Irenaeus's declaration that Matthew wrote in the language (or dialect) of the Hebrews; and (3) Irenaeus's statement that Mark wrote after the departure of Peter and Paul.

Against Heresies 3.1.1

In the following passage, Irenaeus not only addresses the publication sequence of the Gospels, but also indicates the situation surrounding the publication of Matthew, Mark, and John. The long-standing challenge with this passage has been in understanding what Irenaeus actually intended. In his third book of *Against Heresies*, he says:

> We have learned from none others the plan of our salvation, than from those through whom the Gospel has come down to us, which they did at one time proclaim in public, and, at a later period, by the will of God, handed down to us in the Scriptures.... For, after our Lord rose from the dead, [the apostles] were invested with power from on high when the Holy Spirit came down [upon them], were filled from all [his gifts], and had perfect knowledge: they departed to the ends of the earth, preaching the glad tidings of the good things... Matthew also issued a written Gospel among the Hebrews in their own dialect, while Peter and Paul were preaching at Rome, and laying the foundations of the Church. After their departure, Mark, the disciple and interpreter of Peter, did also hand down to us in writing what had been preached by Peter. Luke also.... Afterwards, John, the disciple of the Lord, who also had leaned upon his breast, did himself publish a Gospel during his residence at Ephesus in Asia.[16]

To many scholars, this declaration that Matthew wrote while Peter and Paul were in Rome suggests a publication date in the AD 60s, when their missionary travels and Nero's persecution brought Peter and Paul together before their executions. Thus, this passage has often been cited by those who reject an earlier date for Matthew. For example, John David Michaelis,

---

16. Irenaeus, *Haer.* 3.1.1 (Roberts and Donaldson, *ANF* 1:414).

writing in the 1700s, accepts Matthew as being written first, given the canonical order. And although he acknowledges that "Eusebius affirms that this Gospel was written in the year forty-one," presumably tied to Eusebius's account of an early trip to Rome by Peter during the time of Claudius, Michaelis instead defers to his understanding of Irenaeus, who "dates it [Matthew to] about the year sixty-one."[17] Similarly, Jeremiah Jones cites the Portuguese Jesuit Andradius as agreeing with Irenaeus, largely because this better supported, according to Jones, the "Popish doctrine of the necessity of traditions and the insufficiency of Scripture."[18] In the modern era, Craig Blomberg (who actually holds that Mark was written first) is representative of those who likewise favor a date in the 60s for Matthew, based on his understanding of Irenaeus.[19]

Other modern scholars dismiss even a date in the 60s for the canonical Matthew, asserting that Irenaeus was not referring to a Greek version of Matthew, given Irenaeus's statement that Matthew was written in the Hebrews' own language (or dialect), since "the Greek Gospel of Matthew shows not the slightest sign of having been translated from the Semitic language."[20] Therefore, it is often asserted that the Greek Matthew must have been published sometime later than whatever it is that Irenaeus is referring to here.[21]

Additionally, the statement that Mark was published after the departure of Peter and Paul ("their departure") has been understood by some to euphemistically refer to a time after their death.[22] This euphemism appears in the English translation by Kirsopp Lake, where Eusebius quotes Irenaeus:

> Now Matthew published among the Hebrews a written gospel also in their own tongue, while Peter and Paul were preaching in Rome and founding the church. But after their death Mark also, the disciple and interpreter of Peter, himself handed down to us in writing the things which were preached by Peter.[23]

---

17. Michaelis, *Introductory Lectures*, 212–13.

18. Jones also cites Chemnitius and Mill as subscribing to Irenaeus's date. Jones, *Setting the Canonical Authority*, 3:48–49.

19. Blomberg, *Historical Reliability of the Gospels*, 25.

20. Nolland, *Matthew*, 3.

21. So Blomberg, *Historical Reliability of the Gospels*, 25–26.

22. Wessel, "Mark," 606.

23. Eusebius, *Hist. eccl.* 5.8.2 (Lake, LCL, 1:456). Moreschini and Norelli likewise adopt the "after their death, Mark" euphemism in their English translation of Irenaeus's *Against Heresies*. Irenaeus, *Haer.* 3.1.1; Moreschini and Norelli, *Early Christian Literature*,

However, other translations of Irenaeus reject this euphemism. Rather, the passage is simply rendered "after their departure."[24] Each of these areas of contention will be addressed below.

Matthew Wrote while Peter and Paul Were Preaching at Rome

There are several difficulties with Irenaeus's testimony concerning the origins of Matthew's Gospel, if Irenaeus is indeed suggesting that it was published in the AD 60s, when Peter and Paul were known to be co-resident in Rome, ministering and then suffering martyrdom. First, why would Matthew at this time write a "Gospel among the Hebrews in their own dialect"?[25] Scholars have long struggled with this dilemma. Thomas Birks outright dismisses Irenaeus, as offering "a historical absurdity" in proposing that Matthew would write the first Gospel "thirty-six years after the ascension, and then in Syriac [or Aramaic], just at the beginning of the convulsions that scattered and destroyed the Jews, and when the converts, who spoke Greek, must have been tenfold more than those who knew Hebrew only."[26] Further, Birks reminds us that James had been written decades earlier to believing Jews, "not in Hebrew, but in Greek."[27] Other authors point out that the church in Rome was founded long before the presumed joint residency there of Peter and Paul in the 60s.[28]

Compounding this enigma is the fact that Eusebius, when quoting the passage from Irenaeus, does not take issue with Irenaeus's views on the dating of the Gospel, though Irenaeus's views appear to modern readers to diverge from Eusebius's own.[29] Thomas Townson offers a solution by suggesting that Irenaeus is not actually addressing the question of when Matthew was published; but rather, Irenaeus's objective "was to declare from

---

31.

24. Irenaeus, *Haer.* 3.1.1 (Roberts and Donaldson, *ANF* 1:414). With the parallel in Eusebius, *Hist. eccl.* 5.8.2; (McGiffert, *NPNF*[2], 1:222).

25. Irenaeus, *Haer.* 3.1.1.

26. Birks, *Horae Evangelicae*, 267.

27. Birks, *Horae Evangelicae*, 267.

28. Cockburne, *Historical Dissertation*, 1:192–93; Greswell, *Dissertations on the Gospels*, 1:153. This early visit approach is adopted by Wenham, *Redating Matthew, Mark and Luke*, 146–47.

29. Eusebius, *Hist. eccl.* 5.8.2; Curran and Curran, "St. Irenaeus," 38.

whom and how the churches had received the doctrine which they held."[30] Accordingly, Townson would restructure Irenaeus's statements above and thus translate the passage as, "now Matthew among the Hebrews published also a written Gospel . . . Peter and Paul being the evangelizers at Rome," etc.[31] In 1905, John Chapman offered up this same approach, pointing out that Irenaeus's prior paragraph (as preserved in a Latin manuscript) sets up the question, "How has this preaching [of the principle apostles] come down to us in writing?"[32] Irenaeus's response therefore is simply that "two of the apostles wrote down their own teaching, while [the teaching of] two others were reported by a follower."[33] But this still leaves a difficulty with the passage, in that Paul did not to our knowledge participate in the founding of the church in Rome, although he certainly later ministered there.[34] By the time that Paul wrote to the Roman church in roughly AD 57, it was already well established, such that he was able to address many church leaders by name (Rom 16:3–16).[35]

Fortunately, a contemporary classics scholar has perhaps offered a solution. Michèle Lowrie reminds us that "cities bear a symbolic weight that goes beyond their manifold physical and social structures."[36] Accordingly, Rome was not merely the capital city, but Rome was also the empire to its fullest extent, encompassing those regions under significant Roman influence and dominion. Lowrie cites Ovid and other Latin authors to demonstrate the correspondence between the city of Rome and the empire.[37] For example, Ovid states that, "The land of other nations has a fixed boundary: the circuit of Rome is the circuit of the world."[38] A poem from Horace is also used by Lowrie to demonstrate the concept of Rome as empire:

> Within this poem, Horace prays to the Sun and asks, *possis nihil urbe Roma / uisere maius* ("May you be able to visit nothing greater than the city of Rome," *Carm.* 11–12). Usually, *urbs Roma* denotes

---

30. Townson, *Discourses*, 112. Wall similarly asserts that Irenaeus was not trying to lay out chronological relationships. Wall, *Critical Notes*, 1–2.
31. Townson, *Discourses*, 111–12.
32. Chapman, "St. Irenaeus on the Dates," 564–65.
33. Chapman, "St. Irenaeus on the Dates," 565.
34. Curran, "St. Irenaeus and the Dates—Part 3," 302.
35. Moo, *Romans*, 3–4.
36. Lowrie, "Rome: City and Empire," 57.
37. Lowrie, "Rome: City and Empire," 66.
38. Ovid, *Fasti* 2.684 (Fraser, LCL, 5:106–7).

the city proper, but the context of the Sun's daily travels over the sky opens the possibility of a wider, indeed very wide meaning... (*Carm.* 54-56). The city of Rome is again the Rome of empire.[39]

The passage from Horace is particularly significant to the interpretation of Irenaeus, given that both Horace and the Latin translation of Irenaeus employ forms of the noun for Rome (*Roma* in Horace; *Romae* in Irenaeus).[40] Irenaeus likewise, in the original Greek, employs a form of the noun for Rome (*Rhōmē*). This is significant, as most ancient references to Rome, as the empire, employ a form of the adjective, whether in Latin (*Romanus*) or Greek (*Rhōmaios*). But here we have the Latin noun being employed for referring to the empire.

With respect to Greek authors, instances where the noun for Rome (*Rhōmē*) is used to refer to more than the city are also rare, but there are examples. For instance, Josephus uses the noun to speak of Caesar as bestowing on "Antipater the privilege of a citizen of Rome" (*Antipatrō de politeian en Rhōmē*) in a sense which is broader than the geographically defined city on seven hills.[41] Plutarch correspondingly refers to the allies of Rome who desired "the citizenship of Rome."[42] Herodian, writing perhaps half a century after Irenaeus, also employs the noun for Rome in a sense which appears to encompass more than the city alone, as he downplays Maximinus's military success against the barbarians, given the many who were being "murdered ... in Rome and the subject nations."[43] Again, far more common is the use of the adjective when referring to the Roman Empire, to Roman colonies, to Roman soldiers, to Romans in general, etc., yet the singular noun form is used in these instances.

For those familiar with the Hebrew Bible, the notion that the name of a capital city can also be used to refer to the nation is well established. Samaria refers not only to the city, but also the entire northern kingdom (*en Samareia*; 1 Kgs 13:32 LXX). Damascus could refer to both city and the region (*en Suria*; 2 Sam 8:6), Babylon could refer to both the city and the

---

39. Horace, *Carm.* 11-12; 54-56; Lowrie, "Rome: City and Empire," 64.

40. Irenaeus originally wrote in Greek. However, more of his writings have been preserved in Latin than in Greek.

41. Josephus, *Ant.* 14.137 (Whiston, 374); Josephus, *Flavii Josephi Opera*, 3:264. In contrast, references to Roman citizenship utilizing the adjective are abundant, such as those instances found in the NT (e.g., Luke 16:37-38).

42. τῆς ἐν Ῥώμῃ πολιτείας. Plutarch, *Cato the Younger* 2.1 (Perrin, LCL, 238-39).

43. Herodian, *History of the Empire* 7.3.1 (Whittaker, LCL, 168-69).

country (*ek Babulōnos*; 2 Kgs 20:14), etc. Similarly, to be "in Israel" (*en tō Israēl*; Luke 2:34) could conceptualize more than just a specific territorial region.

Thus, with reference to Irenaeus's challenging statement, I suggest that to preach "at Rome (*en Rhōmē*)" or "in Rome" was not to preach exclusively in the capital but within the empire.[44] Roman colonies, in particular, "were considered extensions of Rome itself," and Caesarea Maritima would later gain that revered status under Vespasian, well before Irenaeus wrote.[45] Notably, Herod had gone to great lengths to honor and please Caesar and the Romans in his development of Caesarea Maritima, as Josephus reports that it included a temple of Caesar, a statue of Caesar, a theater, and an amphitheater.[46] Therefore, insofar as these Roman bastions represented Rome, preaching even in a city like Caesarea Maritima, the administrative headquarters of Pilate, Quirinius, and Agrippa I, was akin to preaching in Rome.[47]

It is also helpful to recognize that the same Greek prepositional word, *en*, stands at the head of both prepositional phrases in Irenaeus: "among [*en*] the Hebrews . . . at [*en*] Rome."[48] While *among* and *at* are both legitimate translations for *en*, it is unusual to select different English words for translating the same Greek word within adjacent phrases which are employing contrasting parallelism. Therefore, the modern English reader must not allow these disparate word choices to drive the understanding of the passage. Perhaps the more balanced translation might have been: "Matthew also issued a written Gospel amidst the Hebrews in their own dialect, while Peter and Paul were preaching amidst Rome."

Regardless, if this understanding of Irenaeus's "at Rome" is accepted, then Irenaeus stands well aligned with the other church fathers, in affirming an early date for Matthew, by stating that Matthew published among the Hebrews even as both Peter and Paul were first preaching in Rome,

---

44. "In Rome" is per Lake's translation of Irenaeus, as presented in Eusebius. Eusebius, *Hist. eccl.* 5.8.2 (Lake, LCL, 1:456). In contrast, Roberts and Donaldson translate this phrase from the Latin version of Irenaeus as "at Rome." Irenaeus, *Haer.* 3.1.1 (Roberts and Donaldson, ANF 1:414).

45. Stambaugh, "Greco-Roman Cities," 1047.

46. Josephus, *Ant.* 15.330-41.

47. Stambaugh and Balch, *New Testament in Its Social Environment*, 26-28.

48. ἐν τοῖς Ἑβραίοις . . . ἐν Ῥώμῃ. Eusebius, *Hist. eccl.* 5.8.2. This approach to the "preposition plus singular noun" construct (ἐν Ῥώμῃ) is comparable to the usage in Mark 6:4, which speaks of Jesus's reception within his homeland (ἐν τῇ πατρίδι αὐτοῦ).

whether in Caesarea Maritima (Acts 10) or elsewhere in the empire, such as in Antioch (Acts 11).[49]

Matthew Wrote with Reference to the Hebrews' Own Language

Irenaeus's statement that Matthew issued a written Gospel among the Hebrews "in their own tongue," "in their own language," or "in their own dialect [*tē idia autōn dialectō*]"—depending on the translation—has fostered much consternation among scholars, as there is little extant evidence of a non-Greek version of our Matthew.[50] Additionally, modern scholars are united in the view that the present Greek version of Matthew is not a simple translation from a Semitic language. Furthermore, if Irenaeus is here explaining the origins of a Hebrew version of Matthew, which is on a par with the Greek versions of the other Gospels, then nowhere does he explain where, when, and from whom the Greek version of Matthew was produced. For these reasons, what are we to make of Irenaeus's statement?

It is also perplexing that in making his claim, Irenaeus does not indicate that he might be in conflict with what Papias had stated half a century earlier, particularly since Irenaeus elsewhere favorably cites Papias.[51] Papias had previously declared that "Matthew collected the oracles in the Hebrew language, and each interpreted [or translated] them as best he could," without any suggestion that the oracles were formally published before being translated.[52] Given that Irenaeus, the apologist, is known for his aggressive responses to those whom he considers to be in error, can it not be assumed that Irenaeus is making a statement which he understands to be consistent with Papias?[53] On this basis, an alternative approach to translating "Mat-

---

49. Accordingly, Birks likewise asserts that the Gospel of Mark was written at Caesarea Maritima, for the Roman converts. Birks, *Horae Evangelicae*, 232.

50. τῇ ἰδίᾳ αὐτῶν διαλέκτῳ. Respectively, these English translations are by Lake, McGiffert, and Roberts and Donaldson. Eusebius, *Hist. eccl.* 5.8.2 (Lake, LCL, 1:297; McGiffert, *NPNF*² 1:222); Irenaeus, *Haer.* 3.1.1 (Roberts and Donaldson, *ANF*, 1:414).

51. Papias wrote in the first half of the second century, while Irenaeus wrote in the latter part of the century. Evans, *Ancient Texts*, 273–74. Irenaeus cites Papias in Irenaeus, *Haer.* 5.33.4.

52. The quote from Papias is found in Eusebius, *Hist. eccl.* 3.39.16 (Lake, LCL, 1:298).

53. Nolland appropriately proposes that "the coming together of διαλέκτῳ and ἡρμήνευσεν in Papias's words suggests that the latter word should be taken here to mean 'translated' rather than 'interpreted.'" Nolland, *Matthew*, 3.

thew published among the Hebrews a written gospel in their own language [*tē idia autōn dialectō*]" is warranted.[54]

A simple solution is available if we remember that in Greek there are many uses of the dative case and that these uses can result in dramatically different translations. As will be argued below, I contend that Irenaeus can be better translated in the sense that "Matthew published among the Hebrews a written gospel *with reference* (or *respect*) *to* their own language," with the sense that it had been translated out of their language. I'll further improve on this translation below.

This proposed translative approach treats the dative forms in *tē idia autōn dialectō* as "dative[s] of reference/respect," a use in which "the dative is used to qualify a statement that would otherwise typically not be true. This dative can thus be called a frame of reference dative, limiting dative, qualifying dative, or contextualizing dative."[55] Daniel Wallace cautions that it is sometimes "easy to confuse a dative of reference/respect with a dative of sphere; however, the resulting ideas frequently have the opposite meaning."[56] As an illustration, Wallace presents Luke 18:31: "all the things written by the prophets *concerning* the son of man."[57] If not for the dative of reference/respect option, this passage might otherwise be improperly translated as "all the things written by the prophets to the son of man," "for the son of man," or "for the benefit of the son of man," rather than "*concerning* the son of man." Words such as *"with reference to," "concerning, about, in regard to, etc."* are commonly used to convey the intended reference/respect relationship with the noun being referenced.[58]

BDF characterizes the "dative of respect" as being "appropriate when contrast is involved either in the text of in the mind."[59] Indeed, this appears to be the problem which has plagued translators and scholars throughout the centuries, in handling Irenaeus. The reference/respect approach to the dative fits well in this passage, if we understand the passage to be asserting that: Matthew published among the Hebrews, that which was *in reference to* their own language, but was not their own language. Note that

---

54. Again, we are leveraging Eusebius's Greek text for this analysis. Eusebius, *Hist. eccl.* 5.8.1–2.

55. Wallace, *Grammar*, 144–45.

56. Wallace, *Grammar*, 145.

57. Wallace, *Grammar*, 145.

58. Wallace, *Grammar*, 145.

59. Blass and DeBrunner, *Greek Grammar of the New Testament*, 106.

Irenaeus is not using the language of Paul per Acts 22:1 (and Acts 26:14), when he spoke to his audience "in the Hebrew language" (*tē Hebraidi dialecti*), where *Hebrew* is a singular adjective modifying *language*, which is a singular noun. Papias likewise uses the Acts 22:1 formulation.[60] Rather, in Irenaeus, "among the Hebrews," is being modified or qualified by the statement concerning the language, and it is for the interpreter to determine the nature of this qualification. Several NT passages likewise employ a *tē idia dialectō* formulation, which are commonly translated as "in their own language" (e.g., Acts 1:19).[61] However, these passages are generally drawing a contrast between words in two different languages and could just as easily be translated as "with respect to their own language," or "in contrast with their own language," akin to the contrast which Irenaeus may be expressing. For example, in Acts 1:19, "And it became known to all the inhabitants of Jerusalem, so that the field was called in their own language," or "with reference to their own language," "Akeldama, that is, Field of Blood." Note that Luke here is contrasting the name—what those other people are calling the field, with what he is calling it in his Greek text.

Accordingly, since Irenaeus is communicating the backstory of the Gospels, my preferred translation is "Matthew also issued a written Gospel among the Hebrews, *in a* language *contrasting with* their own." Thus, Matthew published in Greek, a language which was not the native language of the Hebrews.

Mark Was Published after Peter and Paul Departed to Preach

The final conflict to be addressed, in the writings of Irenaeus, is pertinent to the publication date of Mark. As indicated above, Irenaeus is sometimes translated as "after their departure, Mark [*meta de tēn toutōn exodon Markos*] . . . did also hand down to us in writing what had been preached by Peter," etc.[62] But sometimes, Irenaeus is euphemistically translated into English as "after their death, Mark."[63] Scholars subscribing to this second

---

60. Eusebius, *Hist. eccl.* 3.39.16.

61. Parsons and Culy state that the word which follows διαλέκτῳ "makes it clear that the reference is to the Aramaic language." Parsons and Culy, *Acts*, 17.

62. For example, Irenaeus, *Haer.* 3.1.1 (Roberts and Donaldson, ANF 1:414). Also, Eusebius, *Hist. eccl.* 5.8.3 (McGiffert, NPNF² 1:222).

63. For example, Eusebius, *Hist. eccl.* 5.8.2 (Lake, LCL, 1:456); Moreschini and Norelli, *Early Christian Literature*, 31.

translation tend to place the publication date of Mark's Gospel either in the mid to late AD 60s, or the early 70s, after the death of Peter and Paul.[64] However, I contend that this euphemistic translation is not justified, given the broader literary context.

Earlier in the Latin version of this passage (the Greek text is not available), Irenaeus had already identified to the reader the context for those who were departing, with the use of a virtually synonymous Latin verb. "For after our Lord rose from the dead, [the apostles] were invested with power from on high . . . they departed [Latin: *exierunt*] to the ends of the earth, preaching the glad tidings of the good things . . . Matthew also issued a written Gospel . . . [then] after their departure [Latin: *excessum*], Mark, the disciple and interpreter of Peter," etc.[65]

Normally, if similar words are expressing similar ideas within a context, then a translator should not jump from a non-figurative gloss (translation) to a euphemistic gloss, without any prompts from the text itself which warrant such.[66] Hence, the second departure is not a departure by death, but a departure to preach "in Rome," as discussed earlier.[67] With this interpretation, Mark can be understood as having been written just shortly after Matthew.

Accordingly, since Mark is generally recognized as being written with a Latin audience in view, rather than a more general Greco-Roman audience as per Luke, it may well have been written by Mark to the Latins in Caesarea Maritima, such as Cornelius and friends, who had so recently benefited from Peter's preaching.[68]

---

64. Strauss, *Mark*, 29, 39; Edwards, *Mark*, 6–7; Moreschini and Norelli, *Early Christian Literature*, 45. Curran takes this further, arguing that "after their death" is also intended to apply to Luke. Curran, "St. Irenaeus and the Dates—Part 4," 447.

65. Irenaeus, *Haer.* 3.1.1 (Roberts and Donaldson, ANF 1:414). Latin text is from Irenaeus, *Sancti Irenæi*, 2:2–4. The Latin roots are *exeo* and *excedo*.

66. Compare 2 Macc 5:5 in the Vulgate, where forms of these same two Latin verbs are used to legitimately juxtapose a non-figurative gloss with a similar euphemistic gloss, but there the context warrants such.

67. Clement of Alexandria, as cited by Eusebius, speaks of Mark as having been written "in this manner: When Peter had publicly preached the word at Rome [ἐν Ῥώμῃ] . . . those present, who were many, exhorted Mark, as one who had followed him for a long time and remembered what had been spoken, to make a record of what was said; and that he did this, and distributed the Gospel among those who asked him." This testimony aligns well with a Caesarea Maritima origin, per our earlier ἐν Ῥώμῃ assessment. Eusebius, *Hist. eccl.* 6.14.5–7 (Lake, LCL, 2:47–49).

68. Birks, *Horae Evangelicae*, 232.

In summary, I propose that the central portion of Irenaeus's *Against Heresies* 3.1.1 would be better translated as "Matthew also issued a written Gospel among the Hebrews *in a* language *contrasting with* their own, while Peter and Paul were preaching in Rome, *the empire*, and laying the foundations of the Church. After their departure *to other lands*, Mark, the disciple and interpreter of Peter, did also hand down to us in writing what had been preached by Peter."[69]

RECONCILING IRENAEUS WITH THE OTHER CHURCH FATHERS

In this next section, the writings of several other early church fathers are briefly surveyed, to demonstrate that they can be understood consistent with the approach taken with Irenaeus above. This is not an exhaustive evaluation, but it provides optimism that my approach to Irenaeus is sufficiently coherent with the other church fathers to merit further consideration.

Papias: Matthew and Team Translated from Matthew's Notes

The meaning of Papias's statement that "Matthew collected (*sunetaxato*) the oracles (*ta logia*) in the Hebrew language, and each interpreted (*hērmēneusen*) them as best he could" has been debated.[70] Some scholars claim that Papias's oracles refer to the creation of the "Q" document, as a collection of Jesus sayings which were in circulation among the early churches, and which stand behind the published Gospels of Matthew and Luke.[71] Accordingly, Nolland defends the view that *sunetaxato* should be understood as *translated*, rather than *interpreted* or *collected*, as given above.[72] Instead, Bauckham contends that Papias mistakenly believed that

---

69. Irenaeus, *Against Heresies* 3.1.1.

70. Eusebius, *Hist. eccl.* 3.39.16 (Lake, LCL, 1:298). Various interpretative approaches are surveyed by Carson and Moo, *Introduction to the New Testament*, 142–44; France, "Matthew," 900, 906. Hendriksen also lists several other proposed interpretive options, such as interpreting the phrase to refer to a "Hebrew style." Hendriksen, *Matthew*, 87–90. More recently, Black has similarly translated the passage as "in their own style." Black, *Why Four Gospels?*, 23.

71. So Nolland, *Matthew*, 2–3.

72. While I concur with Nolland's view on how to understand συνετάξατο, he then goes on to assert that the translation effort "suggests the existence of multiple renderings into Greek of the 'oracles' assembled by the apostle Matthew," which he speculates led to

there was an Aramaic or Hebrew version of Matthew's Gospel, which was then translated into Greek.[73]

As an alternative, I am personally fond of Edgar Goodspeed's proposal that Papias is here referring to the Hebrew or Aramaic notes which Matthew took of Jesus's activities and sermons (e.g., the Sermon on the Mount) and that the collaborative translation effort was the preparation of such for an initial publication, which was in Greek.[74] This effort could have been facilitated by the many converts within the earliest years after the resurrection and ascension.

Clement: Mark Wrote at the Request of Those in Caesarea Maritima

Clement of Alexandria is cited by Eusebius as claiming that those who heard Peter preach "at Rome" requested that Mark, "who had followed him [Peter] for a long time and remembered his sayings, should write them out."[75] And further, that "when Peter learned of this, he neither directly forbade nor encouraged it."[76] Two points are noteworthy. First, Clement's "at Rome" uses the same *en Rhōmē* as does Irenaeus, though without the contrast given by Irenaeus's "among the Hebrews," which in Irenaeus helps constrain how *en Rhōmē* should be understood, as discussed above.[77] However, Peter is presented as alive at the time that Mark wrote, though not local. Taken together, Clement can be understood in a manner which does not conflict with our approach to Irenaeus, such that Mark wrote for the benefit of those in Caesarea Maritima, after Peter departed the region.[78]

---

a collection akin to the Gospel of Thomas or the Q document. Nolland, *Matthew*, 2–3.

73. Bauckham, *Jesus and the Eyewitnesses*, 222–27. Likewise, Birks outright rejects Papias, as "the very idea that the first written gospel was left in a dialect, known to a small minority of the Church, and that chance translations were the only resource of all the rest, is highly unnatural, and hard to reconcile with the wisdom of the apostles." Birks, *Horae Evangelicae*, 261.

74. Goodspeed, *Matthew*, 16, 88–89, 108–10. Though, note that Goodspeed himself contends that Mark was written before Matthew. Goodspeed, *Matthew*, 144. Hendriksen also articulates the view that Papias may have been referring to the translation of Matthew's notes, as one of several possible options for understanding Papias. Hendriksen, *Matthew*, 88–90.

75. Eusebius, *Hist. eccl.* 6.14.5–7 (McGiffert, *NPNF*[2] 1:261).

76. Eusebius, *Hist. eccl.* 6.14.5–7 (McGiffert, *NPNF*[2] 1:261).

77. Eusebius, *Hist. eccl.* 6.14.5–7 (McGiffert, *NPNF*[2] 1:261).

78. Whereas the more common assessment is that Clement is fixing the publication of Mark's Gospel in the early to mid-60s, shortly before the traditional date of Peter's

Elsewhere, Eusebius cites Clement as stating that "Matthew, who had at first preached to the Hebrews, when he was about to go to other peoples, committed his Gospel to writing in his native tongue."[79] This passage aligns with what Irenaeus said, likewise using the datives found in Irenaeus, so can also be understood as employing datives of reference/respect.

Origen: Matthew Was Written for the Benefit of the Jews

Origen, as cited by Eusebius, is said to have testified that he "learned by tradition that the first [Gospel] was written by Matthew, who was once a publican, but afterwards an apostle of Jesus Christ, and it was prepared for the converts from Judaism, and published in the Hebrew language."[80] I contend that the English translator has gone beyond what the Greek text says, for the underlying Greek text of the last clause is *grammasin Hebraikois suntetagmenon*, which does not include the word for *language*.[81] Rather, the dative *Hebraikois* can merely indicate that the written document was prescribed *to* or *for* the benefit of the Hebrews. Hence, this statement aligns with our modern perception of Matthew's target audience, without making an assertion concerning the language of Matthew's Gospel.

Justin Martyr and Eusebius: Peter's Early Trip to Rome?

Now we come to a fascinating account in Eusebius, which purports to provide background to the writing of Mark's Gospel. In the second volume of Eusebius's *Ecclesiastical History*, he weaves together the history of the early church, the succession of emperors, the writings of contemporary Jewish authors, and the events in Acts, along with reports from Clement, Irenaeus, and others. It is quite a hodgepodge, or a quilt made of disparate fabrics.

Chapters 1 through 12 follow the history of the church from the appointment of Matthias to the twelve (Acts 1:26–26) to the death of Herod Agrippa and the famine in Judea (Acts 11), with the famine noted as occurring during the reign of Claudius. In chapter 1, Simon Magus is introduced as one who "counterfeited faith in Christ" during the time that Philip was

---

martyrdom. For example, Blomberg, *Historical Reliability of the Gospels*, 25.

79. Eusebius, *Hist. eccl.* 3.24.5–7 (McGiffert, NPNF² 1:153).
80. Eusebius, *Hist. eccl.* 6.25.3–4 (McGiffert, NPNF² 1:273).
81. Eusebius, *Hist. eccl.* 6.25.3–4 (Lake, LCL, 2:74).

preaching in Samaria, and who eventually "received the merited punishment" at the hands of Peter (Acts 8).[82] In chapter 13, Eusebius proclaims that "the enemy of man's salvation [Satan] contrived a plan for seizing the imperial city for himself," to which "he conducted" Simon Magus, who "led many of the inhabitants of Rome astray."[83] Eusebius quotes Justin, in a letter to Antonine, as referring to Simon as one put forward by demons after the ascension: "Simon, a Samaritan of the village of Gitto, who in the reign of Claudius Caesar performed in your imperial city some mighty acts of magic," etc.[84] In chapter 14, Simon flees "across the sea . . . to the city of Rome," to which Peter, "during the reign of Claudius," is led, there to destroy Simon.[85] In chapter 15 then, Eusebius continues the story by reporting that immediately following the destruction of Simon, "Peter's hearers . . . besought Mark . . . that he leave them a written monument of the doctrine which had been orally communicated to them."[86]

This is all quite the saga. Of course, Acts does not explicitly record a trip to the city of Rome by Peter before Paul gets there. Nonetheless, this is the basis which some scholars use to claim that the "another place" in Acts 12:17 refers to a very early trip to the city of Rome by Peter (and Mark) and to substantiate the writing of Mark's Gospel there.[87] At the same time, this is another passage which causes scholars to question the reliability of the church fathers. I can only echo the various arguments presented by E. Schuyler English and others, who assert that it is more reasonable to speculate that Peter traveled to "Bethany, or Caesarea, or Capernaum, or even another part of Jerusalem," then that he made a quick trip to Rome without any record of such in the Scriptures.[88] Hence, I can merely speculate, with

---

82. Eusebius, *Hist. eccl.* 2.1.11–12 (McGiffert, *NPNF*[2] 1:104–5). Irenaeus also speaks of this "Simon the Samaritan" and of Helen, his companion. However, Irenaeus does not report that Simon traveled beyond Samaria and Tyre, though his followers and religion did. Irenaeus, *Haer.* 1.23.

83. Eusebius, *Hist. eccl.* 2.13.1–3 (McGiffert, *NPNF*[2] 1:113–14).

84. Eusebius, *Hist. eccl.* 2.13.3 (McGiffert, *NPNF*[2] 1:114); Justin, *First Apology* 26.

85. Eusebius, *Hist. eccl.* 2.14.4–6 (McGiffert, *NPNF*[2] 1:115). Hippolytus repeats Justin's account that Simon Magus journeyed "as far as Rome," where he continued to cause problems. Hippolytus, *Refutation of All Heresies* 6.15 (MacMahon, *ANF* 5:81).

86. Eusebius, *Hist. eccl.* 2.15.1–2 (McGiffert, *NPNF*[2] 1:115–16).

87. Wenham, *Redating Matthew, Mark and Luke*, 146–48.

88. English, "Was St. Peter Ever in Rome?," 317. As Moo contends, "Luke's language is too indefinite to justify this [a trip to Rome] as an even probable conclusion." Moo, "Gospel Origins,'" 28.

the goal of bringing this account into alignment with my approach to Irenaeus and Clement, and with Scripture, that the second encounter between Peter and Simon Magus perhaps occurred in Caesarea Maritima, rather than across the sea in Rome, as claimed by Justin. And perhaps the purported confrontation in Rome was with regard to Simon Magus's followers, rather than with Simon, but this is not what the text appears to claim.[89]

In summary, the testimonies of Papias, Clement, and Origen can be understood to align with my approach to Irenaeus. Although, the testimony of Justin Martyr must be adjusted to eliminate an improbable early trip to Rome by Peter, in order for the location from which Mark's Gospel was published to align with my paradigm.

CONCLUSION

In this chapter it has been shown that the early church fathers consistently identified Matthew as being published first. In addition, I have argued that reasonable solutions are available for resolving some of the perceived conflicts between these church fathers. First, if *Rome* is understood to refer to Rome as the empire, then Irenaeus can be understood as testifying that Matthew wrote while Peter and Paul were initially preaching to those other than the Jews. Secondly, if the reference to "*in* their own language" is understood rather as being "*contrasting with* their own language," then Irenaeus can be understood as testifying to an early Greek version of Matthew, not to an early Hebrew or Aramaic manuscript. Thirdly, if Papias's reference to the collected oracles is understood as referring to Matthew's collection of notes, for which he had help translating, then Papias can likewise be understood as testifying to the production of an early Greek version of Matthew. Finally, if "after their departure" refers to Peter and Paul's departure to preach to the gentiles, then Irenaeus can be understood as testifying to an early publication of Mark, likely to the Latins such as Cornelius in Caesarea Maritima. Taken together, these solutions allow us to have a renewed respect for the credibility of the church fathers in describing the circumstances surrounding the publication of the Gospels, circumstances which affirm an early publication of both Matthew and Mark.

---

89. Along these lines, Irenaeus recounts "the disciples and successors of Simon Magus of Samaria," who "seduce others" and "teach his doctrines." Irenaeus, *Haer.* 1.27.3 (Roberts and Donaldson, *ANF* 1:353). Also, Irenaeus, *Haer.* 4.33.3.

Arguments from the Early Church Fathers

To be clear, my primary concern in this book is not whether Mark was published second after Matthew (the Augustinian Hypothesis), which I favor, as opposed to Luke being second (the Griesbach/Two Gospel Hypothesis), as is favored by Orchard, Farmer, Peabody, Black, and others.[90] But my primary concern is whether there is sufficient justification for affirming that Matthew was not only the first Gospel, but was published early, within a decade of the resurrection and ascension. This will be our focus. In this, I find common cause with Bernard Orchard, who asked the critical question: "Did the right conditions exist for the composition of the Gospel of Matthew between AD 30–44? And does it fit into the situation revealed in Acts 1–12?"[91] To which he then insightfully observes: "the fact is that the restoration of the priority of Matthew immediately opens up, willy-nilly the possibility of a very early date for the Gospel of Matthew. . . . even before Paul's first missionary journey (47–49), that is, even prior to the departure of Peter about AD 44 (cf. Acts 12)."[92] Most notably, if we can accept the paradigm that the first Gospel, Matthew, was published early, then I contend that this increases the inherent trustworthiness of the witness testimony of all of the Gospels, regardless of the ordering of the subsequent Gospels.

---

90. The most prominent recent advocate of the so-called Augustinian hypothesis of Gospel origins, with the traditional Matthew, Mark, Luke, and John ordering, is John Wenham. Wenham, *Redating Matthew, Mark and Luke*.

91. Orchard and Riley, *Order of the Synoptics*, 232.

92. Orchard and Riley, *Order of the Synoptics*, 233. Also, Black, *Why Four Gospels?*, 3–7, 53. In contrast, in both Farmer's recent "Two Gospel" chapter and Peabody's "Two Gospel" chapter, in their respective contributions to multi-view works, though they assert Matthean priority, they do not broach the critical issue of when Matthew was written. Rather, their emphasis is limited to the literary relationships between the Gospels to show that Mark followed Luke. Farmer, "Case for the Two-Gospel Hypothesis"; Peabody, "Two Gospel Hypothesis."

4

Arguments from Galatians

TWO EXEGETICAL ARGUMENTS FOR an early Gospel will be developed below based on Paul's letter to the Galatians. The first argument begins by observing that Paul evidently found it essential for his ministry to write a circular letter recounting his personal biography and core teachings to the churches of Galatia, shortly after visiting the region; therefore, it is suggested that he would likewise have found it essential for the followers of Jesus to promptly publish a Gospel chronicling Jesus's life and teachings after his death. Accordingly, a comparison between Galatians and Matthew is used to make the case that the Gospel of Matthew is the type of document which would have satisfied this essential need, given the many thematic and pedagogical (teaching method) parallels to Paul's letter. Further, a number of Pauline epistles are examined to show that Paul expected others to follow his ministry example, including the authoring of written materials for the benefit of the church. Together, these reinforce the argument that Paul would have expected for someone to publish something like Matthew.

The second argument is derived from an examination of *proegraphē* within Gal 3:1. Although English Bibles consistently translate this word here as "publicly portrayed," concerning Paul's presentation of Jesus's crucifixion to the Galatians, it is shown below that "previously written" is a better translation, suggesting that the Galatians had something like a Gospel available to them at the time of Paul's first missionary journey.

Arguments from Galatians

PAUL PUBLISHED HIS BIOGRAPHY AND CORE TEACHINGS

Paul, an apostle—not from men nor through man, but through Jesus Christ and God the Father, who raised him from the dead—and all the brothers who are with me, to the churches of Galatia. (Gal 1:1-2)

Why did Paul think it necessary to write a circular letter to the churches of Galatia? Had he not just visited the region and preached the gospel (Acts 13-14), declaring the grace of Christ and recalling his own experience on the road to Damascus, including his calling as an apostle (Gal 1:11-16)?[1] Therefore, when Paul heard that Judaizers were undermining the gospel which he had preached, could he not have simply deferred to those who had heard his sermons to defend his authority and protect the integrity of his message?[2] Or could he not have simply dispatched trusted envoys to present his concerns orally? Would it not have been more effective for Paul to preserve and disseminate his personal life story and his teachings by means of the same orality practices supposedly favored for the preservation of the "Jesus traditions," as characterized by many modern scholars?[3]

For modern students of the Gospels, who have repeatedly encountered scholarly pronouncements that the Jesus traditions persisted for thirty or more years in a predominantly oral form, reliant on the memories of the aging witnesses, Paul's decision to publish his personal life story and teachings in written form appears to stand in stark contrast to the apostles' purported lack of interest in publishing the events of Jesus's life and teachings. How is it that the practice of oral tradition, supported by tradents,

---

1. For this chapter, it is assumed that Galatians is the earliest of Paul's extant letters, written to the region of the churches visited during Paul's first missionary journey (per the Southern Galatian theory), and sent around AD 48, prior to the Jerusalem council of Acts 15:6. Bruce, *Galatians*, 55; Longenecker, *Galatians*, lxx, lxxxvii; Schreiner, *Galatians*, 24, 29, 31.

2. "In biblical criticism, [a tradent is] an individual responsible for passing on oral traditions, especially religious traditions." Murphy, "Tradent," 170.

3. I allude here to the predominant scholarly premise that the Jesus traditions were primarily, if not exclusively, transmitted orally for several decades. For example, scholars such as Dunn assert as a presupposition that "the Galilee of Jesus was an *oral* society," despite "first-century Israel . . . [being] a Torah-shaped society, and thus a literary society." And thus, "the earliest traditions about Jesus were transmitted by word of mouth." Dunn, *Jesus, Paul, and the Gospels*, 8-9.

those who passed on traditions orally within a community, was somehow deemed appropriate for promoting the life story and teachings of Jesus (according to the modern paradigm), but not that of Paul?[4]

And yet, evidently, Paul found it essential for his ministry to publish a letter. This begs the question, if Paul found it essential to publish a letter like that sent to the Galatians, even though he lived in a society with limited literacy, would he not also have found it essential for someone to have put into circulation a document communicating key aspects of Jesus's life and teachings, defending the messianic claims, and proclaiming the gospel message of Jesus?

Consequently, we will now explore the parallels between Paul's letter to the Galatians and Matthew's Gospel, with respect to the types of material which their respective authors sought to communicate via written mediums. Galatians has been chosen for this comparison, as arguably being the earliest of Paul's epistles, and Matthew, as it is often held to be the earliest Gospel, by those rare scholars (mostly of an earlier generation) who argue that a Gospel was published within roughly a decade after the resurrection and ascension.[5]

More specifically, the intent will be to demonstrate thematic and pedagogical parallels, rather than direct citations between the writings. Questions related to the extent of Paul's awareness and utilization of the Jesus traditions, whether as quotations or allusions, will be left unaddressed.[6] In addition, this section will emphasize Paul's expectation that church leaders follow his approach to ministry, including his publication of written materials. And, while the assessment will not prove that Paul had access to a written Gospel at the time that Galatians was written, I will ultimately

---

4. Richard Bauckham admirably argues his view that the tradents who ensured the integrity of the Jesus traditions, until they were published as the canonical Gospels, were the eyewitnesses themselves, centered on the disciples. Bauckham, *Jesus and the Eyewitnesses*, 7–8, 30, 306. Bauckham presumes that Mark was published in the AD 60s, thirty years after the death of Jesus, and that Matthew and Luke were likely published in the AD 80s, with John a little later. Bauckham, 1 *Jesus and the Eyewitnesses*, 4, 19–20, 137.

5. An earlier footnote defended the identification of Galatians as the earliest letter. Some of those who have argued for an early date for the Gospel of Matthew include Wenham, *Redating Matthew, Mark and Luke*, 223; Birks, *Horae Evangelicae*, vii; Townson, *Works of Townson*, 1:29; Owen, *Observations on the Four Gospels*, 22; Fernandes and Larson, *Hijacking the Historical Jesus*, 122; Black, *Why Four Gospels?*, 7.

6. Craig Blomberg surveys many of the prior scholarly assessments for how Paul appeared to draw from the Jesus traditions. Blomberg, "Quotations, Allusions, and Echoes," 129–30, 133–36. See also Allison, "Pattern of the Parallels," 2–4.

Arguments from Galatians

argue in this section that the Gospel of Matthew is consistent with the type of circular document which Paul would have favored and considered as essential for his early ministry.

Why does it matter? Because I am unconvinced by the claim that oral tradition theories provide a satisfactory basis for asserting that the detailed teachings and life story of Jesus were accurately preserved over a period of decades, before the first Gospel was published.[7] If the premise of an early Gospel can be accepted, then we can envision Paul as carrying a copy of Matthew's Gospel with him on his first missionary journey, and perhaps also Mark's Gospel on his subsequent journeys. And we can anticipate that these played a significant role in his presentation of the gospel, as he encouraged those whom he visited to examine the Scriptures (Acts 17:11; compare 17:2), and as he wrote, reminding the churches "that when you received the word of God, which you heard from us, you accepted it not as the word of men but as what it really is, the word of God" (1 Thess 2:13). This should also then impress on us the importance of the written Gospels, as being essential to our ministries. But further, this paradigm allows us to contend for the accuracy of the Gospels without having to first defend the ability of aging witnesses to accurately remember the words and deeds of Jesus.

Thematic Parallels between Galatians and Matthew

Grace to you and peace from God our Father and the Lord Jesus Christ, who gave himself for our sins to deliver us from the present evil age, according to

---

7. Richard Bauckham and Craig Keener have both published significant volumes which seek to bolster the credibility of the Gospels, on the premise that Mark was published in the AD 60s, followed by the other Gospels. These volumes are invaluable. But Robert McIver has effectively argued for what we all know from common experience, that "much can happen to traditions that are preserved in human memories for this length of time," referring to the supposed decades before the Jesus traditions were written down. McIver focuses much of his attention on the frailties of memory in the areas of transience, suggestibility, and hindsight bias. These can drive variations in detail and also drive falsehoods, not only when eyewitness testimony is presented formally, but also when past events are remembered in general. While affirming that eyewitness testimony offers general reliability, he contends that it usually contains a mixture of correct and incorrect recollections, resulting in perhaps 80 percent accuracy. For further discussion of this issue, refer to the chapter below, "Rejecting Bauckham's Eyewitness Memory Theory." Also, Bauckham, *Jesus and the Eyewitnesses*; Keener, *Christobiography*; McIver, *Memory*, 1, 10–11, 20, 22; McIver, "Collective Memory," 132, 143.

the will of our God and Father, to whom be the glory forever and ever. Amen. (Gal 1:3–5)

Commentaries on Galatians emphasize a number of key themes in the letter, including God's grace, the cross, Jesus as both Messiah and the Son of God, justification by faith, the truth of the gospel over and against the Judaizer heresy, the work of the Spirit, freedom from the law, the unity of believers, etc.[8] And not surprisingly, these are themes or topics which also appear in Matthew; although, Paul clearly advances the theological concepts beyond what is expressed in the Gospels.[9] In the following paragraphs, we will examine several of these themes, to identify parallels which can be discerned in the Gospel of Matthew, and will explore how these themes manifest either a similar perspective, a complementary perspective, or what I classify as a developing perspective, when comparing Matthew and Galatians.

Thematic Parallels with Similar Perspectives

Many of Paul's themes, as articulated above, are similarly echoed in Matthew. For example, the theme of God's generous grace is advanced in Matthew: by the angel's declaration that Jesus would save his people from their sins (Matt 1:21), the inclusion of the women in the line of the Messiah (1:3, 5), the parables of both the unforgiving servant (18:27) and the vineyard laborers (20:13–15), etc.[10] These all speak to God's grace. Further, Dale Allison characterizes the whole of the Sermon on the Mount as being "in the middle of a story about God's gracious overture to God's people through his

---

8. This list of themes is based on Stott, *Message of Galatians*, 182–83; Schreiner, *Galatians*, 387–401; Cole, *Galatians*, 43–45; de Boer, *Galatians*, 12–13. Keener aggregates the themes as being the gospel, law, promise, and Spirit. Keener, *Galatians*, 70. Longenecker also highlights the promise to Abraham, faith of Abraham, sons of Abraham, and the like. Longenecker, *Galatians*, 109, 112. The theme of inheritance might likewise be included here, as tied to being sons of Abraham. Bruce, *Galatians*, 192.

9. While not specifically focused on Galatians and Matthew, David Wenham has provided a helpful assessment of the similarities between Jesus and Paul in their understanding of the kingdom, the gospel, Christology, the cross and sacrificial atonement, the community of believers, ethical teaching, eschatology, etc. Wenham, *Paul: Follower or Founder*.

10. Morris, *Matthew*, 23, 30, 475, 505.

Son."[11] Jesus also speaks of God's "gracious will" in revealing the good news of the kingdom through the Son (Matt 11:26).

Furthermore, Matthew parallels Galatians by affirming that Jesus is both the Messiah and the son of God. From the very first verse (Matt 1:1) Jesus is introduced as the Christ, the descendant of David and therefore the rightful king, and the descendent of Abraham as the heir of the promise. And Matthew situates Jesus as the one fulfilling the prophecies of Isaiah (Matt 1:22–23), Micah (2:5–6), Hosea (2:15), and Jeremiah (2:17–18). He is declared to be the son of God by demons (8:29), disciples (14:33), executioners (27:54), by his own testimony (26:63–64), and even by the voice of God (3:17; 17:5). He is affirmed by miracles (4:24; 8:16; 21:14) and by divine power (8:27).

Matthew also exhibits parallels to Paul's foremost theme, that "justification [is] by faith, apart from works of the law" (Rom 3:28; compare Gal 2:16).[12] In Matthew, the focus is grounded in the need to attain a righteous standing before God, beyond what compliance to the law can provide; and this concept is progressively developed as being tied to personal faith in Jesus. This focus on righteousness begins with John the Baptist's call for repentance for entry into the kingdom (Matt 3:1–2) and is then elaborated in the Sermon on the Mount, as Jesus demonstrates the inadequacy of the law or of any other code of conduct for satisfying the requirements of divine perfection (5:48). Matthew first presents Jesus as the necessary object of this faith and as the forgiver of sins during his healing ministry–in the healing of the centurion's servant, as Jesus says, "Let it be done for you as you have believed" (8:13); of the paralytic, where he says, "Your sins are forgiven" (9:2); of the hemorrhaging woman (9:22); and of the two blind men (9:28–29). Completing the package is Matthew's presentation of Jesus as the substitutionary atonement, whose blood provides for the forgiveness of sins (20:28; 26:28).

Thematic Parallels with Complementary Perspectives

Some thematic parallels are more complementary in nature. For example, Paul's concern over defending the truth of the gospel over and against the Judaizer heresy finds a parallel in Jesus's defense of his gospel against Pharisaic legalism. Neither Paul nor Jesus minced words in challenging their

11. Allison and Davies, *Matthew I–VII*, 1:86.
12. Bruce, *Galatians*, 81; Schreiner, *Galatians*, 2.

audiences (Matt 11:16-24; Gal 1:6) and in condemning false teachers (Matt 15:7; 23:13-29; Gal 5:10, 12). Moreover, they both appealed to Scripture in their rebukes (Matt 21:42; 22:29; Gal 3:1, 8).[13] They also argued that one should be more concerned with pleasing God rather than man (Matt 6:1-6; Gal 1:10).

While Paul and Matthew both speak of the Spirit, their thrusts are often complementary, rather than directly aligned. For Paul, the promised Spirit is to be received by faith (Gal 3:2-5, 14) and then believers are to be led by the Spirit, away from fleshly behavior and into a life filled with the fruit of the Spirit (Gal 5:16-25). In contrast, Matthew anticipates a future baptism of the Spirit (Matt 3:5), he speaks of the role of the Spirit in speaking through the disciples (10:20), and he asserts the necessity of baptizing in the name of the Spirit, as part of making disciples (28:19).[14] Hence, there is a shared recognition that the Spirit comes, empowers, and leads, yet there are different aspects which are in view.

Thematic Parallels with Developing Perspectives

And then there are a few themes where Matthew provides material which is then substantially developed in Galatians. For instance, Matthew cites Jesus as declaring that he had not "come to abolish the Law or the Prophets . . . but to fulfill them," and he condemns those who might seek to relax any of the commandments (Matt 5:17-18).[15] In contrast, Paul speaks repeatedly of the freedom which one has in Christ (Gal 2:4; 5:1, 13), whereby one is no longer bound by the law. Of course, it is due to Paul's subsequent teaching that we now understand the sense in which one is no longer bound by the law, in that the law was added "because of transgression," effectively bringing about a consciousness of sin (Gal 3:19; Rom 3:20; 7:7), and that the law "served as a guardian until Christ came" (Gal 3:24-25).[16] Thus, it

---

13. Galatians 3:1 is cited for its use of προεγράφη, which is consistently translated elsewhere in the NT (i.e., Rom 15:4; Eph 3:3; Jude 4) as referring to something which was previously written. It generally (if not exclusively) also carries this meaning in contemporary non-biblical literature. For example, Plutarch, *Camillus* 39.3; Cicero 27.3; 46.2; Josephus, *Ant.* 11.283. Classical examples include Demosthenes, *Against Evergus and Mnesibulus* 47.42; Aeschines, *False Embassy* 60; Aristotle, *Economics* 1352a.1.

14. There are also references to the Spirit in the context of Jesus: his birth (Matt 1:18), baptism (3:16), etc.

15. Other passages which express concern for the law include Matt 7:12; 22:40; 23:23.

16. Scholars debate the meaning of "because of transgression." For the various

is not surprising that some scholars emphasize that "there are significant differences in the ways in which Paul and Matthew handle the subject of the law."[17] Nevertheless, this should not be characterized as a difference, but rather as a further development of a thematic parallel.

In addition, Paul's theme of the unity of Jewish and gentile believers perhaps also falls into this *developing perspective* category.[18] This doctrine is certainly not something which Matthew emphasizes, although he does touch on the principles of gentile inclusion and unity. For example, sometime after Jesus reminds his followers that they "are all brothers" (Matt 23:8–9), he speaks of a future gathering of the nations by the Son of Man (Matt 25:32); and then later he commissions his eleven *Jewish* disciples to go and "make disciples of *all* nations" (Matt 28:19). Nonetheless, the message that the "Gentiles are fellow heirs, members of the same body, and partakers of the promise in Christ Jesus" is a mystery which was uniquely revealed to Paul (Eph 3:1–6). Accordingly, Paul could claim that the gentile inclusive "gospel that was preached by me is not man's gospel, for I did not receive it from any man, nor was I taught it, but I received it through a revelation of Jesus Christ" (Gal 1:11–12). Consequently, one can find hints of this theme in Matthew, but for Paul, it was the direct revelation from Christ which was the basis for his teaching. Again, these thematic parallels suggest that Matthew is the type of publication which Paul would have expected for the followers of Jesus to promptly publish.

Summary

In summary, in this section I have reviewed several of the key themes from Galatians which have parallels in Matthew to show that there are common thematic interests between the two writings. Now certainly, Joel Willits is undoubtedly correct in asserting that "when Matthew and Paul address the same topic . . . they deal with it for different reasons and to accomplish different ends."[19] Nonetheless, my point is that, given that Paul found it essential to write on these themes, it is reasonable to speculate that he would

---

approaches refer to Schreiner, *Galatians*, 239–40; Bruce, *Galatians*, 175; Longenecker, *Galatians*, 138.

17. Foster is not asserting that they are in "dispute . . . [but] neither of course could it be construed as similarity." Foster, "Paul and Matthew: Two Strands," 95.

18. The inclusion of the gentiles was kept as a mystery until Acts 10.

19. Willitts, "Paul and Matthew," 71.

have likewise found value in having similar material available concerning Jesus; and more specifically, a Gospel very like Matthew, which evidences thematic parallels which are similar, complementary, or developing in nature.

Pedagogical Parallels between Galatians and Matthew

For I would have you know, brothers, that the gospel that was preached by me is not man's gospel. For I did not receive it from any man, nor was I taught it, but I received it through a revelation of Jesus Christ. For you have heard of my former life in Judaism, how I persecuted the church of God violently and tried to destroy it. (Gal 1:11–13)

There are also parallels in the methods used in Galatians and Matthew for instructing prospective readers. In this section, we'll briefly note the pedagogical use of the biographical stories and teaching discourses in Galatians and Matthew, and also look at their pedagogical use of Scripture.

Pedagogical Parallels in the Mix of Narrative and Teachings

Paul exhorts his readers based on his life story, "you have heard of my former life" (Gal 1:13), and based on his teachings, "I would have you know brothers, the gospel preached by me" (Gal 1:11), and so on.[20] This mix of personal narrative and teachings is likewise fundamental to the structure of Matthew, as the Gospel alternates between the story of Jesus and the five great discourses.[21] Indeed, this was the approach employed in the Torah itself, as the story of the people of Israel was combined with the discrete teachings of the law.[22]

---

20. Longenecker highlights how Paul uses these two epistolary disclosure formulas, essentially serving as his thesis statement and the introduction to his autobiographical material, as his *narratio*, his "statement of facts," within the letter. Longenecker, *Galatians*, 20.

21. Andrew Lincoln elaborates on how each of Matthew's "five great teaching discourses ... [are] integral to the ... narrative's plot." Rather than disrupting the flow of the narrative, the discourses advance the narratives. Lincoln, "Story for Teachers?," 115–16.

22. As Alan Cole affirms, "if the 'Torah' is the 'instruction' of God to his people, then history, the story of the saving acts of God, has just as much place in the Torah as

Arguments from Galatians

In Galatians and Matthew, the biographical narratives of Paul and of Jesus are used to give authority to their respective truth claims. Paul gains stature in recounting his heritage, his zealous defense of the traditions, the direct intervention of Jesus Christ at his conversion and training, and in the recognition and sanction which he received from the apostles in Jerusalem. Whereas the life story of Jesus enhances his own reputation by highlighting his prophetically anticipated and divinely empowered ministry. Both narratives also emphasize their personal sacrifice and their integrity in standing against wrong practices and false teachings.

On the teaching side, Paul's discourses bear some semblance to Jesus's discourses, with regard to their polemical approach. For instance, Paul confronts his audience concerning their flawed understanding of righteousness using a series of rhetorical questions, chastisement, and an emphasis on the demands of perfection (Gal 2:15—3:14); Jesus similarly confronts a flawed understanding of righteousness in the Sermon on the Mount (Matt 5-7). Elsewhere, Paul draws comparisons between Sarah and Hagar, and between the Jerusalem above and that below, to draw a distinction between those born of the flesh and those born of the spirit (Gal 4:21-31); Jesus likewise employs a series of contrasts within the parabolic discourse, to draw a distinction between those of the kingdom and those not of the kingdom (Matt 13). Paul appeals to the Galatians in how they should live, given their relationships within the "household of faith" (Gal 5:25—6:10); similarly, Jesus appeals to the disciples in how brothers and servants should live together because they are all children of the father, within his discourse on relationships (Matt 18). And though the significance of these parallels should not be overstated, the salient observation is that both writings employ a mix of story and teachings, employing the biographical stories to support the truth claims and leveraging similar persuasive approaches in the teaching discourses.

Pedagogical Parallels in the Deference to Scripture

There are also pedagogical parallels in how Galatians and Matthew defer to Scripture—in its authority, its prophetic nature, and in its use to confront false teachings. Paul invokes Scripture without qualification. He repeatedly draws from both the stories and the teachings of Scripture, and he fully expects that his audience will accept his reasoned conclusions based

---

legislation." Cole, *Galatians*, 179.

on Scripture's authority.[23] He also credits Scripture with prophetically anticipating God's present work through Christ and amongst the gentiles (Gal 3:1, 8).[24] As Moisés Silva notes, "Galatians is only second to Romans, proportionately speaking, in its explicit appeals to Scripture."[25] And with respect to Matthew, it hardly needs to be said that "the Hebrew Scriptures . . . permeate the Gospel," whether as quotations, allusions, or echoes; these occur "roughly twice as often as in Mark, Luke, or John." Matthew vigorously invokes the OT; indeed, "virtually every major theological emphasis of Matthew is reinforced with Old Testament support."[26]

In summary, I have shown that there are pedagogical, or teaching method, parallels between Galatians and Matthew, with respect to the mix of events and teachings, and in their deference to Scripture. This doesn't presume or privilege Matthew as a text which Paul might have known or make a claim that either text was substantively different from other Jewish texts of the era, which leveraged Jewish exegetical methods. However, it does further substantiate the claim that Matthew is of the same type of material as that which Paul thought worthy of publishing, given his authoring of Galatians.

Paul's Expectation that Others Follow His Ministry Approach

I . . . write these things . . . to admonish you as my beloved children. For though you have countless guides in Christ, you do not have many fathers. . . . I urge you, then, be imitators of me. That is why I sent you Timothy, my beloved and faithful child in the Lord, to remind you of my ways in Christ, as I teach them everywhere in every church. (1 Cor 4:14–17)

Paul repeatedly called on the faithful to imitate his example, his traditions, his pattern, his way of life, and his ministry methods. In Galatians, Paul simply encourages his readers to "become as I am" (Gal 4:12), which

---

23. Obvious scriptural citations and allusions include Gal 1:15–16; 2:16; 3:6, 8, 10–13, 16–17; 4:14, 22, 27, 30; 5:14.

24. The reference to Gal 3:1 is defended in chapter 3.

25. Further, even in the first two chapters, where there are "no explicit scriptural citations . . . it is immediately apparent that Paul's discussion . . . moves in the conceptual world of the OT and makes no sense apart from the latter." Silva, "Galatians," 785–86.

26. Blomberg, "Matthew," 1.

broadly speaks to his devotion to the gospel (1:10) and to being free from the law (5:1–2); but in his other letters, his exhortation for imitation is more expansive.[27] He even goes so far, I will demonstrate, as urging the churches to imitate his practice of publishing material for the benefit of the church. In this section, I will survey Paul's admonition that others follow his approach to ministry and will link such to the production of written materials, for the instruction of the church.

To the Corinthians: "I . . . write these things . . . be imitators of me"

To the Corinthians, Paul became more than just a guide in Christ, but a father (1 Cor 4:15). He urged the church to imitate him. "I urge you, then, be imitators of me" (4:16). And he even sent Timothy to remind them of Paul's "ways in Christ" (4:17). For our purposes, it is significant to note that Paul highlights to the Corinthians that he is conveying his admonitions to them in writing. "I do not write these things to make you ashamed, but to admonish you as my beloved children" (4:14). Hence, it may be implied, although not explicitly stated, that Paul's practice of writing admonitions to those whom he considered to be children in the faith falls within the scope of what he was calling the Corinthians themselves to imitate.

Later, Paul reinforces the importance of writing things down for the instruction of others, when he states that the things which happened to Israel were to be understood as examples, "written down for our instruction" (1 Cor 10:11; compare Rom 15:4). And then, he again calls on the Corinthians to "be imitators of me," while commending them for "maintain[ing] the traditions even as I delivered them to you" (1 Cor 11:1–2).[28] Given the above context, I suggest that this "maintaining the traditions" refers not only to maintaining or keeping the content of the traditions, as in "trying to please everyone in everything I do . . . [so] that they may be saved" (1 Cor 10:33), but also to the method of keeping the traditions.[29] If written

---

27. "'Become like me' looks back to the autobiographical accounts of Galatians 1:13—2:14, where Paul speaks of his own loyalty to the truth of the gospel, and to the expositions of 2:15—4:11, where Paul sets out his arguments in defense of the Christian gospel vis-à-vis the Jewish law." Longenecker, *Galatians*, 189.

28. Robert Plummer identifies Paul's evangelistic ministry as the focus of his "imitate me" in this passage, specifically with regard to "evangelistically-motivated self-denial." Plummer, "Imitation of Paul," 222, 225.

29. Κατέχω can refer to either keeping something that is tangible or intangible, and sometimes both can be in view. In 1 Cor 7:30, the term is used of the tangible keeping

materials are truly in view with this reference to traditions, as they are in 2 Thess 2:15, then Paul is also applauding the Corinthians for how they are preserving and using these written materials. Indeed, this linkage between the varied aspects of keeping the traditions has its roots in the Torah, where the king is required to make a copy of the law, to keep it with him ("it shall be with him"), and to read it all the days of his life (Deut 17:18–19). Thus, I am proposing that to the extent to which Paul had delivered traditions or teachings to the church in written form, he expected them to imitate him, in preserving and delivering written traditions to others, such as the traditions of Jesus.

To the Philippians: "To write the same things . . . join in imitating me"

To the Philippians, Paul was their partner in advancing the gospel (Phil 1:5, 12; 4:15). For Paul, being worthy of the gospel included "striving side by side" in unity, while earnestly looking out for others (1:27—2:4). In this context, Paul urges the church to imitate him and to be watchful for those who "walk as enemies of the cross" (3:17–18). And so, as with the Corinthians, Paul situates his call for imitation within the framework of his literary ministry when he says, "to write the same things to you is not trouble to me and is safe for you" (Phil 3:1) and then later exhorts his readers: "brothers, join in imitating me" (Phil 3:17).

In addition, I also want to draw attention to the closing of this letter, where Paul urges the Philippians to "greet every saint in Christ Jesus. The brothers who are with me greet you. All the saints greet you, especially those of Caesar's household" (4:21–22). Often, Paul concludes his letters with an exhortation that the church "greet one another" (e.g., Rom 16:16).[30] However, in this passage, Paul appears to make a broader request, which goes beyond the limits of the Philippian church itself. Rather, his request of the Philippians appears to be similar to his request of the Colossians, who were

---

of goods, whereas in Heb 3:6 it refers to the intangible, to "hold fast our confidence." In the parable of the soils, though, the seed which is kept is a tangible thing, yet serves as a metaphor for the intangible word (Luke 8:15; Matt 21:38). But with regard to 1 Cor 11:2, scholars such as Adele Reinhartz exclusively focus on the "content and goal of imitation," along with related issues such as Paul's "right to exhort" the church, without considering the tangible medium of the traditions which are to be imitated. Reinhartz, "Meaning of the Pauline Exhortation," 398, 403.

30. The "greet one another" requests are found in Rom 16:16; 1 Cor 16:20; 2 Cor 13:12; and 1 Thess 5:26. Hansen, *Philippians*, 329.

urged to extend his greetings to the Laodiceans (Col 4:15). Therefore, I suggest that Paul is hereby encouraging the Philippians to likewise participate in an additional aspect of the ministry with him, by following his example of writing letters of encouragement to other churches.[31] Thus, part of the task of partnering in the gospel, of encouraging, of warning, etc. is to be found in engaging with others via a written medium. This perspective also helps inform our understanding of Paul's earlier statement, when he urged, "what you have learned and received and heard and seen in me—practice these things" (Phil 4:9).

To the Thessalonians: "taught . . . by letter . . . imitate us"

To the Thessalonians, Paul represents himself as a brother who "toiled and labored," that he might not be a burden (2 Thess 3:8). And it is this example which Paul presses the Thessalonians to imitate, as he deals with the issue of those who were refusing to work (3:6–14). "Keep away from any brother who is walking . . . not in accord with the tradition that you received from us. For you yourselves know how you ought to imitate us" (2 Thess 3:6–7). In this passage, the imitation is framed in the context of the received tradition, which Paul characterizes as being taught both orally and in writing, as Paul had earlier said, "stand firm and hold to the traditions that you were taught by us, either by our spoken word or by letter" (2:15).[32] Therefore, this call for imitation reasonably includes both the preservation and the dissemination of the traditions in written form, as suggested earlier.[33]

To recap, I have argued that when Paul urged the churches to imitate his example, it was inclusive of his approach to ministry, including the

---

31. Most commentators, when addressing this closing remark, focus solely on the greeting from Paul and ignore the expectation that the Philippians likewise greet others, arguably via a written medium. For example, Martin, *Philippians*, 189–90.

32. Note that, whereas 1 Cor 11:2 calls for maintaining or keeping (κατέχω) the traditions, 2 Thess 2:15 calls for holding or seizing (κρατέω) the traditions.

33. Ernest Best boldly takes the opposite position, asserting that "while the Thessalonians are urged to receive the traditions, they are not urged to pass them on; this emphasis (cf. 1 Tim 6:14, 20; 2 Tim 2:2; Titus 2:1) belongs to a later age." Best, *Thessalonians*, 318. Yet I contend that his assertion is not rational. Best correctly observes that Paul does not overtly urge the Thessalonians to pass on the traditions in this verse, but certainly Paul expected the Thessalonians to teach those in the church and elsewhere the content of the traditions which Paul was conveying in this letter. Indeed, in Paul's prior letter, Paul had applauded the way in which "the word of the Lord sounded forth from you" (1 Thess 1:8).

issuance of written materials for the benefit of the church. Paul's exhortations to the Corinthians, Philippians, and Thessalonians have been examined, and in each letter, as Paul called on the churches to imitate him, he also pointed out that he was providing his instructions in a written form. This is a noteworthy pattern.

In addition, he applauded or encouraged these churches with regard to maintaining or keeping the traditions. Appropriately, I have suggested that this included the copying and dissemination of these traditions. I have also argued that Paul encouraged the churches, or at least the church of Philippi, to follow his example of writing letters of encouragement and exhortation to other churches. To my broader argument, my point is that it is reasonable to assume that Paul would have expected the church at large to have produced written materials, such as those concerning Jesus, which would likewise serve to strengthen the church and to advance the gospel. Along these lines, Paul certainly demonstrated his own interest in preserving and using written materials, as at one point he requested that Timothy bring him a collection of books and parchments (2 Tim 4:13). Perhaps we can envision the Gospels of Matthew and Mark as being a part of this collection.

Summary

Three propositions have thus far been advanced in this chapter. First is the assertion that there are sufficient thematic parallels between Galatians and Matthew, that one may reasonably speculate that if Paul found it essential to publish a document which addressed the themes found in Galatians, which he obviously did, then he would have likewise found value in having something like Matthew available, given the similar themes, but with a focus on Jesus. This has been supported by an exploration of Matthew, showing parallels to key themes in Galatians. Second is the assertion that Galatians and Matthew share sufficient pedagogical parallels to also justify this speculation. These include a similar usage of biographical narratives and teaching discourses, along with a similar deference to Scripture. And third is the assertion that, when Paul voiced an expectation that his followers imitate him—this included his ministry methods and even the publication of written materials for the mutual encouragement and instruction of the early churches. To this end, excerpts from the letters to the Corinthians, Philippians, and Thessalonians have been assessed.

Arguments from Galatians

Ultimately, I have aspired to show that the Gospel of Matthew is indeed consistent with the type of circular document which Paul would have favored and considered as essential for his early ministry. Next, we will consider the possibility that Galatians itself might explicitly refer to a previously written Gospel.

JESUS'S RESURRECTION WAS "PREVIOUSLY WRITTEN"

O foolish Galatians! Who has bewitched you? It was before your eyes that Jesus Christ was publicly portrayed as crucified. Let me ask you only this: Did you receive the Spirit by works of the law or by hearing with faith? Are you so foolish? Having begun by the Spirit, are you now being perfected by the flesh? (Gal 3:1–3)

With amazement, Paul rebuked the Galatians, accusing them of turning aside from the gospel which he had declared to them. "O foolish Galatians! . . . It was before your eyes that Jesus Christ was publicly portrayed [*proegraphē*] as crucified" (Gal 3:1).[34] These are sharp words. And yet, the modern reader is left with the question, in what sense was the crucifixion portrayed? Was Paul reflecting on his oratorial performance before the Galatians? Or was he alluding to previously written materials, which he had laid before their eyes which spoke of the crucifixion? Following a review of classical, Hellenistic, and New Testament usage, this section will conclude that the *proegraphē* in Gal 3:1 should be translated with the sense of "previously written," such that Paul was referring to a published document, such as a Gospel, which he had put in front of them.[35] This is significant, as Paul's rebuke was therefore not merely focused on their rejection of what he had taught but was also a stinging reprimand of their rejection of what a Gospel taught concerning the work of the crucified Christ.[36]

---

34. . . . οἷς κατ' ὀφθαλμοὺς Ἰησοῦς Χριστὸς προεγράφη ἐσταυρωμένος; (Gal 3:1, SBLGNT). Holmes, *Greek New Testament: SBL Edition*.

35. προεγράφη is the aorist passive indicative third person singular form of προγράφω.

36. It is also significant, as it offers further evidence that Paul's evangelistic ministry was firmly rooted in the mutual examination of written materials with his audiences, rather than merely in the preaching of oral traditions, even during his earliest work in Galatia. Contra Dunn's emphasis on the reception and preservation of each "church's

Diachronic Analysis[37]

The following diachronic analysis considers classical Greek, Hellenistic, and Septuagintal usages of *proegraphē*, in its various forms. The dictionary form of *proegraphē* is *prographō*, which carries three principal meanings according to the LSJ lexicon. These are broadly grouped as "*write before* or *first*," "*set forth as a public notice*," and "*write* a name *at the head of a list*."[38] Two of these meanings are clearly coupled with something which has been written. Yet even the "public notice" meaning presupposes that written materials are in view, as the cited examples from the classical era include a notice to appear for trial, a summons to a meeting, the proclamation of a festival, and so on.[39] Within the Hellenistic period, examples abound within these categories, particularly in the writings of Plutarch, who refers to a posted summons, the placarding of household goods for sale, a listing of people to be put to death, citizen registrations, a posted advertisement of a cure for distemper of the mind, etc.[40] Likewise, Josephus refers to the decree which was published to save the Jews in the time of Esther.[41] And Milligan and Moulton cite an example in which a father posted a public proclamation declaring that he would not be responsible for his son's bad debts.[42]

Within the Septuagint, there is but a single instance of *prographō*, found in a passage from 1 Maccabees, in which King Demetrius wrote to the Jews, releasing them from various taxes and tributes, granting certain liberties, and granting authority for the raising of a standing army (1 Macc 10:22–35): "I *will* further, that there be enrolled [*prographētōsan*] among

---

founding traditions … (in oral form)." Dunn, *Galatians*, 327–28.

37. A diachronic word analysis examines how words "have been used in the past and how they have changed meaning through time." Bock and Fanning, *Interpreting the New Testament*, 141–42.

38. Liddell et al., *Greek-English Lexicon*, 1473. With regard to the New Testament instances of προγράφω, LSJ lists Eph 3:3 under the subcategory of "*write before* or *above*"; Gal 3:1 under "*was proclaimed* or *set forth publicly*"; and Jude 4 under "*those whose names have been registered* for condemnation." The Rom 15:4 instance is not specifically listed.

39. Specific examples include Demosthenes, *Against Evergus and Mnesibulus* 47.42; Aeschines, *False Embassy* 60; Aristotle, *Economics* 1352a.1.

40. Plutarch, *Camillus* 39.3; *Cicero* 27.3; 46.2; *Aemilius Paulus* 38:4; *Vitae decem oratorum* 1.

41. For example, Balz refers to Josephus's account of Esther, in which a written decree was published. Josephus, *Ant.* 11.283; Balz, "Προγράφω," 154.

42. Moulton and Milligan, *Vocabulary of the Greek Testament*, 538.

the king's forces about thirty thousand men of the Jews, unto whom pay shall be given" (10:36).[43] This Septuagintal usage appears to carry the sense of establishing a written enrollment or registration, akin to the use elsewhere of the simple verb *graphō* (1 Macc 8:20; 13:40) and of *apographō* (3 Macc 2:29; 4:14; Luke 2:1).

Verlyn Verbrugge notes that words within the *graphē* word group (within which he includes *graphō*, *prographō*, etc.) encompass not only writing, but also drawing, engraving, painting, inscribing, etc.[44] For example, the BDAG lexicon includes within its discussion of *prographō* instances where *graphō* is used to refer to both magical papyri and decorative statuary artwork.[45] Ultimately, based on the literary evidence, Verbrugge concludes that the "whole range of meaning covered by the *graphē* word group" persisted into the Jewish-Hellenistic era.[46] Hence, based upon the above assessment, it may be claimed that during the NT era *prographō* nominally referred to something which has been previously written, in one form or another, including the use of such when "*set forth as a public notice*."

A passage in Josephus which refers to an emancipation decree issued during the reign of the Ptolemies in Egypt is sometimes cited by biblical commentators as an example of a public notice which supports a "publicly portrayed" translation in Gal 3:1, without requiring a written referent.[47] However, the context in Josephus clearly demonstrates that even this particular "public notice" was in a written form, as the passage indicates that the decree's various dictates were being read aloud.[48]

---

43. Brenton, *Septuagint*. Although Balz refers to this instance as exemplifying the "proclaim publicly" gloss, this seems unwarranted, given that the list is keeping track of those who were to be assigned various duties and be paid. Balz, "Προγράφω," 154.

44. Verbrugge, "Γραφή," 113.

45. However, BDAG does not offer any specific instances where the "public notice" sense exists, without reference to something which is written, drawn, etc. For example, BDAG cites under the "public notice" gloss an example out of Josephus in which γράφω is used to refer to the making of a picture of a god. Josephus, *Against Apion* 2.252; Bauer et al., *Lexicon*, 867.

46. Verbrugge, "Γραφή," 114.

47. For example, Longenecker claims that in this passage, Josephus uses προγράφω "locatively, in the sense of a public announcement," without acknowledging that this public announcement came in the form of something written. Longenecker, *Galatians*, 100. Bruce similarly determines that the "prefix προ- is locative, not temporal," while neglecting that γράφω root still suggests something inscribed, per its classical, Hellenistic, and biblical usage. Bruce, *Galatians*, 148.

48. Josephus, *Ant.* 12.32–33 (Whiston, 310).

Synchronic Analysis[49]

The following synchronic analysis considers the New Testament uses of *proegraphē*, in its various forms. Again, the dictionary form of *proegraphē* is *prographō*. Three instances of *prographō* (in various forms) occur within the New Testament, other than in Gal 3:1. In Rom 15:4, Paul refers to the Scriptures which were "written in former days ... for our instruction." In Eph 3:3, he speaks of the mystery of the church, about which earlier in the letter "I have written briefly." In Jude 4, reference is made to the intrusion of ungodly people into the church, "whose condemnation was written about long ago" (NIV). Thus, *prographō* is used in all of these passages to refer to something previously written, which is being authoritatively referenced in support of the thrust of the author's argument.[50] Further, these writings reflect a consistency of meaning between Paul and Jude.

However, in Gal 3:1, an alternative interpretation of *proegraphē* is typically advanced by translators and commentators, such that the word refers not to what was previously written, but to what was previously spoken—that which was "before your eyes ... publicly portrayed." Hence, when Paul chastises the Galatians for their failure to remember what he had put before their eyes concerning the crucifixion of Christ, it is claimed that it was his act of proclaiming the crucifixion which is ostensibly in view. Here, according to Alan Cole, the preacher is presented "as God's herald, God's town-crier."[51] Here, the Galatians are reminded that they had clearly perceived the truth of the crucifixion, with more than just their physical eyes. Again, according to these scholars, it was the proclamation of the crucifixion which is in view.

In addition, some commentators combine the "public notice" sense of *prographō* and the "draw, paint" sense to speak of the "verbal picture painted" before the Galatians.[52] Again, according to these commentators, this

---

49. A synchronic word analysis studies words "within a given period ... or within the writings of a specific author." Bock and Fanning, *Interpreting the New Testament*, 141–42.

50. Bauckham reviews various competing perspectives before concluding that Jude has in view a combination of OT and apostolic prophesies, which are then (partially) elaborated in Jude 5–19. The other perspectives had argued that what was in view are prophecies from pre-Christian writings, such as the book of Enoch, or lists kept in heavenly books. Bauckham, *2 Peter, Jude*, 35–36.

51. Cole, *Galatians*, 132. Cole also connects this with Paul's self-description in 1 Tim 2:7.

52. Bruce appeals to the "public placard" sense of προγράφω, citing Luther's idea "of a verbal picture painted before the hearer's eyes ... a vivid description of the crucifixion."

Arguments from Galatians

"verbal picture" lacks any physical writing, drawing, or painting.[53] Commentators thus applaud Paul's oral presentation, the "apostolic kerygma which set forth [the crucifixion], like a placard for all to see."[54] Longenecker likewise finds a figurative "public placard [to be] most congruous with the imagery 'before your eyes.'"[55] Similarly, Arichea and Nida assert that the whole expression is a metaphor, describing the "familiar practice of making public announcements by means of bills or posters."[56] And de Boer goes further, to assert that the "mention of the eyes . . . [makes] a possible allusion to unspecified OT passages equally improbable."[57]

Nevertheless, one must consider whether a figurative approach to *prographō*, which lacks any connection to something physically written, is preferable or appropriate. Significantly, the accompanying "before your eyes (*kat ophthalmous*)" idiom refers merely to doing something before someone's face.[58] It does not necessarily restrict that action to an exclusively oral presentation. For example, the idiom is used when the Lord commands Jeremiah to "take great stones and hide them in the entrance . . . in the sight of the men of Judah" (Jer 50:9 LXX). And earlier, the idiom is used when the false prophet "Ananias took the yokes from the neck of Jeremias in the sight of all the people, and broke them to pieces" (Jer 35:10 LXX). In both instances, the idiom is used to emphasize that the action is to be taken before someone, not whether or not something is to be said or read.

More significantly, the commentator-preferred figurative approach to *prographō* is inconsistent with how the term is utilized elsewhere in the NT, especially in Paul's writings. Indeed, this treatment of *prographō*, devoid of any written referent, is effectively a *hapax legomenon* (a unique instance)

Bruce, *Galatians*, 148; Luther, *Galatians*.

53. Bauer et al., *Lexicon*, 867; Balz, "Προγράφω," 154. Kittel and Friedrich affirm the "public proclamation [of the] apostolic preaching" gloss, but resist going so far as embracing the sense of a "vivid description" (see footnote below), as "there is no attestation for this sense" of vividness. Kittel and Friedrich, *Theological Dictionary Abridged*, 133.

54. Fung, *Galatians*, 129.

55. Longenecker, *Galatians*, 100–101.

56. Arichea and Nida, *Paul's Letter to the Galatians*, 53.

57. de Boer, *Galatians*, 171.

58. Bauer et al., *Lexicon*, 744. For example, LSJ translates κατ’ ὀφθαλμοὺς λέγειν τινί as "to tell one *to one's face*," based on Aristophenes, *Frogs* 626. Liddell et al., *Greek-English Lexicon*, 1278. To my knowledge, there are no extent occurrences of ὀφθαλμος with προγράφω, other than in Gal 3:1.

within the NT, if not within all of Greek literature.⁵⁹ Rather than imposing a unique reading, I contend that exegetes should instead be prejudiced towards applying a consistent semantic meaning to the translation of *prographō* in Galatians, similar to that applied in Romans, especially given the often overlapping argumentation and dependance on the OT which is evidenced in these two letters.⁶⁰ Likewise, the broader context within Galatians should also influence the translation, particularly given the reference to the written law in the prior verse (Gal 2:21) and the frequent references to the OT Scriptures in Gal 3:6–29.⁶¹ Paul has a firm interest in literary materials within this letter. Hence, a translation which alludes to the presentation of things "previously written" is more fitting for Gal 3:1. And thus, a more appropriate translation might be, "O foolish Galatians! . . . What was previously written concerning Jesus Christ's crucifixion was presented before your eyes."⁶²

Of course, this then leads to my speculation that this "previously written" document was none other than Matthew's Gospel, for there is no other candidate document that antedates Galatians, which speaks of the crucifixion.⁶³ With this approach, the Galatians are being rebuked, not for ignoring what Paul "publicly portrayed" to them in his teaching, but rather for their neglect of what he had demonstrated to them from Matthew's Gospel.

---

59. Note that Longenecker rejects a contested textual reading in Gal 2:20 primarily because it represents "a *hap. leg.* in Paul," yet is willing to impose this *hap. leg.* gloss onto Gal 3:1. Longenecker, *Galatians*, 94, 100.

60. Bruce, *Galatians*, 2.

61. In addition, it must be acknowledged that Paul had ready recourse to verbs of declaring and commending (e.g., ἀνατίθημι and συνιστάνω, as used in Gal 2:2 and 2:18, respectively), to which he could have turned to remind the Galatians of his oratory performance, if so desired, and thus avoid a word (προγράφω) which has such clear linkage to written materials. Schreiner makes a similar argument about alternative word selections when judging between potential translations elsewhere in Galatians. Schreiner, *Galatians*, 169.

62. Bretscher argues for a similar non-figurative interpretation, emphasizing that Paul had laid out the scriptures before their eyes. Bretscher, "Light," 81. Wendt does likewise, although she speculates that Paul had in view both the OT and contemporary "Judean writings," akin to the Sibylline Oracles. Wendt, "Galatians 3:1 as an Allusion," 371, 379.

63. To be clear, I am not equating the references to "gospel of Christ" in Galatians (e.g., Gal 1:7) to Matthew's Gospel.

CONCLUSION

In this chapter, two arguments have been presented. The first asserted that there are sufficient thematic and pedagogical parallels between Galatians and Matthew, along with similar uses of Scripture, that we may reasonably speculate that if Paul found it essential to his ministry to publish Galatians, then he would have likewise found it essential for someone to have published a document like Matthew. This is also supported by Paul's repeated expectation that others imitate his ministry approach.

The second argument employed diachronic and synchronic assessments to demonstrate that *prographō* was consistently used to refer to what was previously written or drawn, whether as documents, letters, placards, statuary artwork, public notices, etc. Therefore, despite the common practice by English translators and commentators of treating *proegraphē* figuratively in Gal 3:1, as a reference to Paul's oratory performance, we should instead retain the sense that something "previously written" is being referenced. On this basis, I have speculated that this referenced document may well be the Gospel of Matthew, as there are no other candidate documents that antedate Galatians, which overtly refer to the crucifixion. Again, with this understanding, Paul's intent in this particular verse is to chastise the Galatians for not only ignoring his teaching, but also for ignoring the testimony of the Gospel which he had presented "before their eyes." This also suggests that Paul's earliest evangelistic ministry in Galatia was firmly rooted in the mutual examination of Scriptures with his audiences, akin to his later approach in Thessalonica (Acts 17:2) and Berea (Acts 17:11), and that this was inclusive of a Gospel.

5

Arguments from Post-Reformation Era Scholars

FEW AND FAR BETWEEN are the contemporary voices who yet contend that a written Gospel was published and widely disseminated during the first decade of the Christian church.[1] Yet there exists a rich history of post-Reformation era scholars who contended that the first Gospel, Matthew, was published within just a few years or perhaps within a decade of the ascension. While these authors leveraged the writings of the church fathers for this viewpoint, along with internal features of Matthew's Gospel, our primary interest will be in their related arguments concerning the necessity of an early written Gospel for propagating the gospel message and for preserving its contents, as the church expanded beyond Judea. These scholars spoke of the common desire of ancient people to preserve their religious tenets through written materials, the duty of the witnesses to employ a written medium, the need to secure the church against the spread of falsehoods, the additional weight, authority, and certainty which a written record provided, the uniqueness of the Christian message, the advantage of written instructions over oral, etc. The literary efforts of these authors were not merely academic, for many were defending the Christian faith and

---

1. Perhaps the most notable modern advocates, arguing for the publication of the first Gospel, Matthew, within roughly a decade of the resurrection and ascension, are John Wenham, Bernard Orchard, and David Alan Black. Wenham, *Redating Matthew, Mark and Luke*, 146–72; Orchard and Riley, *Order of the Synoptics*, 241; Black, *Why Four Gospels?*, 50–53.

Arguments from Post-Reformation Era Scholars

Scriptures against contemporary challenges to its authenticity and authority, and they believed that the credibility of the Gospel witness was linked to the publication date of Matthew's Gospel.

Accordingly, the ultimate goal of this chapter is to showcase these historical writings and to demonstrate that these scholars considered a publication of Matthew's Gospel within roughly the first decade after the ascension to be defensible based on the perceived situation of the early church.[2] As part of their apologetic defense of the Gospels, these authors articulated a number of reasons why the early church would have been motivated to publish an early Gospel. These motivational arguments remain worthy of consideration as part of a modern defense of the authenticity and authority of the Gospels, even though Christian academia has largely adopted the premise that several decades transpired before the Jesus traditions were widely disseminated in a written form.[3]

For pragmatic reasons, the scope will be limited to just over a dozen English works, published between the mid-1600s and AD 1900, with other works cited as appropriate.

Modern researchers owe a significant debt to the digitization efforts of recent years, which have made these materials more widely accessible. Therefore, I want to acknowledge Google books, the Library of Congress, Hathi Trust, Microsoft's funding of the Internet Archive, and the Early English Books Online project for making this research possible.

---

2. "The first decade" nomenclature is used a bit loosely herein, as the assumed date of the ascension itself varies by a few years between the various post-Reformation era authors. For example, Birks holds to AD 30 for the ascension and AD 42 for the publication of Matthew. Birks, *Horae Evangelicae*, 147, 243.

3. For example, Richard Bauckham presumes that Mark was published in the AD 60s, thirty years after the death and ascension of Jesus, and that Matthew and Luke were likely published in the AD 80s, with John a little later. Bauckham, *Jesus and the Eyewitnesses*, 14, 19–20, 137. Craig Keener places Mark in the mid-60s and Matthew in the 70s. Keener, *Matthew*, 42–44; Keener, *IVP Background*, 44, 126. Craig Blomberg argues that Mark was written sometime in the 60s, and believes that the evidence for Matthew slightly favors a date in the 60s, sometime after Mark. Blomberg, *Jesus and the Gospels*, 1:135, 151. Although, Blomberg does not want to place too much "significance" on whether the date of Matthew is in the 60s or later, given the availability of the "eyewitnesses of Jesus's ministry." Blomberg, *Historical Reliability of the New Testament*, 16.

APOSTOLIC MOTIVATIONS FOR AN EARLY GOSPEL

Fourteen post-Reformation (pR) era writers have been selected who affirm that Matthew was written no later than AD 42, with several arguing that Matthew was published and widely distributed within just a few years of the ascension. Their affirmation of these early dates will be illustrated below, along with their evaluation of the external and internal evidence, and then their arguments for the early necessity of a published Gospel will be elaborated.

Post-Reformation Era Advocates for an Early Matthew

Eight of the surveyed post-Reformation era writers assert that Matthew was written around AD 41–42. These include Richard Ward (1646), William Cave (1676), John Edwards (1693), Jeremiah Jones (1798), Edward Greswell (1837), Richard Watson (1844), Thomas Birks (1852), and Joseph Angus (1866).[4] Four writers propose AD 37–38, including Henry Owen (1764), George Tomline (1822), Thomas Horne (1825), and Francis Upham (1881).[5] Two writers simply insist that Matthew was written within a few years of the ascension; these are Robert Cockburne (1755) and Thomas Townson (1778).[6] Several non-English authors are also reported as having affirmed similar dates, including Baronius, Vossius, Wetstein, Tillemont, Patritius, Reithmeyer, and Du Pin.[7]

---

4. Dates listed for each author are publication dates. Ward, *Theological Questions*, 4; Cave, *Antiquitates Apostolicae*, 180; Edwards, *Discourse concerning the Testaments*, 3:416; Jones, *Setting the Canonical Authority*, 3:162; Greswell, *Dissertations on the Gospels*; Watson, *Exposition of the Gospels*, 8–9; Birks, *Horae Evangelicae*, 243; Angus, *Bible Handbook*. Note that Lardner, contrary to what Cave appears to be saying in the cited work above, attributes an AD 48 date to Cave. Lardner, "History of the Apostles," 40–41.

5. Owen, *Observations on the Four Gospels*, 22; Tomline, *Introduction to the Study*, 1:211; Horne, *Critical Study of the Scriptures*, 4:232; Upham, *Thoughts on the Holy Gospels*, 163, 175.

6. Cockburne, *Historical Dissertation*, 1:191; Townson, *Discourses*, 128. Note that the first work is actually anonymous, but is attributed to Cockburne by Townson. Townson, *Discourses*, 25n5.

7. Lardner reports that Baronius "was of the opinion that this Gospel was published in the year 41, soon after Peter had begun to preach to Gentiles at the house of Cornelius in Caesarea," while Vossius and Wetstein held that Matthew was written eight years after the ascension, and that Tillemont asserts that Matthew "wrote his Gospel about three years after the crucifixion," around AD 36. Lardner, "History of the Apostles," 41. Patritius and Reithmeyer are identified by Heiss as arguing for an early date. Heiss, *Four*

Broadly, their determinations are driven by their understanding of the testimony of the church fathers, the internal evidence within the Gospel itself, and by the perceived needs of the early church. The excerpts provided below are intended to showcase these perspectives, using their words, without necessarily highlighting or aspiring to resolve discrepancies between the various authors.

The External Evidence of the Church Fathers

The historical testimony of the church was of immense importance to seventeenth-century English Protestant apologists, as Anglicans, Puritans, and Nonconformists contended with each other and with papists and atheists.[8] Accordingly, Patristic authorities were frequently invoked, not only when addressing issues of faith and practice, but also when defending the authenticity and authority of the Gospels; this deference to the church fathers continued over subsequent centuries.[9] The conclusions drawn from these extra-biblical sources are surveyed below, regarding the dating of Matthew's Gospel, followed by what they inferred from the biblical evidence. Ultimately, though, these authors primarily defer to a number of perceived motivational arguments as driving the early publication date.

Cockburne is representative of most of these pR authors in leveraging the testimony of Eusebius, as confirmed by Jerome, Epiphanius, and others, when declaring that "it seems to have been generally agreed among ancient writers" that Matthew's Gospel was published first, "a few years after our Savior's ascension, and before the apostles left Jerusalem to execute the commission [which] they had received to proselytize the nations."[10] According to Cockburne, Eusebius testifies that "St. Peter preached the Gospel

---

Gospels, 27. Du Pin indicates that Matthew wrote about AD 39. Du Pin, *New History*, 1:187.

8. Spurr, "Special Kindness for Dead Bishops," 315, 323, 326. Nonconformists included those outside the church of England, such as the Presbyterians, Baptists, and Congregationalists.

9. Spurr, "Special Kindness for Dead Bishops," 314–17. For example, the reverence for the writings of the "primitive" church can be observed in the opening pages in Cave, *Antiquitates Apostolicae*, sec. dedication.

10. Cockburne, *Historical Dissertation*, 1:191–92. Cockburne is presumably deferring to such passages as Eusebius, *Hist. eccl.* 3.24.5–7; 5.8.1–2 (Origen); 6.25.3–6; Jerome, *Commentary on Matthew*, preface; Epiphanius, *Panarion* 51.4.12—51.5.1; Irenaeus, *Against Heresies* 3.1.1.

at Rome, in the reign of Claudius; about which time it was that Matthew published his account . . . when the witnesses . . . were alive."[11] More specifically, it was at the "beginning of the reign of Claudius"; although Cockburne alone makes this precise claim.[12] Therefore, the implication for him is that the Gospel was written no later than AD 41, albeit he himself will ultimately assert an earlier date.[13] At the same time, he does acknowledge that the writings of Irenaeus and others suggest later dates.[14]

Similarly, Edwards and others affirm that Matthew "committed the evangelical transactions to writing . . . about eight years after Christ's ascension," before their departure "to go and preach in foreign regions."[15] Owen and others also cite sixth-century Cosmos of Alexandria as declaring that the Gospel was authored during the persecution which followed "the death of Stephen, which obliged St. Matthew to depart from Judea," before which "the believers entreated him to leave with them a written instruction for the regulation of their lives . . . his Gospel."[16] Cave also cites Epiphanius as reporting that Matthew published "at the command of the apostles, while he was yet in Palestine, about eight years after the death of Christ."[17] Cave

---

11. Cockburne, *Historical Dissertation*, 1:113. For the reference to Peter being in Rome during Claudius, Cockburne cites Eusebius, *Hist. eccl.* 2.14. For the Matthew reference, Cockburne cites Eusebius, *Hist. eccl.* 2.15, which does not directly refer to Matthew. Perhaps Cockburne is suggesting a linkage to Eusebius, *Hist. eccl.* 3.24.5–7. For this time period, the pertinent emperors were Tiberius (14–37), Caligula (37–41), Claudius (41–54), and Nero (54–68). Kruse, *Romans*, 1.

12. Cockburne, *Historical Dissertation*, 1:194n3. Cockburne attributes this to Eusebius, without specifying the reference; perhaps he is alluding to Eusebius, *Hist. eccl.* 2.13–14. Some of our authors also link to a disputed "third year of Caligula" passage in Eusebius. Tomline, *Introduction to the Study*, 1:210n1.

13. Cockburne, *Historical Dissertation*, 1:192–93.

14. Cockburne, *Historical Dissertation*, 1:192; Owen, *Observations on the Four Gospels*, 2–3; Irenaeus, *Haer.* 3.1.1.

15. Edwards does not cite his source, although shortly thereafter he cites Jerome, Eusebius, Saint Augustine, and Chrysostom, when stating that Matthew wrote first in Hebrew, then Greek. Edwards, *Discourse concerning the Testaments*, 3:416. Some of the others who leverage the eight years or so statement include Jones, *Setting the Canonical Authority*, 3:162; Ward, *Theological Questions*, 4.

16. Owen, *Observations on the Four Gospels*, 2, 21–22.

17. Cave, *Antiquitates Apostolicae*, 180. Cave's sidenote identifies Epiphanius's "Haeref. 51" as his source; however, Epiphanius merely reports that "the first issuance of the Gospel was assigned to" Matthew. Thus, Cave may be taking Epiphanius as implying that Matthew was still in Jerusalem while the disciples were still gathered. Epiphanius, *Panarion: Books II and III*, 79:29.

declares that this account is "most plain," as Matthew's Gospel must have been "written before the dispersion of the apostles, seeing [that] St. Bartholomew . . . took it along with him into India," according to Pantaenus.[18]

Additionally, brief reference is made by some of these authors to notes added to various manuscripts, which also attest to this time frame of eight years after the ascension, but this is merely offered as supplemental collaboration, and generally with the full recognition that the attestation of these side notes is unprovenanced.[19] And of course, some of the ancient testimony, particularly that which is several centuries removed from the apostolic age, is likewise of limited value.

The Conflicting External Evidence

The pR authors often tried to address the difficult statements and apparent discrepancies within the writings of the church fathers, beyond just the issue of Matthew's publication date. (Note that in an earlier chapter, I have offered solutions to some of the apparent discrepancies.) For example, one major area of contention concerns the language of the original publication of Matthew's Gospel. Townson, Tomline, and other pR authors cite Papias (as quoted by Eusebius), Irenaeus, Origen, Jerome, and others as asserting that Matthew was initially written in the Hebrew language (or perhaps Aramaic or Syriac) in Judea, and principally for the sake of the believing Jews, before a Greek version was published, despite there being no extant physical evidence of a Hebrew version.[20]

Cockburne is willing to accept the testimony of the church fathers, that Matthew was originally written in Hebrew, lest "their testimony in points of higher consequence" be weakened.[21] At the same time, he speculates that it is probable that the Greek version was written by Matthew himself, still well before Mark was published, and not as a pure translation.[22] Townson like-

18. Cave, *Antiquitates Apostolicae*, 172, 180; Eusebius, *Hist. eccl.* 5.10.2–3; Jerome, *Lives of Illustrious Men* 36.

19. Townson, *Discourses*, 25; Jones, *Setting the Canonical Authority*, 3:162; Du Pin, *Compleat History*, 1699, 2:36.

20. Townson, *Discourses*, 26; Tomline, *Introduction to the Study*, 1:213; Eusebius, *Hist. eccl.* 3.24.5–6; 3.39.16; 6.25.3–4; Irenaeus, *Against Heresies* 3.1.1; Jerome, "Prefaces to the Commentaries," 495; Cyril, "Catechetical Lectures," 98.

21. Cockburne, *Historical Dissertation*, 1:196.

22. Cockburne, *Historical Dissertation*, 1:205–6. Edwards considers it probable that Matthew also wrote the Greek version, adding explanations of "some of the Hebrew

wise proposes that Matthew was initially published in Hebrew, "for the sake of the common people of Jerusalem and Judea," but that "at the same time or very soon after it must have been published also in Greek, which was more familiar than Hebrew to a great body of the [Jewish] dispersion."[23]

In contrast, Horne proposes that the Hebrew version was published in AD 37–38, while the Greek version was published in AD 61; with the latter date proposed as a means of reconciling "the apparently conflicting testimonies of Irenaeus and Eusebius."[24] Greswell echoes this view, dismissing the notion that both versions were published together, as he maintains that the diaspora Jews would have understood the Hebrew version; plus, he reasons that if the Greek version quickly followed, then of necessity it would have begun with an obligatory mention of the Hebrew text, which it does not.[25] Regardless, there is no suggestion by these writers that an initial Hebrew version might have been inferior in scope or quality to a final Greek version, as though a subsequent Greek version improved on what was originally published.[26] Ward and Watson, on the other hand, are skeptical that a Hebrew version ever existed.[27]

---

words." Edwards, *Discourse concerning the Testaments*, 3:416.

23. Townson, *Discourses*, 78. Owen asserts that if the Gospel was not originally in Greek, then it was "very early translated into that language." Owen, *Observations on the Four Gospels*, 83.

24. Horne, *Critical Study of the Scriptures*, 4:234. Horne points out that Josephus also published in two languages, as he "wrote the History of the Jewish War in Hebrew and Greek." Horne, *Critical Study of the Scriptures*, 4:237. Also, Greswell, *Dissertations on the Gospels*, 1:137. Upham merely asserts that Matthew turned the Hebrew (or Aramaic) Gospel into Greek, "some years after." Upham, *Thoughts on the Holy Gospels*, 195.

25. Greswell, *Dissertations on the Gospels*, 1:141–42, 153. Greswell goes further, to suggest that Mark was the primary translator of Matthew's Gospel, and then supplemented it with his own, "either both at Rome, or both about the same time." Greswell, *Dissertations on the Gospels*, 1:154.

26. For example, Blomberg argues that the *logia* referred to by Papias was "probably a precursor to what we call the Gospel of Matthew . . . perhaps a collection of Jesus's teachings." Yet, this fails to recognize that Papias' works themselves were called the "Interpretation of the Oracles [Λογίων] of the Lord," comprising five books. Thus, Papias uses the term to refer to a substantive body of work. Paul likewise uses the term to refer to the large body of OT writings (Rom 3:2). Further, the church fathers, when articulating the order and circumstances of the Gospels, always present the Matthew which was published first as being on a par with the other Gospels. Blomberg, *Historical Reliability of the New Testament*, 6–7. Eusebius, *Hist. eccl.* 3.39.1.

27. Ward, *Theological Questions*, 5; Watson, *Exposition of the Gospels*, 13. It is perhaps worth observing that, while Irenaeus declares that Matthew published in Hebrew, Papias merely reports that "Matthew collected the oracles [τὰ λόγια] in the Hebrew language,"

Arguments from Post-Reformation Era Scholars

The varied accounts from the church fathers are well known to modern students of Gospel origins, as are the weaknesses of these accounts, given their apparent contradictions and the temporal remoteness of the church fathers from the first century. Indeed, the weaknesses of these testimonials were well known to the pR authors themselves, and they openly acknowledged such. However, for the pR authors, what was often more important than the testimonies of the church fathers was what our authors found in the biblical texts themselves and what they understood of the situation of the early church. Owen explains his process of evaluation, as follows, while speaking in the third person:[28]

> In the course of his [Owen's own] enquiry, he followed chiefly the light of Scripture; and where that failed, betook himself to the primitive writers for further instruction. But as these writers differ widely in their accounts, he has only so far adopted their opinions, as they appear conformable to the sacred history, and consistent with each other and even the testimonies alleged are generally to be looked upon as no more than collateral proofs of what had been deduced [by Owen] before from the internal structure of the Gospels. . . . if he has affixed to some of the Gospels, and particularly to Saint Matthew's, an earlier date than others have done, it was because the peculiarities of this Gospel, in conjunction with the circumstances of the Jewish church, evidently point to such a period.[29]

The Internal Evidence within the Scriptures

The pR authors often found evidence for an early date within the text of Matthew's Gospel itself. Lardner, though not himself an advocate of an early date, nicely articulates one argument as he finds it remarkable that "none of the Evangelists [Gospel authors] should give in their account [anything]

---

which I suggest could simply indicate that he was the one who recorded Jesus's sayings in their original language before "each interpreted them as best he could," in order to (exclusively) publish the first Gospel in Greek. Eusebius, *Hist. eccl.* 3.39.16 (Lake, LCL, 1:297); 5.8.2.

28. Note that it was Henry Owen who some credit with originating the Two Gospel Hypothesis, which postulates that Matthew was written first, that Luke then used Matthew, and that Mark then used both Matthew and Mark. Evans, "Two Source Hypothesis Response," 14–15; Osborne and Williams, "Markan Priority," 20–21.

29. Owen, *Observations on the Four Gospels*, iv–v.

of the preaching of the apostles after our Lord's ascension, and the descent of the Holy Ghost upon them," nor of the miracles performed, nor of the many converts.[30] To other authors, this suggests that the earliest Gospel must have been written before substantive time had passed.[31] In particular, the failure to mention the persecution following Stephen's martyrdom is claimed by Owen and others as evidence for a very early date.[32] And Upham elaborates on "Matthew's caution . . . [in referring to] certain persons and events" as evidence that his Gospel was "written as early as" this time of persecution, as he seeks to protect the identities of vulnerable Christians.[33]

In addition, Townson highlights the distinct way in which Matthew references prominent individuals. For example, "Matthew entitles Herod the Great simply [as] Herod the King" (compare Matt 2:1 with Luke 1:5), which to Townson suggests that the disciple wrote before he knew of another king Herod; namely Herod Agrippa, who was not "invested . . . with regal power over Judea" until AD 37.[34] Likewise, in Matthew's account, the most distinguished John is John the Baptist, and therefore Matthew consistently refers to the disciple John as the brother of James, whereas the other Gospels only refer to the disciple as John, given his post-resurrection prominence, except for when he is first introduced. Also in Matthew, Pilate is frequently referred to as being governor, suggesting that Pilate still held that post at the time Matthew was written, in advance of his recall to Rome before Tiberius's death in AD 37.[35]

Greswell simply notes that Matthew's Gospel "exhibits plain indications that it was composed expressly for a Hebrew community of Christians, and in Palestine, and very probably, early in the Christian history."[36]

---

30. Lardner, "History of the Apostles," 164.

31. For example, Tomline, *Introduction to the Study*, 1:211.

32. Owen, *Observations on the Four Gospels*, 22; Upham, *Thoughts on the Holy Gospels*, 163, 178.

33. For example, Matthew's Gospel appears particularly discrete, in comparison with the other Gospels, in its treatment of the family of Lazarus and of Jesus's mother, who may have been at particular risk. There are likewise others whom he does not refer to by name, such as Jairus, Bartimaeus, and Zacchaeus. Upham, *Thoughts on the Holy Gospels*, 163, 170, 178–79.

34. Townson, *Discourses*, 106–7.

35. Townson, *Discourses*, 105, 107–8; Horne, *Critical Study of the Scriptures*, 4:232. Birks makes the same argument concerning John and Pilate. Birks, *Horae Evangelicae*, 244–45, 251.

36. Greswell, *Dissertations on the Gospels*, 1:16.

Arguments from Post-Reformation Era Scholars

Twelve Motivational Arguments for an Early Matthew

Most significantly, these authors argued that the situation of the early church, the need to propagate and defend the gospel message as the church expanded beyond Judea, and to accurately preserve an account of the life and teachings of Jesus, would have motivated Matthew to publish his Gospel within the earliest years of the church. Twelve motivational arguments for the necessity of an early Gospel publication are elaborated below.

1) Because All People Seek to Preserve Their Religion

Cockburne observes that people of "all civilized nations" seek "to preserve their religion and to transmit it to [their] posterity."[37] Indeed, the custom of writing religious tenets was evident among the Jews, the followers of Confucius, the Persians, the Arabians, and the Romans.[38] Therefore, it is reasonable to assume that the Jewish Christians would likewise seek to expeditiously preserve their religion through written means. Correspondingly, Greswell finds it "reasonable to assume that the necessities of later ages [for written religious material] would ... immediately" be in view.[39]

2) Due to the Demand for an Authentic Record by Judean and Diaspora Jews

Owen contends, with regard to the time of the first Gospel publication, that "it may be sufficient to observe at present, that the circumstances of things, and the necessities of the church, seem to plead in favor of the earliest, rather than the latest [proposed] dates. For we can hardly suppose that the church would be left [for many years] ... without any authentic account in writing of facts so highly important not only to its edification, but also to its very being."[40] More specifically, Cave reports that after the ascension, Matthew was "entreated by the converted Jews to commit to writing the history of our Savior's life and actions, and to leave it among them as the standing record of what he had preached to them."[41]

---

37. Cockburne, *Historical Dissertation*, 1:iii.
38. Cockburne, *Historical Dissertation*, 1:v–vi.
39. Greswell, *Dissertations on the Gospels*, 1:68.
40. Owen, *Observations on the Four Gospels*, 7.
41. Cave, *Antiquitates Apostolicae*, 178.

Townson, having determined that the Hebrew and Greek versions of Matthew were written for the Jews of Judea and the diaspora before a large number of gentiles were integrated into the church, resolves that "Matthew was published when the situation of the church . . . required" a Gospel, "within just a few years of the ascension" while the apostles were still in Judea, and certainly by the beginning of AD 37.[42] Birks identifies the conversion of Cornelius as the "motive for recording the discourses and miracles of Jesus, both for the use of the converts in Palestine and for a testimony to the unbelieving Jews."[43]

3) To Provide Greater Weight and Authority to the Christian Message

Tomline asserts that the apostles would lose "no time in writing an account of the miracles which Jesus performed, and of the discourses which he delivered, because the sooner such an account was published, the easier it would be to enquire into its truth and accuracy; and consequently, when these points were satisfactorily ascertained, the greater would be its weight and authority."[44] This is reminiscent of Paul's evangelistic approach during his journeys, as he would often reason from the written Scriptures (Acts 17:2, 11).

Horne is of the same opinion, "for as the Jews . . . [would] endeavor to render suspected, the oral declarations of the apostles concerning the life, transactions, and resurrection of our Savior, it would not a little tend to strengthen the faith and courage of the first Christians, if the most important events in the history of Jesus Christ were committed to writing in a narrative which should set forth his dignity and divine majesty."[45] Townson also points out that since the Jerusalem counsel deemed it necessary to convey their message to Antioch in writing, "we cannot suppose" that they would find it any less necessary to convey the "life and doctrine of their blessed Lord" in a similar authoritative manner.[46]

---

42. Townson, *Discourses*, 113, 128.

43. Birks, *Horae Evangelicae*, 243.

44. Tomline, *Introduction to the Study*, 1:211. Horne affirms Bishop Tomline's assessment. Horne, *Critical Study of the Scriptures*, 4:229–30.

45. Horne, *Critical Study of the Scriptures*, 4:226.

46. Townson, *Discourses*, 75.

Arguments from Post-Reformation Era Scholars

4) As a Duty of Those Called to Be Witnesses

Given the use of "the Scriptures on every Sabbath . . . the witnesses could secure the precision and permanency of their witness only by putting it in writing."[47] Per Upham, many within the church would surely have started writing out their recollections of Jesus at an early date, particularly after the conversion of thousands within Jerusalem and so, "the witnesses must then have seen . . . that it was their duty to have the Gospel properly written out."[48]

5) To Secure the Church against the Spread of Falsehoods

Given the widespread interest in Jesus, and the likely emergence of "apocryphal and imperfect gospels," Birks argues that placing the "facts on record" was imperative, in order "to secure the church against the spread of falsehoods" or the publication of materials by writers "of secondary and more remote authority."[49] This is reminiscent of Quintilian's lament that students "made frequent annotations [against his orations] that sometimes circulated in public and reproduced a teacher's work to its detriment."[50]

6) Due to the Apostle's Zeal and the Uniqueness of the Christian Message

Jones goes further, by pointing out that "the zeal of the apostles and first Christians for propagating Christianity" was so great that it cannot be imagined that they would "be so negligent" as to not promptly employ a written medium as a "means to promote it":[51]

> Christianity, in its very infancy, made a very great noise in the world: the doctrines of it were new and surprising; vast numbers continually embraced it: one would think therefore, that, had there been nothing else, men's curiosity would have influenced them to procure those authentic accounts, which the Gospels contain; that

---

47. Upham, *Thoughts on the Holy Gospels*, 40.
48. Upham, *Thoughts on the Holy Gospels*, 44–45.
49. Birks, *Horae Evangelicae*, 55.
50. Quintilian, *Institutes of Oratory* 1 Pr 7–8 and 2.11.7, as cited by Cribiore, *Gymnastics of the Mind*, 144.
51. Jones, *Setting the Canonical Authority*, 3:164, 172.

so they might know the history of a person's life and doctrines, who had been so remarkable, and made so great a figure in the world.[52]

7) To Facilitate Training in Christian Belief and Practice

Edwards contends that, when Paul reminded Timothy of the training which he had received as a child, Matthew's Gospel was one of the Scriptures which guided Timothy in the development of his Christian faith and practice (2 Tim 3:14–16).[53] The early dissemination of these written material could be used for private edification.

8) To Support the General Edification and Public Reading within the Church

Church leaders were expected to publicly read and exhort from the Christian Scriptures (1 Tim 4:13), reflecting the synagogue practice. Accordingly, Watson asserts as presumptive that Matthew would have been published early, if only to satisfy the public reading and general education needs of the Christian assemblies:

> Still many became Christians in Judea, and other countries, who could only be generally and vaguely acquainted with the public life and discourses of their Redeemer; persons brought to faith and salvation by the impression of the miracles of the apostles, the convincing native energy of truth, and the secret influences of grace upon their hearts, for whose confirmation in faith, and the holy comfort of the Gospel, that history of Christ, that exhibition of his doctrine, that powerful impression of his whole extraordinary character, which every single gospel contains, was essential. The Gospels were books to be read in their assemblies, as being placed upon a level with the sacred books of the Old Testament by their inspiration, and as being also the key to the law and the prophets.... All these present strong reasons for an early composition of an authorized history of Christ, and favor, as a presumptive

---

52. Jones, *Setting the Canonical Authority*, 3:164.
53. Edwards, *Discourse concerning the Testaments*, 3:29.

argument, the early dates ascribed to that of St. Matthew, which was undoubtedly the first published.[54]

9) To Help Christian Faith Be More Certain

Ward asserts that the Gospels were written "for the help of our knowledge, lest that in process of time, there should either have been no remembrance, or a false remembrance, of our salvation and redemption by grace"; thus, God has committed such to writing, "that the truth might remain . . . unto all ages."[55] Further, the "Lord would have our memories to retain truth, not lies, and therefore commands the Gospel to be written that the truth may not be corrupted."[56] Ward claims that

> The gospel was written for the help of our faith, lest it should have been uncertain. If the history of Christ's conception, birth, life, temptation, sufferings, obedience, and the like, had only been by tradition delivered from father to son; in process of time, we should have questioned the truth of it, and so our faith would have been the more shaken and less sure: to redress which, the Lord commends all these things to writing, that so our faith might be firm and working, not frail, and wavering. If the gospel had been related unto us by others, not by the apostles, we should have been prone to have called the truth and certainty of it in question: as the Sadducees, who will neither receive nor embrace any other Scripture, but only the Pentateuch, or five books of Moses, because none were written by him, but them: and therefore the Lord will have the gospel written, and the canon and rule of faith taught, confirmed, and sealed by his apostles, who were eye and ear witnesses, of what they wrote, that we might the more undoubtedly believe the infallible truth of it.[57]

10) Due to a Concern over the Loss of the Eyewitnesses

Cockburne dismisses the late dates which Irenaeus seems to suggest, lest "the memory of these extraordinary facts" be "impaired by the death of

54. Watson, *Exposition of the Gospels*, 9.
55. Ward, *Theological Questions*, 3.
56. Ward, *Theological Questions*, 3.
57. Ward, *Theological Questions*, 3–4.

so many eyewitnesses."[58] By the AD 60s, countless witnesses would have already died both by natural causes and by means of persecution.

11) Due to Concerns That Oral Traditions Are Liable to Uncertainty and Resistance

Jones reminds his readers that "Matthew has delivered to us not only the actions, but the discourse of Christ; and this he must needs be able to do with greater certainty, while they were fresh in his memory, than when through length of time he began to lose the impressions of them."[59] Indeed, the consensus of these authors was that oral traditions were liable to great uncertainty and corruption, and offered a basis for others to impeach the accuracy of the Gospels.[60] This view aligns with that of ancient Greco-Roman authors, such as Cicero, Livy, Philo, Plutarch, Quintilian, and others who likewise expressed concerns over the reliability of aging memories and admonished orators to be active writers.[61] But Watson also points out that many of the "sayings of Jesus" were "designedly enigmatical, and could not be understood until after his ascension," and then only with the help of the Holy Spirit (John 14:26). Thus, many of the discourses were "floating, so to speak . . . all correct as to substance, but more or less confused" as to their impact and character; again, adding impetus to moving beyond merely preserving such via oral traditions.[62] It was also observed that the oral tradition practices of the Jews were condemned by the Lord Himself (Matt 15:2–9); therefore, the pR authors expressed little sympathy to the prospect that the church would have followed a similar oral tradition model.[63]

Further, it was believed by the pR authors that only by recording the rules of a religion could it successfully be promulgated, particularly since there is "an innate propension to licentiousness" and indulging the passions, which resists constraints; thus, "it would not have been safe for this reason to trust to their memory that which they did not care practice."[64]

---

58. Cockburne, *Historical Dissertation*, 1:193.

59. Jones, *Setting the Canonical Authority*, 3:50; Birks, *Horae Evangelicae*, 60.

60. Cockburne, *Historical Dissertation*, 1:iii; Birks, *Horae Evangelicae*, 39; Townson, *Discourses*, 76.

61. Refer to the next chapter.

62. Watson, *Exposition of the Gospels*, 15.

63. Angus, *Bible Handbook*, 90.

64. Cockburne, *Historical Dissertation*, 1:iv. "So incessant is the influence of man's

Arguments from Post-Reformation Era Scholars

12) To Facilitate Propagation into Other Languages

Angus points out that "the public reading of these books [Scripture] in a language intelligible to the people, was appointed by God both among the Jews and in the Christian church."[65] Therefore, it may be assumed (although Angus doesn't explicitly state such), that the bilingual disciples, who were ministering in regions where Syriac, Latin, and other languages were prominent, would recognize the inherent value in having a written source from which translations could be made.

Summary

In summary, the authors cited above emphatically argued that the apostles would have been motivated to promptly publish a Gospel, soon after the ascension and before the church expanded much beyond Judea. The prompt publishing of a Gospel would preserve Jesus's ministry and teachings for both present and future believers, would make them available for both private and public use, and would facilitate the propagation of the message into other lands and languages. And it would secure the accuracy of such against the death of the witnesses, the inaccuracies of less credible witnesses, the frailties of memory, the natural propensity to soften the teachings, and the attacks of outsiders. For these and other reasons, our authors fully believed that an early publication date was both reasonable and defensible based on the perceived situation of the early church.[66]

Half a century ago, a similar argument was advanced by Bernard Orchard.

> Our Matthew therefore came into existence because those leading the Church in the first decade after the Resurrection needed the support of a document that would (1) set out clearly the credentials

---

moral state upon his judgment and perceptions, that any unwritten revelation must have undergone essential, though, perhaps, insensible modifications." Angus, *Bible Handbook*, 81.

65. Angus, *Bible Handbook*, 88.

66. In the modern era, John Wenham has echoed many of these concerns. "Good reasons for making a written record are likely to have arisen quite soon. For instance, a reliable source of instruction would be needed when no qualified teacher was available; it would be felt necessary to secure accuracy in . . . what was being taught . . . [and] a need would be felt for a form of witness to those outside the church." Wenham, *Redating Matthew, Mark and Luke*, 200.

of Jesus its Founder in a manner cogent for Jews of that period, i.e. the reasons for his claim to be the Messiah, the Son of David and the Son of God, (2) furnish the written record of his fulfilment of the prophetical writings of the Old Testament to counter the accusations of the Church's enemies in Jerusalem, (3) provide the record and the proof of the Church as the new Israel of God, itself a fulfilment of OT prophecy, and (4) provide an official record or handbook of Jesus' teaching in a compact and handy form. The Gospel of St. Matthew does all this, and is therefore to be seen as the necessary Christian response and reaction to the hostile environment that it had inherited from the moment of Jesus' Death on the Cross. But it is also the basic manifesto of the Good News already made known to the Jews and now to be made known also to the Gentiles (Mt 28:16–20).[67]

AN APOLOGETIC CONCERN FOR THE AUTHORITY OF SCRIPTURE

But why did these post-Reformation era writers themselves publish their own books? Many of these authors saw a need to respond to contemporary challenges to the authenticity and authority of the Gospels. For example, in the seventeenth century, in the English preface to Du Pin's treatise it is warned that "such a Spirit of atheism, skepticism, and infidelity has of late prevailed, that 'tis high time for every honest man and good Christian to look about him. . . . [For] they chiefly aim to strike at the genuineness and authority of the Holy Scriptures . . . [raising] objections against the truth and authority . . . of Holy Writ."[68] Du Pin's apologetic treatise defends against this challenge by declaring that "the Gospels were from the first infancy of the church in the hands of all the Christians and read publicly in all the church."[69] Likewise, Cave regrets that "we live in a time, wherein religion is almost wholly disputed into talk and clamor, men wrangle eternally about useless and insignificant notions . . . how much these evils have contributed to the atheism and impiety of the present age, I shall not take upon me to determine."[70] And his apologetic writings aspire to counter such.

---

67. Orchard, "Why Three Synoptic Gospels?," 242.
68. "Translator's Preface," i.
69. Du Pin, *Compleat History*, 1699, 1:226.
70. Cave, *Antiquitates Apostolicae*, dedication.

Arguments from Post-Reformation Era Scholars

In the eighteenth century, Jones was responding to challenges from a recent book which asserted that the Gospels were for a long while unknown and concealed.[71] While Cockburne was countering those who "have endeavored by subtle evasions to reason us out of the most important doctrines of the Christian faith, which they have represented with their usual modesty, as contradictory and absurd, or have explained away, by their artificial comments, the plain sense of the text, and the common belief of Christians, in order to accommodate them to certain schemes of moderation."[72]

In the nineteenth century, Birks begins his work by speaking of contemporaries who claim that the Gospels "are not real histories, but a collection of early legends," whose "composition must be referred to a date very considerably removed from the events they profess to record," with the "earliest barely preceding the fall of Jerusalem."[73] Thus, the Gospels are accused of "infidelity," charges are made against the accuracy of numerous accounts, and the German critics even go so far as speaking of the "inventive fertility of the writer of the third gospel."[74] Upham understood that he had a duty to respond to "the insolence . . . of infidels" who claimed that the church "knows nothing of her own records," that the "Gospels are later than the time of the disciples . . . their character [being] legendary and superstitious," that they are later than the epistles, that "the disciples never thought of any written memorial to their Lord," etc.[75] Accordingly, Upham endeavors to provide answers to "the time, the writers, and the inspiration of the Gospels."[76]

To recap, these authors were motivated to defend the authenticity and authority of the Gospels, part of which was accomplished by defending an early date for the first written Gospel. And unsurprisingly, these same attacks on the veracity of the Gospels continue even to this day, with one modern author asserting that the Gospels are perhaps 80 percent accurate.[77] Others

---

71. Jones refers to a *Notion of the Gospels* written by Hobbes, Toland, and Dodwell. Jones, *Setting the Canonical Authority*, 3:160, 163. Also, Cockburne, *Historical Dissertation*, 1:58–59.

72. Cockburne, *Historical Dissertation*, 1:liv.

73. Birks, *Horae Evangelicae*, 1–2.

74. The assertions of Strauss, Schleiermacher, Neander, and others are repeatedly countered by Birks. Birks, *Horae Evangelicae*, 37, 330–31.

75. Upham, *Thoughts on the Holy Gospels*, 14.

76. Upham, *Thoughts on the Holy Gospels*, 14.

77. McIver, *Memory*, 20, 22; McIver, "Collective Memory," 132, 143.

skeptically speak of the Gospels as "refracted memories of Jesus, bent or skewed in a certain direction. But if we can recognize what these bents are . . . we can still get back to probably authentic information about Jesus."[78] And one modern textbook critically highlights the issue: "we should not assume that the Gospel accounts are necessarily unreliable simply because they are late, but the dates should give us pause."[79] This skeptical assessment illustrates the apologetic value which an early Gospels proposition provides, if embraced. Thus, the need to continue defending the Gospels yet remains.

Appropriately, Phil Fernandes has challenged evangelical apologists to reject popular modern dating theories and instead press the question, "how early could the four Gospels have been written?"[80] Perhaps, therefore, it is time to recognize that our apologetic forebears had it right, that the early dates must be defended and that the motivational argument is central to such, supported by internal evidence and a careful reading of the church fathers.

CONCLUSION

There is indeed a rich history of post-Reformation era scholars who contended that the first Gospel, Matthew, was published within a few years or perhaps within roughly a decade of the ascension. They leveraged both the writings of the church fathers and internal evidence to make their case; but more significantly, they argued that the situation and needs of the early church served to motivate the early publication of Matthew. This chapter has aspired to allow the present reader to hear these authors on their own terms. And in their own words, these authors have demonstrated that they considered an early publication of Matthew to be defensible based on the perceived situation of the early church. Future research might investigate how their arguments were contested by their antagonists.

This view that Matthew was published within a decade was widely disseminated in the United States during the 1800s, with many Bible editions including a chart: "Account of the Dates or Time of Writing the Books of the

---

78. Blomberg and Seal, "Recent Scholarship," 50. This is a paraphrase of the conclusion in Donne, *Historiographical Jesus*, 268.

79. Ehrman, *New Testament*, 44.

80. Fernandes, "Redating the Gospels," 488.

New Testament."[81] The chart, according to research by the New York Bible Society and New York Library, was composed by Dr. John Witherspoon and first appeared in a Bible in 1791, as English language Bibles began to be printed in America.[82] Per Witherspoon, Matthew's Gospel was written thirty-nine years after the birth of Christ, and Mark's Gospel forty-three years after the birth of Christ.[83] Although, at least one Bible in 1807 deferred instead to Lardner's dates, placing Matthew and Mark in the AD 60s.[84] The early Scofield Bibles (1909 and 1919) continued to promote to the public this view that Matthew was written early, in AD 37, but that Mark was written between AD 57 and 63.[85] In the United Kingdom, a more limited selection of Bible printings included date assessments, such as Bishop Wilson's statement in a 1785 printing that "St. Matthew wrote within eight, St. Mark within ten [years] . . . after the ascension."[86] And the Newcome Bible (1808) listed three potential Gospel publication dates—from Lardner, Owen, and Townson.[87] Hence, the opinions of our post-Reformation era scholars, with regard to the early dating of Matthew, were widely propagated particularly in America.

We owe a debt of gratitude to these apologists, as they defended the credibility of the Gospels against contemporary attacks, attacks which leveraged the narrative that the first Gospel was not published until decades after the ascension. Nor should it be surprising that attacks on biblical integrity yet persist into the modern era, despite numerous apologetic efforts seeking to advance the speculative proposition that oral tradition was capable of preserving the integrity of the Gospel contents over multiple decades, until evangelists were finally motivated to publish the life story and teachings of Jesus. Therefore, I suggest that the arguments of these post-Reformation era writers ought to be incorporated into our modern Gospel origins dialogue. Let us grant that this *motivational argument* for the early publication of Matthew offers a coherent and reasonable perspective on

81. For example, *Holy Bible (Greenough)*.

82. Hills, *English Bible in America*, 7.

83. I've collected images of Bibles from 1810, 1815, 1817, 1823, 1828, 1834, 1840, 1842, 1850, 1852, 1862, and 1870, all from different printers, which employed the Witherspoon chart. A Bible published in 1847 had its own chart, listing Matthew as AD 37 and Mark as AD 65. Nourse, *Holy Bible*.

84. Etheridge, *Holy Bible*.

85. Scofield and Schuyler, *Scofield Reference Bible*.

86. Cruttwell, *Holy Bible*.

87. Newcome, *New Testament*, xxv–xxvi.

Gospel origins. Indeed, some contemporary authors, such as Michael Bird, have recognized the legitimacy of elements of the argument as "a conserving force" behind the preservation and transmission of the Jesus tradition, though without recognizing that the motivational argument drives not merely to an oral preservation of the tradition over decades, but to publications in the near proximity of the ascension itself.[88]

Nevertheless, regardless of one's view of the Gospel dates, the arguments advanced by these writers are helpful for explaining the motivation behind the eventual publication of the Gospels.

---

88. Bird, *Gospel of the Lord*, 66. Craig Blomberg nicely summarizes Bird's reasons for wanting to accurately preserve the traditions. "These include practical guidance for Christian living, help for defining the Jesus-movement over against other forms of Judaism in the polemical environment of those early years, biographical interest in the movement's founder, authentication of its beliefs and practices in the context of all the various religious and philosophical alternatives of the day, the desire to imitate Jesus' example, and sheer curiosity and interest in the figure of Jesus." Blomberg, *Historical Reliability of the Gospels*, 66.

6

Arguments from the Ancients on Memory and Orators

Rejecting Bauckham's Eyewitness Memory Theory

And the mind, being like wax, having received the impression, keeps it carefully in itself until forgetfulness, the enemy of memory, has smoothed off the edges of the impression, or else has rendered it dim, or perhaps has completely effaced it.[1]

THESE TIMELESS WORDS OF Philo, a contemporary of both Jesus and the apostles, reflect a reality of the human condition which has been conceded throughout the ages, that memory is fleeting. Storytellers and audiences alike recognize that memories fade, with time, with age, with the retelling of the stories, and as the stories are passed down through others. Where literacy is available this frailty is resisted, as notes are taken, speeches are transcribed, and books are published. Otherwise, societies must rely on individual and community memories for preserving both stories and speeches.

With respect to the epic saga of Jesus, the limitations of memory are a central concern in gauging the reliability of the Gospel accounts, as many

---

1. Philo has in view here a wax writing tablet. Philo, *That God Is Unchangeable* 43 (Yonge, 161).

modern scholars maintain that the earliest Gospels were not published until thirty to fifty years after the resurrection of Jesus.[2] Some scholars assert that this delay did not adversely affect the integrity of the Gospel accounts. For example, Richard Bauckham has argued that Jesus's life and teachings were faithfully preserved due to the personal memories of those who were eyewitnesses of Jesus's ministry.[3] Other scholars discount Bauckham's proposition, contending that eyewitness memories should not be considered as reliable over an extended period. Academic journals and textbooks happily debate this topic.[4] Yet, what both Bauckham and his critics fail to consider are the perspectives of the first-century audiences, and how their attitudes concerning the reliability of long-term memories might have affected their response to the gospel message, under the premise that decades transpired before the first Gospel was published.

In fact, contemporary Greco-Roman authors expressed concern over the reliability of memory, particularly as witnesses aged.[5] And, at the same time, they taught that those practicing the art of oration should be active writers. Correspondingly, these attitudes may well have been shared by those receiving the earliest published Gospels.[6] Even the eyewitnesses, who were motivated to preserve and promote the Jesus traditions (John 20:30–31; 1 Cor 11:2, 23), would have been cognizant of these cultural biases.[7] Consequently, if those of the first century were nominally predisposed against a reliance on long-term memory, then this would undermine the historical credibility of Bauckham's present theory, that the church was satisfied to wait decades before publishing the earliest Gospels, because the

---

2. The bibliography below lists several useful texts which speak to the preservation of the oral traditions.

3. "They [the eyewitnesses] are the obvious people to have controlled this [the tradition] in the interest of faithful preservation." Bauckham, *Jesus and the Eyewitnesses*, 306. Bauckham presumes that Mark was published in the AD 60s, thirty years after the death of Jesus, and that Matthew and Luke were likely published in the AD 80s, with John a little later. Bauckham, *Jesus and the Eyewitnesses*, 14, 19–20, 137.

4. A number of these publications will be cited herein.

5. "Ancient" will be used herein as a synonymous term to refer to these Greco-Roman authors who were roughly contemporary with Jesus and the eyewitnesses.

6. For discussions of ancient publication methods, refer to Alexander and Winsbury. Alexander, "Book Production," 71–105; Winsbury, *Roman Book*.

7. With regard to preserving the traditions, Bauckham affirms, "the early Christian movement had an interest in preserving the traditions about Jesus faithfully." Bauckham, "Gospel Traditions," 389.

eyewitnesses were capable of preserving the integrity of the Gospels primarily through their personal memories.

Therefore, rather than debating whether eyewitness memories were capable of reliably preserving the Jesus tradition over an extended period, the more interesting question is whether the eyewitnesses and original audiences would have agreed that this approach would be advantageous, from an apologetic perspective. How did those of the first century view long-term memory and the use of writing for preserving speeches, history, and witness testimony? This question is important, as Bauckham's theory is currently being used to provide modern apologetic support for Gospel reliability, and hence authority, and yet it is not clear that the theory has adequate merit when these ancient perspectives are considered.

GRECO-ROMAN VERSUS MODERN PERSPECTIVES ON MEMORY

In this chapter, after elaborating on Bauckham's proposition and the modern challenges to such, we will consider contemporary Greco-Roman perspectives on the frailties of memory, particularly due to aging. Likewise, we will consider their perspectives on the relationship between reading, writing, and oratory practices, and particularly the expectations which were placed on orators to put their orations in writing. Whereas much of the recent Gospel-related orality debate has been leveraging research on rabbinic Jewish traditions of the second century, this chapter will instead focus on Greco-Roman perspectives, while also including the perspectives of a few hellenized Jews who operated outside of Palestine. It is the voice of Greco-Roman authors who were roughly contemporary with Jesus and the eyewitnesses which this chapter seeks to hear. From Cicero in the mid-first century BC to Plutarch in the early second century AD, these writers help to inform our understanding of the period.[8]

---

8. Between Cicero and Plutarch, we will also listen to Sallust, from the mid to late first century BC, to Livy and Philo, from the late first century BC to the early first century AD, and to Pliny the elder and Quintilian, from the mid to late first century AD. Josephus and Tacitus, contemporaries with Plutarch, will also make brief appearances, as will others. Approximate dating is per Evans, *Ancient Texts*, 168, 173–74, 287–98; Ulery Jr., "Sallust," 300. Ultimately, we will argue that, while the ancients valued eyewitness testimony, the original audiences of the Gospels would have been skeptical of long-term eyewitness memory as the primary means for reliably preserving the Jesus traditions. Given this skepticism, it can be inferred that the contemporary audiences would have neither

Ultimately, the research will not categorically disprove Bauckham's theory, as we lack sufficient historical records to make confident claims about Gospel origins. That said, in this chapter I will argue, based on the perspectives of the contemporary authors, that many among the original Gospel audiences would likely have found the Gospels to be less reliable and convincing, if the content was known to have been preserved over several decades primarily based on the long-term memories of aging eyewitnesses, without corresponding written or even published materials. This realization should lead us to question whether it is reasonable to assume that the early church would indeed have waited for decades before publishing.

Several Assumptions

Several assumptions will be leveraged in this chapter. First, it will be assumed that the early church sufficiently interacted with the literate segments of Greco-Roman society to be sensitive to their perspectives. Second, it will be assumed that many of those who applauded the oratory performances, whether in the courtrooms or theaters, were aware of and respected the opinions of the famous orators. Expressed another way, it will be assumed that the great orators and writers not only communicated their views to their literary heirs, but also spoke their views into contemporary society. This is not a claim that a preponderance of the population necessarily subscribed to this viewpoint. But it is a claim that, as the early church presented the Jesus traditions to those of the various socioeconomic classes, particularly outside of Judea, they would have encountered a meaningful and influential segment of society who shared the views expressed by contemporary authors. These assumptions are elaborated below. However, before addressing these historical assumptions, I will presuppose that the present reader is generally familiar with the scholarly debates concerning the origins of the Gospels.

---

desired nor expected the eyewitnesses to primarily preserve the Gospel accounts in their personal memories, without writing out and publishing the story of Jesus.

Arguments from the Ancients on Memory and Orators

Assumption #1: Readers Are Familiar with the Orality Debate regarding the Preservation of the Jesus Traditions

It is assumed in this chapter that the present reader has some knowledge of modern Gospel origin theories and of the corresponding orality debate, which speculates as to how the oral traditions (sometimes characterized as "oral history") concerning Jesus were developed and preserved by the Christian community until the traditions were inscribed into what became the canonical Gospels. Birger Gerhardsson, Kenneth Bailey, Werner Kelber, Samuel Byrskog, Jan Vansina, and others have made substantial contributions in this field in recent decades.[9] In addition, a variety of scholarly dissertations have surveyed the range of proposed theories for how the gospel traditions might have been preserved, by way of introducing their more targeted research.[10] Our present study will not retrace the proponents and movements of this debate but will narrowly focus on Bauckham's theory. Several of the pertinent writings are listed in the bibliography.

Assumption #2: The Early Church Interacted with Literate Segments of Society

The New Testament indicates that the early Christian evangelists and apostles engaged directly with the elites of Greco-Roman society, with those who were most likely to be literate or to have had ready access to professional scribes. Within this circle of literacy, I include not only governmental officials and their administrative subordinates but also nobles and those of the upper classes who managed substantive commercial enterprises and property holdings. Indeed, Roger Bagnall has shown that there was a ubiquitous use of written records, such as contracts and property records, across the eastern Hellenistic world, and by extension across the whole of the Roman republic, which was in proportion to an individual's economic status and needs.[11] Almost inevitably, as the gospel was preached, the early

---

9. The following texts speculate as to how the oral traditions may have been preserved. Bailey, "Informal Controlled Oral Tradition," 4–11; Byrskog, *Story as History*; Gerhardsson, *Memory and Manuscript*; Vansina, *Oral Tradition as History*; Kelber, "Rethinking the Transmission," 500, 503.

10. Brewer, "Models for the Oral Transmission," 9–273; Christian, "Restoring the Unique Voices," 13–24; Ewing, "Preference for Oral Tradition," 57–71.

11. Bagnall, *Everyday Writing*, 52. Botha, with reference to Roman Egypt, likewise speaks of a class of local or minor gentry, based out of the thirty administrative capitals,

church interacted with this elite community. Even within Judea, Philip was led to speak with an Ethiopian eunuch, a court official and chief treasurer of the queen, who was heard reading from the prophet Isaiah (Acts 8:27–29), and Peter was directed to witness to Cornelius, a military official of the Roman cohort, who was based in the provincial capital, along with Cornelius's friends and those of his household (Acts 10:1, 24). On Cyprus, as Paul began his missionary activity, he was summoned for a private audience by the proconsul in Paphos, "a man of intelligence" (13:7 ESV). In Berea, it was not only the "more noble" Jews who believed, after examining the Scriptures, but also a number of Greeks "of high standing" (17:11–12). Arguably, many of the synagogue leaders with whom Paul interacted, and particularly those based in the larger Greco-Roman cities, such as in Philippi, Ephesus, Corinth, and Athens, were literate, as they held prestigious positions and presumably had their own collections of religious scrolls. And, being well removed from the heartland of Judaism, these leaders no doubt shared many of the literary-related sentiments of their pagan neighbors.[12] In Athens, Paul also interacted with the philosophers of the various schools (17:18), schools which were known as having their own sacred texts. In Corinth, Paul lectured in the hall of Tyrannus for two years, during which he certainly interacted with some of the local elites, who might be envisioned as taking notes on tablets and scrolls during his oral performances (19:9–10). Given these examples, it should not be necessary to belabor this point further. Clearly, the apostles directly engaged with the literate elites of Greco-Roman society, including those who would have had little regard for any provincial Jewish proclivity for an exclusively oral preservation of religious traditions.[13]

---

who "used their wealth in ways that combined conspicuous consumption with social prestige . . . who, generally speaking, could read and write." Botha, "Greco-Roman Literacy as Setting," 204.

12. "Jews became exposed to and thoroughly engaged with the Greek culture that prevailed in the various communities in which they settled [in the diaspora]." Gruen, "Hellenistic Judaism," 22.

13. Gerhardsson is a key proponent of the theory that the early church would have been averse to publishing the Jesus traditions, due to rabbinic influences. He argues that the disciples were "from that section of [the Jewish] people who looked to the learned Pharisees as its teachers and spiritual leaders . . . Pharisaic Judaism stressed energetically the distinction between written and oral Torah, and opposed tendencies, towards both the written transmission of the oral Torah, and the recognition of copies of such material as official books." Gerhardsson, *Memory and Manuscript*, 201–2. This is a view which Bauckham challenges, although he also notes that elsewhere Gerhardsson does

Of course, it was also this literate class who facilitated the public reading of the NT writings; surely, this would have included many who were steeped in Greco-Roman literary traditions. In this context, Philemon and those of his household immediately come to mind, as representing presumably non-Jewish church leaders who were necessarily literate (Phlm 1:1). Indeed, Timothy himself, having a Greek father, may well have been raised and trained on the masters of Greco-Roman literature (Acts 16:1).

Some scholars may contest the implications of these Christian engagements with the literate segments of Greco-Roman society. Therefore, for our purposes, we will merely take this as a reasoned assumption that, given these direct interactions, the early church would have been sensitive to perspectives regarding memory and the publishing of materials, as expressed by the contemporary authors whose voices we will hear below.

Assumption #3: Contemporary Writers Spoke into the Contemporary Milieu

At the heart of much of the modern orality debate is the debate over Christian literacy. A number of scholars conceive of the early Jesus movement as living "in a milieu that was largely illiterate." They believe that, not only was "Christianity birthed, and its traditions first circulated, in a predominantly oral culture," but that this oral culture was markedly disconnected from the Greco-Roman literary culture which had existed for half a millennium.[14] We are told by these scholars that to make progress in biblical studies, one must "'imagine the oral period' for the sake of historical authenticity."[15] Needless to say, the challenge in this approach is that it largely denies to the modern researcher the utility of the very documents left behind by the great writers of the era, who provide insight into the era. While we will touch on this dichotomy later, this chapter will resist the contention that the early church was disconnected from contemporary literary influences, but will rather take it as a reasoned assumption that the contemporary Greco-Roman writers not only spoke about the contemporary milieu, but

---

acknowledge that the rabbis allowed for the use of private notebooks. Bauckham, *Jesus and the Eyewitnesses*, 251–52.

14. Iverson, "Orality and Gospels," 71–72.

15. Iverson, while lamenting the lack of progress in advancing the orality paradigm, acknowledges "the challenge of hypothesizing about oral traditions from textual artifacts—a daunting task by any standard." Iverson, "Orality and Gospels," 72.

also spoke *into* that milieu through stage performances and the influence of cultural elites, much as modern television programming both describes and impresses itself on modern society, impacting even those who don't invest endless daylight hours in staring at their screens and monitors.

Theaters and amphitheaters existed throughout the empire. Accordingly, Rex Winsbury reminds us that "Cicero identified the stage with the people ... [and] Strabo tells us that poetry can fill theatres." Indeed, "it was the sheer orality of Roman life that provided the context for the movement of styles and stories to and from and between elite and popular cultures ... the themes, stories and moralities that informed [the] literature spanned all classes and indeed all or most of the many ethnicities within the empire."[16] Thus, even though the masses did not share the literary capabilities of the elite and bureaucratic classes, they were exposed to the literary world and to the perspectives of its most influential voices. This naturally had parallels within the early Christian experience, as the literature of the church was publicly read (or performed), to an audience which was expected to adopt the expressed themes and convictions (Col 4:16; 1 Thess 5:27; 1 Tim 4:13). In this context, my assumption does not presume that the predominantly non-literate society uniformly adopted the perspectives expressed in the public performances of contemporary authors, but merely that some did.

Eyewitness Controlled Transmission

Bauckham's Eyewitness Memory Theory

In *Jesus and the Eyewitnesses*, Richard Bauckham argues that the Gospels consist of oral traditions which were carefully guarded by the eyewitnesses, based on their personal memories.[17] This approach purports to offer a reputable basis for reading the Gospels both "in a properly historical way and a properly theological way," and postures the Gospels for providing authentic "access to the historical reality of Jesus."[18] In this, Bauckham admirably participates in the apologetic efforts of the church fathers whom he cites, in defending the authority of the Gospels, and many modern Christian

---

16. Further, "it is this theatrical link that demonstrates the essential continuity between the oral-written culture of the literate upper-class minority, and the oral-visual culture of the rest ... of the semi-literate or illiterate Roman populace." Winsbury, *Roman Book*, 151–52, 171.

17. Bauckham, *Jesus and the Eyewitnesses*, 259.

18. Bauckham, *Jesus and the Eyewitnesses*, 5–6.

apologists have subsequently embraced his reasoning.[19] In making this claim, his theory seeks to portray the Gospels as worthy of being treated as eyewitness testimony and thus afforded the same credibility which eyewitness testimony typically warrants. Certainly, the New Testament authors often asserted their role and authority as eyewitnesses to Jesus's ministry (e.g., Luke 1:2; John 19:35; 21:24; Acts 1:8; 1 Pet 5:1; 1 John 1:1), so Bauckham's conjecture naturally aligns with this dynamic.

Bauckham's chapter on Eyewitness Memory begins with an acknowledgment that there is popular skepticism concerning personal memories, as "we all know from experience that memory is fallible."[20] But, he then explains that *recollective memory*, which is personal memory of certain types of events, is capable of very accurate reconstruction of the events.[21] Thus, he positions the witnesses to serve as guarantors of the Jesus traditions, guarding the reliability of what would become the written Gospels.[22] According to Bauckham, the following factors generally contribute to which events are remembered best: (1) the unusual nature of the events, (2) the consequence of the events, (3) the emotional involvement of the participant, and (4) the frequent rehearsal of the events.[23] These factors are explored further in his subsequent writings.[24]

Bauckham attributes the variations found in the Gospels to five factors unrelated to memory deficiencies.[25] For example, he emphasizes the role which the Gospel authors had in selecting and integrating the life story and teachings of Jesus into a literary whole and in constructing an overall

---

19. Bauckham, *Jesus and the Eyewitnesses*, 428. Modern apologists who have embraced Bauckham's proposition include Norman Geisler, Douglas Groothuis, Andreas Köstenberger and Michael Kruger, and J. Warner Wallace. Geisler, *Christian Apologetics*, 348–49; Groothuis, *Christian Apologetics*, 452; Wallace, *Cold-Case Christianity*, 266; Köstenberger and Kruger, *Heresy of Orthodoxy*, 71–72.

20. Bauckham, *Jesus and the Eyewitnesses*, 319.

21. Bauckham, *Jesus and the Eyewitnesses*, 324, 329–30.

22. Bauckham, *Jesus and the Eyewitnesses*, 262, 346.

23. Bauckham also identifies several characterizations which may indicate which of the memories are likely more accurate; although, he then explains why many of these characteristics are not generally found in the Gospels, due to the limitations of publishing written accounts. Bauckham, *Jesus and the Eyewitnesses*, 330–35, 341–46. Also, Bauckham, "General and Particular in Memory," 43.

24. Note that Bauckham's *Jesus and the Eyewitnesses* was first published in 2006. A second edition was published in 2017.

25. Bauckham, "Eyewitnesses and Critical History," 229.

theological interpretation.²⁶ His point is that there are legitimate reasons for variations between the Gospels, which are not indicative of memory lapses or unauthorized changes to the traditions. Thus, he expresses more confidence in the reliability of the Gospels than is anticipated by other popular theories for the preservation of the oral traditions, including Gerhardsson's rabbinic memorization approach and Byrskog's theory of uncontrolled transmission.²⁷

Although he does acknowledge that some quantity of written notes and formal memorization were involved in the early preservation of the traditions, and that tradents in the various communities also contributed, yet according to Bauckham, "among them the eyewitnesses would surely have been the most important" for guarding the traditions and ensuring their reliability.²⁸ As part of a "formal process of tradition," it was the "authorized tradents, who, from their own familiarity with the tradition, would be competent to make" changes, such as "deliberate interpretative alterations or additions" to the "sayings material."²⁹

Elsewhere, Bauckham cites several ancient authors in order to demonstrate that they recognized that factual credibility was important to their audiences, as also was the use of eyewitness sources.³⁰ This is indeed well supported by the contemporary literature. However, while citing ancient authors in making his case, he fails to address their related concerns regarding the accuracy of the witnesses themselves, particularly as time passed and as the witnesses became elderly.

---

26. Bauckham, "Eyewitnesses and Critical History," 229–30; Bauckham, *Jesus and the Eyewitnesses*, 286.

27. For example, Gerhardsson points out that "even the rabbis could rework their traditions, changing formulations, cancel elements, and insert additions and new layers." Gerhardsson, *Memory and Manuscript*, xix. But Gerhardsson goes further, "Despite careful transmission, the occurrence of certain small alterations as a result of faulty memorization cannot be excluded." Gerhardsson, *Memory and Manuscript*, 335.

28. Bauckham, *Jesus and the Eyewitnesses*, 259, 283–85, 289, 292, 306. Ewing suggests that, rather than the twelve, perhaps the Seventy (or Seventy-Two) per Luke 10:1 should be visualized as the circle of eyewitnesses who carried the authority for preserving the traditions. Ewing, "Preference for Oral Tradition," 59–60.

29. Bauckham, "Eyewitnesses and Critical History," 286.

30. Bauckham, "Response to the Respondents," 529–31.

Arguments from the Ancients on Memory and Orators

A Challenge to Bauckham's Eyewitnesses Memory Theory

Robert McIver has published a useful counterpoint to Bauckham's presentation of eyewitness memory, in *Memory, Jesus, and the Synoptic Gospel*. In his introduction, he makes an initial assessment that, "much can happen to traditions that are preserved in human memories for this length of time," referring to the supposed decades before the Jesus traditions were written down.[31] McIver focuses much of his attention on the frailties of memory, in the areas of transience, suggestibility, and hindsight bias. These can drive variations in details and also drive falsehoods, not only when eyewitness testimony is presented in court, but also when past events are remembered in general.[32] While affirming that eyewitness testimony offers general reliability, he contends that it usually contains a mixture of correct and incorrect recollections, resulting in perhaps 80 percent accuracy.[33]

The applicability of some of the studies referenced by McIver may legitimately be discounted, as Bauckham shows in his responses to other critics.[34] For example, McIver's referencing of studies which involve the memorization of lists and the recollection of a foreign language learned in high school or college hardly seems equivalent to the significance of one's personal involvement in the ministry of Jesus.[35] However, McIver also presents studies in which the test subjects were allowed to be selective in the details which they volunteered against their own *flashbulb* memories, which he defines as a particularly strong memory of a momentous event which

---

31. McIver, *Memory*, 1.

32. McIver, *Memory*, 10–11.

33. McIver, *Memory*, 20, 22. Also, McIver, "Collective Memory," 132, 143. One must be amused by Craig Blomberg's positive spin on McIver's study, as he asserts that "McIver has certainly shown that, even without [a belief in inspiration], a strong case can be made for the trustworthiness of the Gospels in their main contours and doubtless in many details, even if we can't always be quite sure as to which ones," as though this leaves one with a view of the Gospels which is of any use for founding one's faith on. Blomberg, "Memory, Jesus, and the Synoptic Gospels," 326. Blomberg and Seal also paraphrase another skeptical researcher, "what we have are refracted memories of Jesus, bent or skewed in a certain direction. But if we can recognize what these bents are ... we can still get back to probable authentic information about Jesus." Blomberg and Seal, "Recent Scholarship," 50; Donne, *Historiographical Jesus*, 268.

34. Bauckham, "General and Particular in Memory," 37–40, 50–51. Similar objections to the application to certain kinds of memory studies is raised in Bauckham, "Psychology of Memory."

35. McIver, *Memory*, 23, 25; McIver, "Collective Memory," 140.

"combines surprise, indiscriminate illumination, and brevity."[36] These studies demonstrate that memories of even personally meaningful events tend to fade at a rate similar to everyday memories. At the same time, it was found that the test subjects assigned inappropriate levels of confidence to these memories.

Ultimately, McIver applies his concerns to the question of the preservation of the Jesus traditions.[37] Given the role of memory, he is willing to affirm that the Gospels are "generally reliable," while being unconvinced about the accuracy of any particular detail. The introduction of errors is possible "at every stage in the formation, transmission, and preservation of the tradition."[38] As we shall establish, these modern attitudes are not unlike the ancient concerns regarding memory, as expressed by writers who were roughly contemporary with the eyewitnesses and the original audiences. These contemporary writers likewise declared concern over the frailties and transience of memory.

THE ANCIENTS WERE CONCERNED ABOUT MEMORY

In this section, a variety of concerns over memory are highlighted in order to demonstrate that ancient authors, who were roughly contemporary with Jesus and the eyewitnesses, were attentive to mankind's general forgetfulness and the virtually inevitable loss of memory with aging.[39]

36. McIver, *Memory*, 42–46. Unfortunately, for the casual participant in these memory dialogues, Bauckham and McIver focus on slightly different aspects of memory research, and hence use slightly different terms. In Rubin's introduction to his edited work, he cites his contributors as defining *recollective memory* as "a recollection of a particular episode from an individual's past . . . [which] includes a 'reliving' . . . visual imagery . . . and a belief that the remembered episode was personally experienced." In contrast, a *flashbulb memory* leverages "the metaphor of taking a picture," with a focus on "what makes vivid memories vivid." It is these extra details which makes the "memories seem more accurate, thoughtful, and believable." Rubin, "Introduction," 2–3.

37. In his view, the traditions gradually shifted from being preserved by eyewitness to being preserved by the collective, well before the Gospels were written. McIver, *Memory*, 123.

38. McIver, *Memory*, 185. Others take this further. Crossan states, "Memory is as much or more creative reconstruction as accurate recollection, and, unfortunately, it is often impossible to tell where one ends and the other begins." He adds, "Fact and fiction, memory and fantasy, recollection and fabrication are intertwined in remembering." John Dominic Crossan, *Birth of Christianity*, 59–60, as cited in Bird, "Formation of the Gospels," 132.

39. "Loss of mental prowess was one negative feature of old age that was recognized"

Cicero

Marcus Tullius Cicero is considered "the undisputed master of oratory in ancient Rome."[40] In *Cato the Elder on Old Age* (*De senectute*), Cicero presents his reflections on aging and death in a hypothetical discourse between Cato and his younger associates. His statements illustrate well the concern which the ancients had with regard to the mind, as he urges his readers to take action to prevent the degradation which normally occurs with aging:[41]

> But it is our duty, my young friends, to resist old age; to compensate for its defects by a watchful care; to fight against it as we would fight against disease . . . . Nor, indeed, are we to give our attention solely to the body; much greater care is due to the mind and soul; for they, too, like lamps, grow dim with time, unless we keep them supplied with oil . . . . Just as waywardness and lust are more often found in the young man than in the old, yet not in all who are young, but only in those naturally base; so that senile debility, usually called dotage, is a characteristic, not of all old men, but only of those who are weak in mind and will.[42]

Note that while Cicero is arguing that senile debility is the fault of those who are "weak in mind and will," his very comparison with the defects which are characteristic of youth suggests that dotage is likewise more characteristic of the elderly.[43] The effects of aging on the mind are sufficiently prevalent that Cicero is broadly concerned over such.

Through Cato, Cicero opines that, "old men can retain their mental faculties, provided their interest and application continue"; further, they particularly remember those who owe them money, along with their creditors.[44] Accordingly, Cato urges his friends to compensate for the defects of old age, and to not allow themselves to be characterized by the "credulity, forgetfulness and carelessness . . . [and] senile debility" of old age, where "the mind and soul . . . like lamps, grow dim with time."[45] But then, in a

---

during the Roman imperial period. Parkin, *Old Age*, 228.

40. Cicero, *Cicero*, 5. This treatise was written in 45 or 44 BC. May, "Cicero," 80.

41. May, "Cicero," 20.

42. Cicero, *Sen.* 35–36 (Falconer, LCL, 45).

43. Parkin affirms that "Cicero attributes . . . 'that senile foolishness which they call dotage' to a character fault in some old people, but he does not deny its existence." Parkin, *Old Age*, 229.

44. Cicero, *Sen.* 21–23.

45. Cicero, *Sen.* 35–36.

separate letter to Atticus, he expresses more resignation to the inevitable, as "it is still an old man's way to be a trifle forgetful!"[46] Thus, he offers hope for preserving one's mental faculties, but it is clear that old age is generally assumed to bring a growing darkness of mind and the lengthening shadows of forgetfulness, to elaborate on his metaphor.

Sallust

In *The Jugurthine War*, Sallust offers an anecdotal reminder of the impact of age on the mind and the intellect. In the conflict between King Jugurtha of Namibia and the Romans, it is the catalyst which brought Jugurtha to power that is of interest. Jugurtha's adoptive benefactor, the king of Namibia, had in his final years bequeathed the kingdom to Jugurtha, while "being debilitated by age and disease," according to Sallust.[47] Accordingly, on the king's death, the Namibian princes had revoked all of the decrees made in his final several years, as the king was deemed to have "been enfeebled by age, and scarcely sound in intellect."[48] Jugurtha's subsequent retribution against these princes was brutal. Thus, Sallust's tale brought into the Greco-Roman consciousness the deadly consequences which enfeebled minds can precipitate for both men and nations.

Livy

In his fifth book on the *History of Rome*, Livy recounts the reelection of the experienced, but elderly, Publius Licinius Calvus as tribune of soldiers, when Publius had not sought the office.[49] Publius declines the post, given the decay of his body, memory, and mind:

> In me you see no longer the same Publius Licinius, of whom but the shadow and the name are left. My strength of body is decayed, my sight and hearing dulled, memory fails me, and the vigour of

---

46. Cicero, *Att.* 12.1 (Shuckburgh, 3:148).

47. Sallust, *Bell. Jug.* 1, 9.

48. Sallust, *Bell. Jug.* 11. Finley affirms, "the law invalidated contracts and other legal acts performed by anyone suffering from mental incapacity." Finley, "Elderly in Classical Antiquity," 169.

49. The following comment does not affect the point being made above, but Richardson contends that Livy's claim concerning Licinius as the first plebian to be elected consular tribune is false. Richardson, "Complications of Quellenforschung," 178.

> my mind is impaired. Here, he cried, laying hold of his son, here is a young man, the effigy and likeness of him you formerly chose for military tribune first of all plebeians.[50]

In contrast, in a later book, Livy praises Marcus Poscius Cato for retaining his mental acuity, as one who

> had a soul unconquerable by appetites, an unwavering integrity, and a contempt for influence and wealth. In his economy, in his endurance of toil and danger, he was of almost iron-like body and mind, and his mind not even old age, which weakens everything, could break down, since at the age of eighty-six he pleaded a case, spoke and wrote in his own defense.[51]

Thus, in one narrative Livy recalls one who recognized the infirmities of his own age and, in another, one who defied the effects of old age, which are yet reckoned to "weaken everything."

Philo

Concerns regarding old age and memory loss are scattered across Philo's musings.[52] In one passage, he reflects on the arrogance of the human mind, which proudly claims knowledge as its own possession; yet, over the course of time, even the mind has its own thoughts driven from its memory, displaced by other thoughts or by the impact of infirmity or old age.[53] Philo maintains that even the mind's claim that "reasoned thoughts" are its own is absurd:

> When you say they [your thoughts] are yours are you sane or mad to suppose such a thing? Fits of melancholy and insanity, bursts of frenzy, baseless conjectures, false impressions of things . . . loss of memory, the curse which so besets the soul, and other things more numerous than these, sap the security of your [the mind's] lordship, and show that these things are not your possessions but another's.[54]

---

50. Livy, *Ab urbe cond.* 5.18.4–5 (Foster, LCL, 5–7:63).

51. Livy, *Ab urbe cond.* 39.40.7 (Sage, LCL, 38–39:351).

52. In addition to the examples cited, also refer to Philo, *Who Is the Heir?* 249; Philo, *Prelim. Studies* 39–42.

53. Philo, *On the Cherubim* 65–68.

54. Philo, *Cherubim* 69 (Colson et al., LCL, 2:49).

And later, in the same monologue, after asserting that all the qualities of the mind and body are God's gifts and possessions, Philo uses a rhetorical question to make his point.⁵⁵ "Is my mind my own possession? That parent of false conjectures, that purveyor of delusion, the delirious, the fatuous, and in frenzy or melancholy or senility proved to be the very negation of mind.... A little sickness is a cause sufficient to cripple the tongue and sew up the lips of the most eloquent."⁵⁶

Pliny, the Elder

In his books on *The Natural History*, which cover nature and humanity, Pliny offers brief chapters on memory and the mind. After celebrating several men who were reputed to have had splendid memories, Pliny offers the following dose of reality:

> Nothing whatever, in man, is of so frail a nature as the memory; for it is affected by disease, by injuries, and even by fright; being sometimes partially lost, and at other times entirely so. A man, who received a blow from a stone, forgot the names of the letters only; while, on the other hand, another person . . . and so it is, that very often the memory appears to attempt, as it were, to make its escape from us, even while the body is at rest and in perfect health.⁵⁷

Plutarch

As with the others, Plutarch laments the consequences of lost health and of old age, and the accompanying disordering of the senses. This includes the loss of the "assurance and firmness" of memories and even the forgetting of "Dion sneezing or Theon playing at ball"; elsewhere, he describes age as having all of the symptoms of drunkenness—the "faltering of the tongue, babbling . . . forgetfulness, and distraction of the mind."⁵⁸ Thus, he is very aware of the transience of memory. Interestingly, whereas

---

55. Philo, *Cherubim* 65, 84, 118.
56. Philo, *Cherubim* 116 (Colson et al., LCL, 2:77).
57. Pliny, *Naturalis historia* 7.24 (Bostock and Riley, 2:2165).
58. Plutarch, *Plutarch's Morals*, 377. Plutarch, *De communibus notitiis contra stoicos* 7; Plutarch, *Quaestionum convivalum* 3.3.1.

ARGUMENTS FROM THE ANCIENTS ON MEMORY AND ORATORS

Plutarch admires the extraordinary memories of those of the ancient past for passing down history and mythology, he appreciates the fact that written materials were now available, given the difficulty of retaining the earlier works in memory.[59]

Summary

In summary, this section has aspired to illustrate the sentiments of several ancient authors who were roughly contemporary with Jesus and the apostles, who voiced concerns regarding memory, and particularly that of the aged. The voices of Juvenal and others might be added to the chorus.[60] Under the premise that these views were present in the contemporary society, whether dominant or as an under-current, they would arguably influence the reliability with which the Gospel audiences might naturally assign to the stories of Jesus and of his teachings, under Bauckham's paradigm. Consequently, in the context of the sentiments expressed above, Gospel audiences can be envisioned as naturally being skeptical about reliance on long-term witness memories for accurately preserving the traditions.

THE GREAT ORATORS ENCOURAGED WRITING

In this section, my ambition is to illustrate the perspectives of ancient authors regarding the interplay between reading, writing, and oration. As we shall see, this includes the use of writing for preserving history and testimony. This chapter will show, at least from the perspective of the cited authors, that there were both reading and writing expectations of orators in the Greco-Roman culture, of those who were roughly contemporary with Jesus and the early church. Historians had similar expectations. The point being, that those proclaiming Jesus's events and teachings, and desiring to preserve such, would feel pressured to write such down promptly. Correspondingly, it will be shown that it is reasonable to argue that a first-century audience would expect the apostles and other eyewitnesses, as orators and

---

59. Plutarch, *De Pythiae oraculis* 27.

60. For example, "But worse than all bodily loss is dementia, which recognizes neither the names of servants nor the face of a friend with whom she dined last night, nor those she bore, those she reared." Juvenal, *Satires* 10.232–236; Ulery Jr., "De Senectute Studiorum," 232.

guardians of the traditions, to both draft out their messages in writing and to distribute their speeches.

Cicero

In *On the Orator*, Cicero crafts a hypothetical discourse between several famous orators in order to instruct future statesmen on the art and techniques of oration.[61] Within the dialogue, Cicero speaks to the function of oratory, the expectations of the orator, etc. For Cicero, an orator must do more than just develop graceful eloquence and practice in speaking *ex tempore* or *in the moment*. Rather, Cicero asserts the importance of the careful drafting of the message. "Write as much as possible. The pen is the best and most eminent author and teacher of eloquence . . . all the thoughts and expressions . . . needs flow up in succession to the point of our pen . . . the actual marshalling and arrangement of words is made perfect in the course of writing, in a rhythm and measure proper to oratory as distinct from poetry."[62] Accordingly, Cicero admires Plato as one who died "pen in hand."[63] Cicero also demonstrates an implied expectation that speeches should be preserved in writing, as he frequently refers to the publication of both his own speeches and to those of others.[64]

Many of Cicero's writings have been preserved. In his several orations against Catiline, Cicero writes of a trial in which he was a protagonist,

---

61. Cicero, *De or.*, 1–2:xi.

62. Cicero, *De or.* 1.3, 1.32–33. Also, Cicero, *De or.* 2.84, 3.44. More broadly, the orator must also devote himself to constant reading and writing, "for the genuine orator must have investigated and heard and read and discussed and handled and debated the whole of the contents of the life of mankind, inasmuch as that is the field of the orator's activity, the subject matter of his study." Cicero, *De or.* 3.14. Also, Cicero, *De or.* 1.21.

63. Cicero, *Sen.* 13. Plato himself was conflicted over the invention of writing, lamenting its destructive impact on the human memory and on the development of "true wisdom," which requires not only reading, but also instruction and experience (Plato, *Phaedrus* 274c–275c). For, as the written text is fixed, it cannot interact with the arguments raised by the student, and thus "cannot teach the truth effectually" (Plato, *Phaedrus* 275d–276c). Yet, at the same time, he valued it as a means of "reminding," that one might "treasure up reminders for himself, when he comes to the forgetfulness of old age, and for others who follow the same path" (Plato, *Phaedrus* 275a, 276d). And to this end, he wrote extensively, "in the form of dialogues, preserving to some degree the active, living relationship between teacher and student." Botha, *Orality and Literacy*, 29–30.

64. Cicero, *Att.* 1.16; 2.20; 14.20; Cicero, *Epistulae ad familiares* 5.4; 15.6; Cicero, *Amic.* 96.

where several conspirators were condemned based on their intercepted letters, which were submitted as principal evidence in the trial.[65] Not only did Cicero publish his own words and the play by play of the trial, but he also had copies of the extracted confessions dispersed throughout all of Italy and the provinces.[66] This illustrates not only Cicero's propensity for publishing, but also provides insight into the use of written materials in the legal proceedings of Rome, as written statements (both the letters and recorded confessions) were deemed sufficiently authoritative for the rendering of judgment. It also demonstrates the society's high regard for written accounts of recent events and dialogues; this speaks to the anticipated interest in the events and dialogues preserved concerning Jesus.[67]

For another one of his books, *Laelius on Friendship*, Cicero claims to have recounted from memory the main points of a series of dialogues which he had with Laelius, which then became the basis for a hypothetical discourse between Laelius and several others.[68] This example demonstrates not only Cicero's capable memory, but also the importance which this great orator placed in subsequently moving his work to a written format.[69]

Philo

For Philo, those whom he considered to be orators were the prophets, sages, and kings of Israel, who spoke the oracles of God: "our witnesses are the oracles which Moses wrote in the sacred books."[70] While Philo does not generally delineate expectations of orators, relative to reading and writing, the Jewish history which he elaborates is filled with orators whose writings were published and with orators who clearly read from their predecessors. In one passage, he speaks of the training of the Levites, whom Moses established as the guardians of the oracles of God (compare Rom 3:2).

---

65. Cicero, *In Catalinum* 3.5. The official records of the trial had not yet been published. Cicero, *Cat.* 3.6.

66. Cicero, *Cicero Orations*, 302.

67. The legal appeal to written commissions and documentary evidence is also illustrated in Cicero, *Pro Archia* 4.8; Cicero, *Pro Flacco* 16.39.

68. Cicero, *Amic.* 1, 3.

69. With regard to his speeches, not only did he write out many of his speeches for distribution, but when he had a "lapse in memory" during an oration, he would have the distributed copies corrected. Cicero, *De Officiis* 2.3; Cicero, *Att.* 13.44.

70. Philo, *Cherubim* 124. Similarly, in Philo, *On the Life of Moses* 2.188; Philo, *On the Rewards and Punishments* 1; Philo, *On Giants* 49; Philo, *On Planting* 137–38.

According to Philo, at twenty-five years of age the Levites were appointed to active service in the Tabernacle of Witness, while studying and being taught the "doctrines and principles of wisdom."[71] Then, at fifty years of age, the Levites ceased this work and become the trusted "guardians of the words and covenant of God," having entrusted these words to memory, and now being prepared to speak forth God's judgments and laws.[72] Thus, he shows that those who would speak on behalf of God must be intimate with the written Scriptures and that it was these written Scriptures which were to be committed to memory.

Quintilian

In his *Institutes of Oratory*, Quintilian methodically breaks down the art of oratory and shows the close relationship between reading, writing, and oratory. In his introduction he asserts that a student may have a good voice, endurance and grace, but, "they are of no profit in themselves unless cultivated by skillful teaching, persistent study and continuous and extensive practice in writing, reading and speaking."[73] Quintilian declares that the art "consists of five parts—invention, arrangement, expression, memory, and delivery."[74] *Invention* is focused on the orator's strategy for persuading the judge or audience, their arguments and proofs, and whether these involve documents, forced confessions, or witness testimony, submitted in writing or in person.[75] *Arrangement* involves the methods of division, preparation, and proof. According to Quintilian, "our pen must be slow yet sure, we must search for what is best . . . and then, once approved, arrange them with care. For we must select both thoughts and words and weigh them one by one. This done, we must consider the order . . . [and] thus secure a better connection between what follows and what precedes."[76] Likewise, he states

---

71. Philo, *That the Worse Attacks the Better* 63–66.
72. Philo, *That the Worse Attacks the Better* 65–68.
73. Quintilian, *Inst.* 1.0.1; 1.0.27. Quintilian adds that a father who has high hopes for his son must train him intentionally, from an early age, steadily improving his skills in reading, writing, and in the use of his memory. Quintilian, *Inst.* 1.1.1, 15–19, 27–37. The importance of preparing, rather than on just speaking extempore is discussed further in Montefusco, "Quintilian and the Function," 619–20.
74. Quintilian, *Inst.* 3.3.1.
75. Quintilian, *Inst.* 4.1.1–3; 5.7.1–3; 5.7.25.
76. Quintilian, *Inst.* 10.2.106; 10.3.5–6.

that *expression*, including eloquence, style, and rhythm, are best developed through diligent practice in writing, modeling what is found by reading.[77] Indeed, the orator must also acquire a great "stock of words... and we shall attain our aim by reading and listening to the best writers and orators."[78]

Next, the *memorization* of the speech is best developed by reading repeatedly; "we can reread a passage again and again if we are in doubt about it or wish to fix it in the memory."[79] Quintilian even recommends a memorization technique which many of us employ today (albeit with modern white boards):

> One thing which will be of assistance to everyone, namely, to learn a passage by heart from the same tablets on which he has committed it to writing. For he will have certain tracks to guide him in his pursuit of memory, and the mind's eye will be fixed not merely on the pages on which the words were written, but on individual lines, and at times he will speak as though he were reading aloud.[80]

When *delivering* a speech, Quintilian encourages the use of notes or even of a fully written out text.[81] He states that the published notes of some orators align with this recommended approach, as though "jotted down previous to a speech," while the more elaborate published speeches of other orators appear to reflect modifications for posterity.[82] While Quintilian only claims to have published one of his own speeches, he repeatedly refers to the speeches of others, both ancient and more recent.[83]

---

77. Quintilian, *Inst.* 9.5.4; 10.1.1–2. Likewise, "it is in writing that eloquence has its roots and foundations, it is writing that provides that holy of holies where the wealth or oratory is stored." Quintilian, *Inst.* 10.3.3.

78. Quintilian, *Inst.* 10.1.8–9.

79. Quintilian, *Inst.* 10.1.19.

80. Quintilian, *Inst.* 11.6.32 (Butler, LCL, 229, 231).

81. Michael Bird cites both the poet Martial and Quintilian in summarizing that, "In Mediterranean schools of rhetoric, orators often used notes, and hearers of speeches often took notes to capture the gist of the delivery." Bird, *Gospel of the Lord*, 46.

82. Quintilian, *Inst.* 10.7.30–33.

83. He also speaks with frustration, regarding those in the audience who published inaccurate renderings of his orations based on the short-hand notes which were taken, "with a view to making money out of them." Quintilian's claim to have only published one speech, along with his complaint about others publishing his speeches, is in Quintilian, *Inst.* 7.2.24. Examples of speeches to which he refers are found in Quintilian, *Inst.* 3.5.2; 4.0.25; 6.3.42–44; 6.5.9; 11.4.73.

Plutarch

Plutarch likewise speaks frequently of those who wrote out their orations, as though it was a common thing to do, either in advance of the performance, to support memorization, or following the orator's performance, often for distribution to those who were remote.[84] He notes that some orators would even write out speeches for direct distribution, without first performing them.[85] At other times, Plutarch notes that speeches were written with the express purpose of having another present it.[86] This is not unlike some of Paul's letters, such as that to the Colossians, where the bearer of the letter was expected to both orally deliver and then expound on the letter (Col 4:7; also, Eph 6:21).

Livy

Livy likewise valued published materials, but he approaches such from the perspective of a historian. He expresses his high esteem for written records as he laments that more wasn't written in the earliest days of Rome, as "there was but slightly and scanty use of writing," which he identifies as, "the sole trustworthy guardian of the memory of past events."[87]

Livy's concern for accurately guarding history, as he refers to this "sole trustworthy guardian of the memory" (*una custodia fidelis memoriae*) bears some resemblance to Paul's concern for the careful guarding of his teachings and his gospel, as he admonishes Timothy to "guard the deposit"

---

84. There are many examples. Plutarch, *Adversus Colotem* 1; Plutarch, *Agesilaus* 20.3; Plutarch, *Antonius* 20.2; Plutarch, *Caesar* 2.2; Plutarch, *Cicero* 24.2; Plutarch, *De Garrulltate* 5; Plutarch, *Dem.* 8.4; Plutarch, *Lysander* 25.1; Plutarch, *Mulierum virtutes* 0; Plutarch, *Pompeius* 79.2; Plutarch, *Quomodo adolescens poetas audire debeat* 1. The Greek Stoic philosopher Epictetus also spoke approvingly of the well-prepared orator. "When the rhetorician knows what he has written well, that he has committed to memory what he has written, and brings an agreeable voice, why is he anxious?" Epictetus, *Diatribai* 2.16 (Long, 147).

85. Plutarch, *Comparatio Demosthenis et Ciceronis* 2.2; Plutarch, *Pomp.* 64.4.

86. Plutarch, *Dem.* 15.1–2; Plutarch, *Galba* 14.4; with respect to Isocrates, Plutarch, *Vitae decem oratorum* 4.

87. Livy, *Ab urbe cond.* 6.1.1–2. Of course, our acknowledgment of Livy's opinion on the topic of accuracy is offered with some reservation, as subsequent historians have not judged Livy himself to have prioritized accuracy over a well dramatized story. Keefer, "Livy," 178.

(*depositum custodi*, per 1 Tim 6:20 VUL).⁸⁸ Surely, Timothy's entrusted deposit encompassed the historical realities of Jesus. Therefore, the guarding of historical truth, which was so important to Livy, was not unlike the concern shared by the apostles and the early church leaders.

Paul

The term *orator* is not used in the New Testament, beyond the reference to the Jewish lawyer Tertullus (Acts 24:1). However, Paul is regularly before governors, judges, and crowds arguing for the gospel, seeking to persuade and convince, and thus performing the role of an orator.⁸⁹ Not surprisingly, his letters evidence oratory techniques, even if some dispute whether he was classically trained.⁹⁰ Accordingly, we find in Paul's writings a close connection between reading, writing, and oratory. As Paul visits the synagogues, where "Moses . . . is read every Sabbath" (Acts 15:21; also, 13:15), he deftly reasons with them "from the Scriptures" (17:2, 11), and he leverages the Scriptures in his preaching, saying, "what has been written . . . we also believe, and so we also speak" (2 Cor 4:13; compare 1 Cor 15:1–4).⁹¹ In this context, when Paul then writes to Timothy, encouraging him to integrate the public reading of Scripture into his preaching and teaching (1 Tim 4:13), we have modeled for us, within the church, practices which are consistent with the contemporary oratory expectations illustrated above,

---

88. Towner, *Timothy and Titus*, 431; Mounce, *Pastoral*, 371. The language is also similar in 2 Tim 1:14.

89. Laurent Pernot characterizes religious discourses consisting of narratives and eulogies concerning the gods as forms of oratory rhetoric, along with preaching, prayers and hymns. Pernot, "Rhetoric of Religion," 235, 237–38.

90. Richards, *Letter Writing*, 133–40; Schellenberg, "Private Word of the Apostle," 359–61, 368. (The interpretation of patristic testimony has become an important part of the ongoing debate regarding Paul's formal knowledge of ancient rhetorical theory. As early as 1898, E. Norden observed that Paul's earliest readers frequently commented on his innocence of Greco-Roman paideia. And yet, as Margaret Mitchell more recently has shown, these very readers often praised the power of Pauline persuasion, and, what is more, identified numerous rhetorical figures and tropes in Paul's letters. This article provides a reevaluation of the patristic testimony as well as its apologetic context. In so doing, it calls into question Mitchell's own explanation of the apparently contradictory evidence.)

91. Examples from Romans include Rom 1:2; 10:14–17; 15:4.

that the one who speaks should not only be well read, but should also communicate their message via both the spoken and written word.[92]

The linkage between reading, writing, and oration is particularly strong in Rom 10, where Deut 30 is cited. Moses exhorted the people to "obey the voice of the Lord . . . written in this Book of the Law" (Deut 30:10), as "the word [the commandment] is very near you . . . in your mouth and in your heart, so that you can do it" (30:14). Thus, the oral voice of the Lord had been written, and now Moses expected it to be read (orated by the priests), and then orally confessed, believed, and obeyed by Israel.[93] In a similar manner, the gospel which Paul was eager to preach in person (Rom 1:9–15; 15:15–16) had been written, and now Paul expected it to be read (orated), and then orally confessed, believed, and obeyed by the Romans (Rom 10:5–11). In Rom 10, Paul argues that the "righteousness based on faith" has replaced "the righteousness that is based on the law" (10:4–6). Whereas Moses asserted that God's word was near, present in the commandments, Paul asserts that God's word is now even nearer, in the person of Christ. Therefore, Paul can claim that "the word [of faith] is near you, in your mouth and in your heart . . . because, if you confess with your mouth that Jesus is Lord and believe in your heart that God raised him from the dead, you will be saved" (10:8–9). In making his appeal, Paul has readily turned to a written medium to preach the word of faith which he would normally orate in person.

It should not be surprising in the context of the orality debate that some modern scholars, such as Akio Ito, find evidence of "a tension between orality and literacy/textuality standing behind these references to Scripture in Romans 10. Ito argues that Paul is actually drawing a contrast between the writings of Moses and his own work; such that, whereas Μωϋσῆς . . . γράφει [Moses writes], Paul emphasizes the oral nature and oral communication of the gospel consistently in 10:6–21."[94] In this, Ito's perspective echoes those who assert that at the time there was "a general reticence towards writing, varying from mere indifference to active skepticism . . . a

---

92. Valeriy Alikin shows that the public reading of Scripture within the Christian gatherings "is likely to have followed the model of reading literature in first-century Graeco-Roman culture at large." Alikin, *Earliest Christian Gathering*, 157.

93. Moses tasked the priests with reading the law at least every seven years, at the Feast of Booths (Deut 31:9–13) and to teach it (Lev 10:11). He also expected the future king to copy and read the law (Deut 17:18–20).

94. Ito, "Written Torah and Oral Gospel," 240.

dichotomization between the spoken and the written."[95] But Ito goes further and ultimately concludes that "Paul stresses the orality of his gospel because he views himself as a 'prophet'; orality is congenial to prophecy."[96] While I find this perspective insightful, I would counter that the most significant OT prophets were those who wrote and left a legacy; hence, literacy/textuality is even more congenial to prophecy than orality![97] Elsewhere, Ito insightfully describes the fluidity which existed between the written and orally presented text.[98] My own attempt here has been to show that there was indeed a flow from the written to the oral to the written, which does not reflect the reticence that some claim. And the great literate orators, like Paul, were themselves comfortable in transmitting in written form the messages which they were also communicating orally, whether teaching "either by our spoken word or by our letter" (2 Thess 2:15; compare 2:1–5).

Summary

In an earlier section, I presented the concerns expressed by ancient authors over the reliability of long-term memory, particularly that of the aged. Now in this section, I have demonstrated the corresponding expectation that orators should be both active readers and writers. Given my stated assumption that a segment of the audience would have shared the perspectives expressed by these authors and orators, my obvious inference is that the audiences first receiving a published Gospel would have neither desired nor expected the eyewitnesses to primarily preserve the Gospel accounts in their personal memories, without writing out and publishing an account of Jesus. Given these perspectives, it can be argued that there would have been an increasingly adverse apologetic impact, the longer that the witnesses waited before producing a written Gospel account. Consequently, in so far as the church delayed the publication of the Gospels, the audiences were being asked to not only believe in the remarkable assertion of the

---

95. Botha, *Orality and Literacy*, 37.
96. Ito, "Written Torah and Oral Gospel," 258.
97. Either by their own hand or that of their scribe.
98. Ito, "Written Torah and Oral Gospel," 246. Ito goes on to say that: "It may be the case that people did not consciously distinguish the written medium from the oral medium." While there is some truth to this statement, in that both the written and oral may be referred to as what someone says, it is also clear that at times Paul and others were very clear in identifying certain words as written.

resurrection as a historical reality, but also to believe in the reliability of the memories of a community of aging witnesses, concerning the events of Jesus's life and his teachings.

CONCLUSION

As modern students of history and of the biblical texts, we are truly fortunate for the substantial amount of Greco-Roman literature which is currently available for us to sift through when investigating certain topics. Many ancient authors were concerned with the frailties of memory and the loss of memory which came with aging. They used apt metaphors for the memory, likening it to wax or a dimming lamp. They also spoke admiringly of those of the past who had extraordinary memories, yet they were also appreciative of written materials, given the limitations of memory. In addition, those who were orators encouraged their students and readers to read and write prolifically, and they also encouraged the drafting and distribution of speeches. Written materials were important to the cultural elites of the first century, who generated most of this literature.

While these ancient authors predominantly came from the upper and political classes, we can surmise that their sentiments were likely present within the greater society, especially among those who were literate and among those of the public who followed the theater, even if the sentiments merely existed as societal undercurrents. We can thus reasonably assume that the eyewitnesses to Jesus's ministry and teachings would have been sensitive to these sentiments, as they traveled about the empire, and as they sought to preach and preserve the Jesus traditions.

To this end, Craig Keener rightly affirms that "Jesus' disciples, as disciples, would be expected to learn and pass on his teachings."[99] But to my point, a contemporary audience, whenever they were ultimately presented with a written account of Jesus's teachings and ministry, would have expected to find the material truthful and accurate, and not compromised by the kinds of memory lapses about which both the ancients and Robert McIver express concern. Certainly, the audiences would have been more favorably predisposed towards receiving the written accounts if perceived as eyewitness testimony. But, as I have argued, these accounts would be *most* favorably received if based on early memories, rather than based on wax-worn and dimly lit memories. Bauckham's expectation that the Gospel

99. Keener, *Christobiography*, 416.

Arguments from the Ancients on Memory and Orators

authors had a role in selecting and integrating the traditions, in dialogue with the eyewitnesses and the community, remains valid. Yet, the perspectives of the intended audiences must also be considered, in postulating a theory for the preservation of the Jesus traditions.

In conclusion, this chapter has presented contemporary concerns over aging memory and the expectations of orators for being active writers. My thesis has been that while the ancients valued eyewitness testimony, the original audiences of the Gospels would have been skeptical of long-term eyewitness memory as the primary means for reliably preserving the Jesus traditions due to concerns over the aging memories of the eyewitnesses, particularly in an environment where contemporary orators encouraged the drafting and distribution of speeches. Given this skepticism, it can be inferred that the contemporary audiences would have neither desired nor expected the eyewitnesses to primarily preserve the Gospel accounts in their personal memories, without writing out and publishing the account of Jesus. On this basis, it is reasonable for modern apologists to be hesitant to accept Bauckham's proposition that eyewitness memory was primarily responsible for preserving the integrity of the Gospels over thirty to fifty years after the resurrection of Jesus.

The Christian apologist must, I suggest, reconsider whether Bauckham's eyewitness memory theory has more merit in explaining how the Jesus traditions were preserved than the various other competing propositions, while recognizing that many of the competing theories accept the introduction of large measures of invention and corruption into the traditions. The issue is not whether the Holy Spirit may have divinely preserved the memories of the witnesses, as some understand John 14:26 to claim, but whether this claim would have carried weight with the ancient skeptics.[100] If we are indeed motivated to defend Gospel accuracy, reliability, and authority, then an alternative theory is necessary, which does not accept the premise that decades transpired before the earliest Gospels were published, even though this would be to go against the grain of popular

---

100. Though not specifically arguing for long-delayed Gospels, Farnell, Blomberg, and MacArthur all leverage John 14:26 to argue that the Holy Spirit ensured that the NT authors recalled what they needed to. Farnell, "Independence View," 263, 272–73; Blomberg, *Historical Reliability of the Gospels*, 73; MacArthur, *Inerrant Word*, 193. In contrast, Stein emphasizes the Spirit's role per John 14:26 in guiding the tradents of the oral traditions, such that "they felt free to paraphrase and interpret the sayings of Jesus . . . in the body of the tradition itself." Stein, *Synoptic Gospels*, 221. Compare Bauckham, *Jesus and the Eyewitnesses*, 507–8. Refer to my comments relative to John 14:26 in chapter 2.

modern scholarship.[101] Nonetheless, and regardless of our disillusionment relative to Bauckham's eyewitness memory theory, his *Jesus and the Eyewitnesses* still remains a prized resource for contending for the reliability of the Gospels with respect to his handling of Papias, names in the Gospels, inclusios, the deficiencies of form criticism, early Christian concerns over preserving their traditions, etc.

I close this chapter with the following quote from Josephus, in which he praises those who responsibly write their history:

> The ancient historians set themselves severally to write the history of their own times, a task in which their connection with the events added lucidity to their record; while mendacity brought an author into disgrace with readers who knew the facts. In fact, the work of committing to writing events which have not previously been recorded and of commending to posterity the history of one's own time is one which merits praise and acknowledgement.[102]

---

101. Personally, I favor T. R. Birks' proposition that Matthew was written in support of the Jews of the Christian diaspora (compare Acts 8:1–4; 11:19–20), and that Mark was written for the Latin "military readers" of Caesarea Maritima, following the conversion of Cornelius and associates (compare Acts 10), and prior to the influx of a large number of non-Latin gentiles from Asia Minor and Greece. Birks, *Horae Evangelicae*, 281–82, 293, 313.

102. Josephus, *J. W.* 1.14–15 (Thackeray, LCL, 9). It might also be beneficial for the modern apologist to further explore the ancient interest in guarding history and preserving tradition through written means, and to assess how their views aligned with Jewish and Christian interests (e.g., Exod 34:27; Jer 36:2). Kruger has touched on this to a limited extent. Kruger, *Question of Canon*, 47–48.

7

Arguments from the Ancients on Written Materials

Rejecting the Modern Preference for Oral Traditions

IN THIS CHAPTER WE continue highlighting Greco-Roman perspectives which were contemporary with Jesus and the eyewitnesses. Whereas the previous chapter challenged the sufficiency of Richard Bauckham's paradigm that Jesus's life story and teachings were faithfully preserved over several decades due to the personal memories of those who were eyewitnesses of Jesus's ministry, given ancient concerns over aging memories and the expectations of orators, this chapter will more broadly challenge the modern notion that the ancients preferred oral traditions so significantly that they largely denigrated the value of Christian writings concerning the Jesus traditions.

To begin with, we will review Craig Keener's assessment that the Gospels fall within the contemporary genre of historically oriented biographies. He argues that the contemporary audiences would have expected the Gospels, whenever they were published, to present a truthful historical presentation of the Jesus events and teachings. This will be followed by a survey of contemporary Jewish, New Testament, and secular perspectives to show that they valued written witness testimony and treated such as authoritative. Based on these considerations, I will then highlight the implicit (and more explicit) biases found in some of the modern literature which elevate the importance of oral traditions over written materials, at a level which I contend is not reflective of the ancient literature.

ANCIENT AUDIENCE PERSPECTIVES ON WRITTEN MATERIALS

Expectations for Accuracy in Biographies and Histories

"What did first-century audiences expect of biographies?"[1] This question sets the stage for Craig Keener's *Christobiography*, which offers an in-depth and well documented inquiry into the nature of biographical narrative literature during the period of the Roman empire in which the Gospels were written. He establishes that biographers, especially during this era, "intended their works to be more historical than novelistic," and therefore he classifies biography as a sub-type of historical literature, a form of literature in which "historians envisioned their genre as based on facts."[2] There was an overall concern for accuracy, as "ancient historians and audiences expected . . . history-writing, notwithstanding rhetorical embellishments . . . to be truthful" and free of intentional and unintentional falsehoods.[3] Historical literature was also to be the result of careful investigation, which consisted "especially of interviewing people, critically evaluating reports, and accepting what prove to be the most reliable sources." Historians who failed in this were condemned.[4]

Keener identifies a variety of criteria which discerning historical writers employed for evaluating their sources. These included coherence with other sources, historical plausibility, reasonableness, consistency with

---

1. Keener, *Christobiography*, 121.

2. Keener, *Christobiography*, 156–57, 187. Bird likewise concludes that the Gospels follow the mode of Greco-Roman biography, meant to stand as "authoritative guides to the story of Jesus as a companion to Israel's sacred literature," although he does not consider whether these biographies should be classified as a sub-type of historical literature. Bird, *Gospel of the Lord*, 275, 280.

3. Keener, *Christobiography*, 203–4. Byrskog concurs, "In antiquity, no one was more concerned about eyewitness testimony and historical truth than the historians." However, Byrskog then goes on to discriminate between the various types of historical writings, and to characterize the Gospels more as encomiastic (flattering rhetorical) biographical genre than as history writing. Byrskog, "'Truer,'" 483, 488–89.

4. Keener, *Christobiography*, 209–11. Potter likewise affirms that "good and bad history was evaluated in terms of its relationship to the truth" and he cites several classical historians in supporting this argument. Potter, *Literary Texts*, 12.

the person's character, etc.[5] Based on ancient concerns over memory, as cited in the prior chapter, I suggest that the historians' source criteria also included consideration of the reliability of an aging witness's memory. Indeed, Keener acknowledges that:

> Eyewitnesses are not a perfect source . . . he or she will not remember every detail. Whether because of bias, memory lapse, or sometimes even incompetence, even eyewitnesses did not always agree on details, requiring some weighing of individual testimony. Merely four decades after Galba's death, for example, sources offered no unanimity regarding who assassinated him.[6]

Correspondingly, Keener cites Josephus, who took credit for composing "his account while witnesses remained alive who could verify or falsify his claims, and he complained about a rival who had waited twenty years to publish, till after the eyewitnesses, who could have verified or falsified his claims, were dead."[7] This underscores the importance of publishing earlier versus later and, by extension, to publishing well before the mental decline of an aging witness might undermine their ability to verify a claim.

Keener's intent is to portray the Gospels as standing within the tradition of contemporary biographies, such that the substance and variation found in the Gospels are well "within the bounds expected in ancient narratives about actual persons and events."[8] With regard to the oral transmission process which led up to the authoring of the Gospels, Keener identifies Jesus's chief associates as the recognized authorities for what Jesus actually said and did, consistent with Bauckham's theory; however, outside of Jerusalem, Keener envisions a less structured method of preserving the Jesus traditions, such as that which is articulated in Bailey's Informal Controlled Transmission theory, which observed that in certain modern Middle Eastern villages it was the broader community, rather than specific authorized tradents, who provided a corrective influence against any misstatements in the retelling of the collective oral traditions.[9]

Whether or not Keener has correctly surmised the means by which the Jesus traditions were preserved, prior to their publication in the Gospels, is

---

5. Keener, *Christobiography*, 217–18.
6. Keener, *Christobiography*, 244, citing Tacitus, *Historiae* 1.41.3.
7. Josephus, *Life* 359–66; Josephus, *Ant.* 20.266; Keener, *Christobiography*, 245.
8. Keener, *Christobiography*, 21.
9. Keener, *Christobiography*, 472–75; Bailey, "Informal Controlled Oral Tradition," 4–11.

beyond the scope of this chapter. However, what Keener has substantiated is the interest which the Gospel audiences would have had in the truthfulness of the Jesus traditions, whenever they were ultimately published, along with potential concerns over the credibility of the memories of the sources who contributed.

Reception of Written Witness Testimony

How favorably did the first-century Jewish and Christian communities esteem witness testimony, when presented in written form? I pose this question in the context of Gerhardsson's assertion, as summarized by Samuel Byrskog, that "the writing down of [the Gospels] was an emergency measure . . . reflecting the ancient skepticism toward the written word."[10] Neither Gerhardsson nor Byrskog elaborate on the perceived "emergency," but presumably this was due to a pending lack of qualified tradents to continue the oral preservation of the traditions, given Gerhardsson's subsequent statement that, "we have reason to suppose the Jesus-tradition to have been originally passed on by word of mouth—for ideological as well as for practical reasons."[11] While these suppositions concerning what drove the ultimate publication of the Gospels may or may not be factually true, they also presuppose that the ancients were inherently biased against producing a written version of the Jesus traditions, even aggressively resisting such until they had no other choice. Pieter Botha goes even further, based on the writings of Plato and a few others, in disparaging the role of written materials: "written speeches do exist, but their use is deprecated . . . [given] the primacy of the live performance."[12] Rather, I contend that these views distort the relationship between oral and written materials within the culture. With regard to Botha, he is missing the distinction which Plato and others made between the role of written materials to assist with remembering and the inherent value of hearing directly from teachers and live witnesses.[13]

---

10. Byrskog, "Introduction," 8. Botha also seizes on Gerhardsson's statement, in framing the background for his study on orality and literacy. Botha, *Orality and Literacy*, 23; Gerhardsson, *Memory and Manuscript*, 196–97.

11. Gerhardsson, *Memory and Manuscript*, 334.

12. Botha, *Orality and Literacy*, 32. Botha appears to be drawing from Loveday Alexander's assessment of the term "living voice" in Greco-Roman texts, where she characterizes the use of "written texts of speeches . . . [as] deprecated." This will be touched on in chapter 5 below. Alexander, "Living Voice," 227.

13. Refer to the earlier footnote regarding Plato, *Phaedrus* 275a, 276d.

Jewish Hellenistic Perspectives

Philo and Josephus both make arguments based on the "witnesses" whom they cite in their writings. With regard to the declarations of God, Philo affirms that "a clear testimony [*marturiai*] is recorded in the Holy Scriptures ... if, he says, you keep the divine commandment in obedience to his ordinances ... the first boon you will have is victory over your enemies."[14] With regard to Abraham's mourning over the loss of Sarah, Philo states that, "the testimonies [*marturiai*] for this are to be found in the holy books which may never be convicted of false witness [*pseudomarturiōn*]."[15] Hence, the written words are to be accepted as valid testimony, as a true and authoritative witness. Elsewhere, in a more legal sense, Philo makes a similar point, concerning the written testimony of physicians and philosophers:

> If, just as in a court of law, we are to make use, not only of the logical or dialectical proofs, but also of the modes of persuasion that are called "inartistic," one of which is that which employs evidence, we shall call as witnesses many distinguished physicians and philosophers, who ratify their evidence by writings as well as by words.[16]

More broadly, Josephus refers to the works of authors, who were familiar to the contemporary society, as authoritative witnesses. For example, "I have produced numerous ancient witnesses, who mention us [the Jews] in their works."[17] There are numerous statements of this type in the writings of both Philo and Josephus.[18]

---

14. Philo, *Rewards* 79 (Colson et al., LCL, 2:361).
15. Philo, *On the Life of Abraham* 258 (Colson et al., LCL, 6:127).
16. Philo, *Planting* 173 (Colson et al., LCL, 3:303).
17. Josephus, *Against Apion* 2.289 (Thackeray, LCL, 409).
18. Other examples include Philo, *Cherubim* 124; Philo, *Allegorical Interpretation* 3.4; 3.142; Josephus *Ant.* 12.144.

New Testament Perspectives

From the perspective of Jesus, the written Scriptures themselves were of foremost importance to the Jewish nation. In speaking to hostile Jews, Jesus reminds them of the authority which the written Scriptures carried as witness testimony: "you search the Scriptures because you think that in them you have eternal life; and it is they that bear witness about me" (John 5:39). Indeed, it is within the Scriptures that even God's testimony can be found (Acts 13:22). And the very words of Scripture are to be considered as testimony, even when specific individuals are not being cited (e.g., Rom 3:21; Heb 7:17). From the perspective of the apostles, it was the Jewish preservation of these living oracles, these living words, which both Luke and Paul applauded (Acts 7:38; Rom 3:2). In the same vein, the apostles expected for their written words to be accepted as valid witness testimony, to be taken as authoritative and true (John 19:35–36; 21:24–25; also, 3 John 1:12). And John's Revelation boldly declares that its contents were to be taken as a "faithful and true witness" (Rev 3:14).

Secular Perspectives

The acceptance of written materials as authoritative witness testimony by Jewish Hellenistic and Christian writers is consistent with what is found in contemporary secular literature. Pliny, in composing his *Natural History*, defers to the *witness* of many of his sources, as does Strabo, in writing his *Geography*.[19] Plutarch references the *testimony* of Aristotle as being present in his writings.[20] Tacitus, in proclaiming the "eloquence of old," refers to the *witness* of Demosthenes and Cicero.[21] These are but a few examples.

To recap, the intent of this section has been to repudiate any possible preconception that first-century audiences might have tended to dismiss testimony as being authoritative and valid, if presented in written form. Rather, what I have shown is that, particularly in non-legal contexts, it was common to accept written materials as witness testimony.

---

19. Pliny, *Natural History* 8.3; 22.43; 33.36; Similarly, in Strabo, *Geography* 12.4.8; 15.1.30; etc.

20. Plutarch, *Solon* 11.1.

21. Tacitus, *Dialoges de oratoribus* 32 (Hutton and Peterson, LCL, 101).

ARGUMENTS FROM THE ANCIENTS ON WRITTEN MATERIALS

EXCESSIVE PRIORITIZATION OF THE ORAL OVER THE WRITTEN VOICE

Over the past century, a substantial volume of literature has been published to explain how the Jesus traditions might have been preserved before the Gospels were published, within the context of a marginally literate culture. Modern theories vary in the deference which they give to the influence of the eyewitnesses, to the controls exercised over the form and content of the traditions (or the lack thereof), to the role of local tradents who might have memorized the traditions, and to the reworking of the traditions to suit local needs. While the early church might have had recourse to a limited number of written notes, these written materials are rarely characterized as more than a handful of wax tablets or scroll fragments, which an orator might occasionally reference. Rather, the early church is often characterized as having had such a high esteem for the oral form of the traditions that there was little desire for a written record. Yet, within these modern speculations there is little, if any, recognition of ancient concerns over memory degradation, and how this might affect the historical accuracy of the traditions, and only token recognition of the expectation that orators should write and distribute their orations. Indeed, one might question whether modern scholars sustain a higher degree of confidence in ancient memory than the ancients themselves did.

Therefore, the intent of the balance of this chapter is to directly engage with and challenge some of these modern opinions. Against Terence Mournet's assertion that the "living voice" of the oral traditions had precedence over written materials within the early church, I will instead contend that early apostolic publications served to inform and bring stability to the message which was orally conveyed. Against Richard Bauckham's claim that ancient writing primarily supplemented and supported oral forms of remembering and teaching, I will contend that this is not supported by the evidence. Against Craig Keener's implication that the ancients valued memorization over writing, I will contend that the ancients actually valued both. Against those scholars who contend that the church principally employed rabbinic methods (e.g., memorization) for preserving and passing on the Jesus traditions and therefore had little interest in publishing, I will contend that this approach would have been foreign to the many Greco-Roman converts (including Hellenistic Jews) who dominated the early church.

All about the Living Voice?

Terence Mournet particularly emphasizes the priority of the evolving oral traditions concerning Jesus over any written records. In his chapter on "The Jesus Tradition as Oral Tradition," he builds a conceptual model which rejects both the "rabbinical model" and the "literary model," in favor of a more complex "circular process of tradition transmission," with "the oral tradition informing and perhaps modifying the textual tradition and the textual tradition informing and perhaps modifying the textual tradition."[22] Against Gerhardsson's rabbinic model, Mournet argues that it is inappropriate to superimpose on the Christian movement the "methods of pedagogy and tradition transmission" (e.g., extensive memorization) which were developed within Judaism after the destruction of the temple.[23] In this, I agree with him. However, he also condemns the literary model as inappropriately imposing a modern bias in which texts are seen as offering a superior "vehicle for accurate and reliable communications" over oral means, a bias which he contends did not exist in the ancient world.[24] In this, I believe that he fails to acknowledge the testimony of the ancients themselves, with regard to the significance of written texts and the role of these texts in constraining the future evolution of oral traditions.[25]

Mournet builds his conceptual model by echoing the "strong consensus" of modern academia that the vast majority of those in the ancient world were illiterate and that a "small percentage of people were at best, even marginally literate," and hence, "very few people in antiquity were able to interact directly with texts."[26] In support of this claim, he cites a literacy study by William Harris.[27] Yet others challenge this study, given its minimalistic characterization of functional literacy within the ancient world, particularly within the Christian community. For example, Eddy and Boyd assert that "there is evidence that certain written texts . . . would inform all segments of society."[28] Nonetheless, Mournet continues, "and even when

22. Mournet, "As Oral Tradition," 41–42.
23. Mournet, "As Oral Tradition," 46–48.
24. Mournet, "As Oral Tradition," 43–44.
25. Mournet, "As Oral Tradition," 51, 60–61.
26. Mournet, "As Oral Tradition," 50–51.
27. Harris, *Ancient Literacy*, 114, 250, 328. Mournet likewise cites a related study by Catherine Hezser, *Jewish Literacy in Roman Palestine*, 81:496–504, cited in Mournet, "As Oral Tradition," 51, 51n45.
28. Eddy and Boyd, *Jesus Legend*, 241–42. Kruger also pushes back against the

traditions were inscribed in textual form, they were not always valued in the same way that we take for granted today."[29]

Mournet next cites Loveday Alexander's assertion that written texts were "secondary to and subordinate to oral instruction—it is the 'living voice' of the teacher that has priority: the text both follows that voice (as a record of teaching already given) and stands in a subordinate position to it."[30] Mournet clarifies what he understands the *living voice* to encompass: "while texts were indeed commonplace during the time of Jesus, they were often composed in conjunction with or informed by a living oral tradition."[31] According to Mournet, the early Christian texts (including the *Didache*, *Acts of Paul*, and *Q*) all exhibited "their indebtedness" to this developing "living oral tradition," as it advanced from one community to the next, and as it found root in non-Jewish contexts.[32] Then, "when the Gospel writers proceeded to write their respective accounts of the life of Jesus, they were drawing from a river of tradition which itself was formed from the combined input of the diverse steams of Christian thought."[33]

This view aligns with how some scholars understand Papias's stated preference for the "living voice," over written reports.[34] Alexander understands Papias as expressing the same sentiment which she observes in the Hellenistic philosophical schools, in which the latest philosophical developments had priority.[35] However, I contend that this is a misreading of Papias, as Richard Bauckham has effectively shown.[36] Papias is better understood as affirming the value of primary over secondary sources for

---

underlying study by Harris which is cited by Mournet, and the related work by Kelber, for being overly dismissive of early Christian literacy and for suggesting that early Christians might have had a deep seated opposition to writing. While Kruger concurs that the vast majority of Christians could not read or write, he envisions "early Christianity as a culture of 'textuality,'" having "an interest in, and dependence on, written texts." Kruger, *Question of Canon*, 85–86, 85n39, 91, 103.

29. Mournet, "As Oral Tradition," 51.
30. Mournet, "As Oral Tradition," 51.
31. Mournet, "As Oral Tradition," 51.
32. Mournet, "As Oral Tradition," 51.
33. Mournet, "As Oral Tradition," 61.
34. Eusebius, *Hist. eccl.* 3.39.4.
35. Overall, Alexander is striving to show that "in the highly literate world of the first and second centuries" there are "certain cultural contexts in which the written word is treated with a marked degree of skepticism." Alexander, "Living Voice," 242–43.
36. Bauckham, *Jesus and the Eyewitnesses*, 15–17, 21–27.

the writing of history, given Papias's specific interest in the eyewitnesses and their immediate successors, and his interest in their knowledge of what Jesus actually said.[37] Further, "Papias uniquely expands the usual cliché 'living voice' to 'living and surviving voice,'" making it clear that his interest is in original witnesses, not the tradents of developing oral traditions.[38]

Yet, even in the context of the philosophical schools referenced by Alexander, her implication that the older texts carried almost negligible value goes too far. While attentive students would doubtless give heed to the living voice of a physically present teacher over a scroll lying before them, this is not to say that the writings of the earlier teacher were altogether deprecated. Otherwise, what motivation would there have been for any great philosopher to have had their words transcribed and distributed, if the oral musings of their disciples would immediately supersede such? To this point, why would orators express frustration that there were sometimes in circulation written versions of their orations which were unflattering? For Quintilian laments that students "made frequent annotations that sometimes circulated in public and reproduced a teacher's work to its detriment."[39] Thus, even written words falsely attributed to a teacher or orator carried weight for those who read or listened to the reading of such, prevailing even over the objections of the authentic "living voice."[40]

In a society where the writings of the great philosophers were cherished to the point of being studied and memorized by their students, we ought not presume that these writings did not continue to have value and directly influence the next class of students. As Alexander the Great studied

---

37. Bauckham, *Jesus and the Eyewitnesses*, 15–17, 21–27. Similarly, David Potter offers a more balanced discussion of the interplay of written and oral sources when it comes to the work of the historian. He notes that Tacitus "plainly had a sense of the value of the written documents as a historical source, but he was not wedded to the notion that history could, or should, be based solely on a documentary record." Further, he "does not appear to have privileged documents over eyewitnesses." However, note here that it is the eyewitnesses whom Tacitus would privilege; that privilege is not extended (by Potter) to their successors. Potter, *Literary Texts*, 84.

38. Bauckham, *Jesus and the Eyewitnesses*, 27.

39. Quintilian *Inst.* 1 Pr 7–8 and 2.11.7, as cited by Cribiore, *Gymnastics of the Mind*, 144.

40. Also refer to the earlier footnote, where Quintilian complains about those who had illicitly transcribed and distributed some of his speeches. Quintilian, *Inst.* 7.2.24. The implication is that the illicit copies persisted, even though he had released authorized versions, thereby also showing that the authoritative "living voice," even of the originating voice, did not always prevail over the accounts, once written.

under Aristotle, let us not assume that he only learned from Aristotle's interpretation of Plato, without engaging the writings of Plato directly. Nor should we assume that Timothy's Greco-Roman disciples failed to study Paul's letters, merely because Timothy assuredly had them memorized. Rather, we should envision that while oral traditions might have served to inform texts as they were written, these texts would then serve to inform and bring stability to the message which was orally conveyed. Indeed, throughout the writings of the NT and of the church fathers, the earlier apostolic writings were frequently cited as authoritative teachings. Yes, the progressive teachings of the apostles during the first century were valued, but so were the earliest NT writings.

Did a Memorized Account Carry More Authority Than the Reading of a Text?

In a similar fashion, Bauckham also needs to be challenged as he appears to give too much priority to texts held in memory, over and above texts which existed in written form. In this, he characterizes the relationship between reading, writing, and oration (and orality) in a manner which deviates from the voices which I've presented in the prior chapter. While he acknowledges that "in the predominantly oral culture of the ancient world, including the early Christian movement, writing and orality were not alternatives but complimentary," he then asserts that "for the most part, writing existed to supplement and to support oral forms of remembering and teaching . . . as a supplement to orality, more for the sake of reminding than of remembering."[41] As such, he seemingly discounts the value which the ancients placed in the written texts themselves for preserving authentic history (as illustrated by Livy and Plutarch above) or of written testimony itself.[42] His apparent assertion, that the ancients favored the history which was preserved in the memories of students and orators over that which was written, goes beyond what he has demonstrated.

41. Bauckham, *Jesus and the Eyewitnesses*, 287–88. In making this statement, Bauckham aligns with Werner Kelber, who asserts that "very frequently, the inscribing of words on clay, parchment, and papyri . . . was merely creating reference material for purposes of recitation and memorization" and with Samuel Byrskog, as cited by Bauckham. Kelber, "Rethinking the Transmission," 521; Byrskog, *Story as History*, 116.

42. Cribiore points out that books were not only "'reminders' of direct teaching," but also "in philosophical teaching, books were useful in transmitting the doctrines of the past." Cribiore, *Gymnastics of the Mind*, 145.

Clearly, the memorized oral performance of a text was generally preferred by ancient audiences over the simple public reading of such, for its "communicative power."[43] Likewise, Bauckham has aptly shown that historians and Christian apologists, such as Papias, preferred to use firsthand sources and to interview participants and witnesses, when available.[44] However, this is not to say that written texts or those which were publicly read were considered less reliable or authoritative than the equivalent content, when held in memory. For example, Cicero reports that when Sophocles was in his extreme old age and his sons aspired to divest him of control over their estate on a charge of imbecility, "the old man read to the jury" the play which he had just written and was in the process of revising. On hearing the quality of the work, the jury dismissed the case.[45] It was not pertinent that he had not yet memorized the work.

Indeed, the outcome of many Roman court cases turned on the written evidence which was presented, as did cases brought before Jewish courts.[46] While Quintilian speaks of the "tacit prejudice" which existed against written witness depositions in civil trials, he does not suggest that the prejudice is tied to their legitimacy or authority, but with the fact that the one giving the written testimony may be "less ashamed of himself in the presence of a small number of witnesses," and so "his absence from court is attacked as indicating a lack of confidence."[47] But, if the credibility of the absent witness can be established, then there can be parity between the testimony

---

43. Bauckham, *Jesus and the Eyewitnesses*, 22.

44. Bauckham, *Jesus and the Eyewitnesses*, 8–9, 21–27. David Potter points out that while the ancients preferred eyewitness accounts, the "ancient historians . . . realize that eyewitness accounts are liable to deep corruption," plus eyewitness accounts were subject to dramatic differences in perspective. Thus, historians would naturally compare eyewitness accounts with each other and with other records. Potter, *Literary Texts*, 28. Also, Bauckham, *Jesus and the Eyewitnesses*, 479–80. Concern over the accuracy of witnesses is abundant. For example, Sallust, *Bellum catalinae* 16; Livy, *Ab urbe cond.* 39.8.3–8; Josephus, *J. W.* 1.2–3.

45. Cicero, *Sen.* 22–23.

46. For example, Livy, *Ab urbe cond.* 2.4.4–6; Philo, *On the Decalogue* 138–40. Trials also turned on the documentation which could not be produced. Cicero, *Pro Archia* 4.8.

47. Quintilian, *Inst.* 5.7.1–2. For criminal trials, however, there was a requirement that the defendant be physically present, and that evidence be presented, "not indirectly or by affidavit, but personally and by word of mouth." Tacitus, *Dialogues* 36. Canfield adds though, that while "attendance of witnesses was compulsory . . . depositions could be taken." Canfield, "Roman Lawyer," 561.

of those present and those absent.[48] What is notable about the Gospel accounts is that they benefit from a vast number of witnesses and participants; therefore, there should be little concern that a written format might suggest a lack of confidence on the part of the author. Regardless, there is nothing in Quintilian's dialogue which suggests that it is the memory itself which carried heavier weight than a comparable written version of an account by the one possessing the memory, as Bauckham seems to suggest.

With respect to the New Testament, it seems fair to claim that there is likewise no hint that memorized material carried more (or less) authority than material which was written and merely read.[49] For example, when Jesus himself read from the Isaiah scroll in the Nazareth synagogue (Luke 4:17), there is no indication that this event somehow carried less significance, given that he did not recite the Scriptures from memory, as Jesus often did in less formal settings.[50] Similarly, when Paul encouraged Timothy to regularly share the Scriptures with the Christian community (1 Tim 4:13), he commanded that they be publicly read rather than recited from memory.[51]

Better to Inscribe on Your Mind Than on Paper?

Keener offers a pointed anecdote from Antisthenes to demonstrate the high value which ancient teachers and philosophers placed on memory. "To an associate who had lost his notes, one philosopher reportedly replied, 'You should have inscribed them ... on your mind instead of on paper.'"[52] Thus,

---

48. Quintilian indicates that conflicts between evidence given in writing and that given orally "may be turned to advantage by either side," by reference to the witness signatories and the oaths taken. Ultimately, the debate turns to "which [of the witnesses] are the more respectable in character ... [and] which have given the more credible evidence," etc. Quintilian, *Inst.* 5.7.1–2, 5.7.32–34.

49. Bauckham has already convincingly dismissed any *a priori* understanding of the term *tradition* as solely referring to memorized oral teachings or history. He refers to Josephus to make his case. Bauckham, *Jesus and the Eyewitnesses*, 36–38, 269–70.

50. The Essenes also followed a practice of both reading and exegeting in their worship. Philo, *That Every Good Person Is Free* 82.

51. David Aune also points out that, "there is no evidence that Paul, unlike the framers of the Mishnah, wrote his letters with the intention that they be subject to oral transmission." Rather, they were intended to be publicly read. Aune, "Jesus Tradition and the Pauline Letters," 66–67.

52. Keener, *Christobiography*, 475–76. Citation is from Diogenes Laertius, *Lives of Eminent Philosophers* 6.1.5.

Keener's excerpt not only emphasizes that the ancients valued memorization, but also leaves the modern reader with the impression that the ancients emphasized memorization over writing. Yet, this is an inadequate representation of Antisthenes's views, given that almost immediately beforehand he is cited in the ancient literature as emphasizing the expected task of a student: "When a lad from Pontus was about to attend his lectures, and asked him what he required, the answer was, 'Come with a new book, a new pen, and new tablets.'"[53] Indeed, Antisthenes himself is credited with writing ten volumes of material. And the work by Diogenes Laertius, which preserves these anecdotes and summarizes the earlier work, is itself an anthology and catalog of ancient philosophers, particularly celebrating the endless volumes which they produced. Thus, Antisthenes should be an example of but one in a long line of philosophers who valued both memorization and writing.

Greco-Roman Memory Techniques or Not?

Ancient writers celebrated those who had superb memories. They admired the accomplishments of both their predecessors and their peers, who could memorize large works and then present such, in court or on the stage. And, no doubt, there were many within the early churches who were likewise celebrated for their ability to recall and elaborate on the details of Jesus's life and teachings—the beatitudes, the highlights of the passion story, favorite parables or miracles, etc. And certainly, citizens of the ancient world filled their memories with far more useful content than we do in our modern world, including family histories, local folklore, etc. Therefore, it is easy to envision Peter and the other eyewitnesses as rehearsing the Jesus narratives from memory and leveraging anecdotes as part of their preaching, as Bauckham supposes.[54] Nonetheless, there is a discipline required when memorizing extended narratives, especially of the scale of a Gospel. As the church grew outside of Judea, there would have been a constant need to develop additional tradents or other suitably equipped teachers. What would have been their approach for mastering the traditions, to support their oral presentations?

As I have shown above, ancient writings demonstrate that those with the most celebrated memories within the Greco-Roman world generally

---

53. Laertius, *Lives* 6.1.3 (Hicks, LCL, 2:5).
54. Bauckham, *Jesus and the Eyewitnesses*, 216–17.

had an intimate relationship with written materials and relied on such for their feats of memorization. This would seem the obvious pattern for the expanding church to employ for passing on the Jesus traditions, at least to those Greco-Roman teachers who were literate. In contrast, some modern scholars contend that the church principally employed the use of rabbinic methods for preserving and passing on the Jesus traditions, as were used for memorizing the Oral Torah, for which the use of written materials was discouraged. Alan Kirk takes this to the extreme when he asserts, "in rabbinic practice and ideology its manuscript embodiment recedes, virtually to a vanishing point." And further, "because the mnemonic formalization of the Mishnah was quite methodical and its memorization and recitation the focused concern of the rabbinic discipleship circles, there may have been little need for accessory written versions to support its transmission."[55] Other orality theories allow for a few scattered sheets of papyrus to assist the student. However, as we consider the many Greco-Roman converts from the major cities of the empire, including those who were literate and those who were accomplished at memorizing works of philosophy, history, the written Torah, etc., it is difficult to envision that they would have set aside their familiar memorization techniques, as practiced by their literary role models, in favor of these rabbinic methods.

McIver's perspective on large scale memorization is relevant to this discussion, when he asserts that "verbatim memorization of longer texts is only possible with the ability to reference a written text." To illustrate this, he refers to the practice utilized for the memorization of Homeric poems during the Greco-Roman era, which leveraged the use of written texts.[56] Of course, his skeptical contention is not that Christian texts were available in support of extensive memorization, but that Jesus's disciples and their successors only memorized the core meanings of Jesus's teachings. This then contributes to his lack of confidence in the reliability of specific details within the Gospel accounts.[57]

Further complicating the various orality paradigms is the difficulty faced as local tradents aged. Parkin notes a particular challenge faced by

---

55. Kirk, "Memory," 163.

56. McIver, "Collective Memory," 135.

57. Nonetheless, McIver's view is that, while the Gospels contain "inaccurate details . . . the gist of the gospel traditions is reliable and provides a sound general picture of Jesus' sayings and doings." McIver, "Collective Memory," 140–43.

oral cultures, which ultimately serves to reduce the contribution of aging tradents for passing on traditions orally:

> In an oral culture, older generations might enjoy increased prestige while still alive as repositories of traditional wisdom, to be passed on to the young, whereas in a more literate culture written records might increasingly take their place. On the other hand, failing powers of memory and weakened performance skills in old age could mean that the very aged had no oral role to play.[58]

Again, one must ask, as the church spread and came to be dominated by gentiles and Hellenistic Jews, would they not be most strongly influenced by a Greco-Roman affinity to written materials, for memorizing large works, rather than rabbinic methods?

CONCLUSION

In this chapter, I have uncritically accepted Craig Keener's portrayal of the Gospels as historical biography, a genre which was concerned with accuracy, with the truthfulness of biographical accounts. While I recognize that there can be issues with grouping the Gospels with secular works, and then using that genre classification to influence our reading of Scripture, Keener's research has shown that authors of historical biographies evaluated their sources for reliability, and it is this concern for reliability which I contend would have served as a motivating factor to ensure that the Gospel accounts were published early, well before memory degradation became an issue. I have also cited Jewish, Christian, and secular writers to make the case that written witness testimony was indeed valued within contemporary society, by those who would be receiving the first Gospel.

Accordingly, I have pushed back against modern theories of Gospel origins which excessively prioritize oral traditions over written traditions, the oral voice over the written voice. For, the ancients valued their written texts and they continued to influence the readers and societies to whom they were given.

---

58. Parkin, *Old Age*, 66.

8

The Impacts of an Early Matthew on NT Exegesis

READERS OF THE NEW Testament interpret each passage based on an understanding of the historical-cultural context of the passage, the genre of the literature, the larger canonical context, the theological emphasis of the author, the lexical meaning of phrases and words, etc.[1] Naturally, presuppositions and some amount of speculation are used to reconstruct the history of the early church, and this influences the interpretation of both individual passages and interrelated passages.[2] For example, an awareness that 2 Timothy was likely Paul's last letter enables the modern reader to roughly identify the set of oral and written teachings which Paul had in view when instructing Timothy to teach and pass on to the next generation what "you have heard from me" (2 Tim 2:2; 3:10).

In an earlier chapter it was argued that there were means, motive, and opportunity for the early publication of Gospels in support of the expanding church, as it spread following Pentecost, then spread further due to the persecution after Stephen's death, and then spread further yet after the conversion of the Romans in Caesarea Maritima. Subsequent chapters have employed the testimony of the church fathers, along with exegetical, apologetic, and historical arguments, to contend that an early date for Matthew's

---

1. Köstenberger and Patterson, *Invitation to Biblical Interpretation*, 80, 82, 383, 495–96, 502.

2. Carson offers a useful treatise on the issue of presuppositional and historical fallacies. Carson, *Exegetical Fallacies*, 126–34.

Gospel is not only reasonable, but also likely. As a result, we can envision Matthew as being published in support of the apostles' earliest missionary endeavors outside of Palestine, followed shortly by Mark. Given this proposition, it would be valuable to assess whether our understanding of the New Testament is coherent and perhaps enhanced, if read from this perspective.

This present chapter performs an assessment of several portions of the New Testament, based on an early Gospel presupposition. But whereas prior chapters aspired to build the case for an early publication of Matthew, this chapter will instead assume that this was indeed the historic reality and will then assess the implications of such. The survey begins with a review of the Pastoral Epistles, where it will be inferred, based on the above presupposition and other arguments, that terms such as *Scripture* and *the Word* can be understood as inclusive of the early Gospels, unless the context dictates otherwise. It will also be shown that Paul uses the technique of *broad reference* to link his writings with passages from Matthew.[3] These understandings will then underlie a review of Acts, as Paul reasons from the Scriptures, followed by a brief review of one of Paul's other epistles. Again, the purpose of this assessment is to demonstrate that an early Gospel proposition offers coherent and profitable results, when used as an exegetical framework for studying other portions of the NT.

PASTORAL REFERENCES TO SCRIPTURE

Given the presupposition that Matthew was published in the 30s or early 40s, in support of and at the request of an expanding church, it is inferred that this Gospel would have immediately been recognized as authoritative Scripture, suitable for being read and preached in Christian assemblies.[4] This is with the premise that believers would recognize that the writings,

---

3. The concept of *broad reference* is defined by Ian Turner as "the intertextual phenomena where a NT author signals his audience to refer to the wider context of the precursor (OT) text cited." In the present section, the phenomena will be observed to link Paul's writings to the Gospels. Turner, "Going Beyond," 578. Beale provides a more exhaustive methodology for identifying and assessing the connections between NT and OT texts; however, I appreciate the broad reference terminology employed by Turner. Beale, *Handbook on New Testament Use*, 29–36.

4. By accepting these early dates, I contend that we avoid the debates over how long it took for the Gospels, and Matthew in particular, to go through what Francis Watson calls "a process of reception," by which he envisions the four Gospels as being gradually "differentiated from other" Christian writings (i.e., "the mass of available literature") for inclusion in the authoritative canon. Watson, *Gospel Writing*, 3, 7.

covering the life and teachings of Jesus Christ, carried not only the witness and authority of the apostolic leadership in Jerusalem, but also the guidance and authority of the Holy Spirit. Therefore, Pastoral passages such as, "until I come, devote yourself to the public reading of Scripture, to exhortation, to teaching" (1 Tim 4:13), would be understood as being inclusive of both Gospels and other apostolic writings which had been published prior to Paul's letter to Timothy. And, the assertion that "*all* Scripture is . . . profitable for teaching, for reproof, for correction, and for training . . . that the [Christian] man of God may be complete, equipped for every good work" (2 Tim 3:16–17) would likewise be understood by the reader to expand the definition of *Scripture* to be inclusive of not only the Jewish "sacred writings" (2 Tim 3:15), but also the available Gospels and other apostolic writings which address the Christian condition. Accordingly, Timothy Swinson explains:

> Since Paul has already referred to the "holy writings" collectively, affirming their worth as a whole, he now uses *graphē* modified by *pas* so as to convey that this referent is broader and even more inclusive than all of *ta hiera grammata*; it includes as well the *hois emathes kai epistōthēs* [2 Tim 3:14] that so occupy his attention through the letter.[5]

Further, the companion passage, "preach the word . . . reprove, rebuke, and exhort, with complete patience and teaching" (2 Tim 4:2), would also be understood to include the content of available Gospels, particularly given that "the Roman oratory practice involved the use of a written text" to support oral performances.[6] Other references to the preaching and teaching of the word, such as "he must hold firm to the trustworthy word as taught" (Titus 1:9) and "rightly handling the word of truth" (2 Tim 2:15) would also be reasonably understood as inclusive of available Gospels.

In a sense, these perspectives are not novel. For within the local church, these Pastoral passages are often taught as though *Scripture* and *the Word* are indeed inclusive of the whole of the Bible, as these passages are often leveraged to teach doctrines of inspiration, scriptural authority, and church

---

5. Hence, *all* is to be understood in an inclusive or expansive sense. Swinson, *What Is Scripture?*, 151–52, 182. The expectation that Paul's writings be read and exhorted with authority is asserted in several passages (Col 4:16; 1 Thess 5:27; 2 Thess. 3:14). Second Peter 3:16 also affirms that Paul's writings were considered as scripture.

6. Winsbury, *Roman Book*, 105, 122.

practice.[7] Scholars, on the other hand, will often insist that these passages originally had only the OT writings in view, along with oral traditions, per the common academic belief that Gospels were published relatively late and recognized as Scripture even later.[8] Likewise, systematic theologies are typically careful to constrain these specific passages (along with 2 Pet 1:20) to an OT focus, as these passages are used to develop doctrines of inspiration and authority, before the doctrines are subsequently extended as to be inclusive of NT writings.[9] Hence, one advantage of the early Gospel proposition is that it offers a basis for perceiving the *authorial intent* of these passages in a manner which is consistent with the *modern application* of these passages.[10] Namely, that both then and now, these references to *Scripture* and *the Word* should be understood as being inclusive of NT literature.

Given my characterization of statements concerning the preaching and teaching of *the Word* as potentially inclusive of the Gospels, related Pastoral statements must also be evaluated. The familiar "Scripture says" passage calling for the honoring of elders "who labor in preaching and teaching" (1 Tim 5:17) is often already understood to have in view the preaching and teaching of Gospels, given the subsequent "the laborer deserves his wages" quote (1 Tim 5:18), which is apparently from Luke 10:7 (or perhaps is a paraphrase of Matt 10:10).[11] More intriguing are Paul's statements which refer to his preaching mission, such as, "in hope of eternal life . . . at the

---

7. For example, MacArthur, Hendrikson, Knight, and Grudem. MacArthur, *1 Timothy*, 175–78; MacArthur, *2 Timothy*, 144–46, 171–74; Hendriksen and Kistemaker, *Matthew*, 158, 301; Knight, *Pastoral Epistles*, 207; Grudem, *Systematic Theology*, 127–28.

8. For example, Guthrie and Towner treat *scripture* as referring to Old Testament writings only and *the word* as referring to oral tradition, with perhaps some written records. Although, Towner treats *the word* in 2 Tim 4:2 and Titus 1:9 as focused on Paul's teachings and his gospel message. Guthrie, *Pastoral Epistles*, 111, 181, 207; Towner, *Timothy and Titus*, 317, 585–88, 600, 691.

9. For example, Erickson, *Theology*, 171; Grudem, *Systematic Theology*, 75–76; Boice, *Foundations of the Christian Faith*, 38, 494; MacArthur and Mayhue, *Biblical Doctrine*, 80.

10. It may be counterintuitive that unifying scholarly perspectives around a popularized modern teaching is perceived as an advantage. Yet, the theological doctrine of biblical clarity asserts that "the Bible is written in such a way that its teachings are able to be understood by all who will read it seeking God's help and willing to follow it." Grudem, *Systematic Theology*, 105–8, 1238. When the non-scholarly modern Bible reader interacts with words such as *scripture* and *the word*, these terms are naturally understood in terms of the Bible as an integrated whole. Hence, there is value in aspiring to align scholarly consensus with this perspective, if justifiable.

11. Knight, *Pastoral Epistles*, 233.

proper time manifested in *his word* through the preaching with which I have been entrusted by the command of God our Savior" (Titus 1:2–3). In this passage, "his word" is commonly taken as referring to the gospel *message*; however, in the context of the above analysis, it might be inferred that this statement is inclusive of a written Gospel(s), which Paul had been entrusted to preach.[12] The difficulty with this particular speculation is that Paul elsewhere speaks of *the gospel mystery* which he had been called to preach, as being primarily concerned with the mystery of the multi-racial Jewish-gentile church (e.g., Rom 2:16; 16:25; Eph 3:6), a theme which is not overtly addressed by the Gospels (although, note the discussion in the "Arguments from Galatians" chapter above).[13] Consequently, the conjecture that "his word" in Titus 1:3 encompasses available Gospels must be advanced only tentatively.

PASTORAL USE OF BROAD REFERENCE

New Testament authors skillfully used the technique of *broad reference* to establish connections to particular OT passages.[14] This is to say that when writing a passage, a NT author may have had in view not only the specific quotes and obvious allusions which are made to a specific OT passage, but may be more broadly referencing the contexts, themes, and concepts of that OT passage. The author may thus "be inviting readers to make further sense of the passage by bringing more into play from the wider OT context."[15] Hence, the modern reader must be sensitive to the possibility, whenever quotations or allusions connect a NT passage with an OT passage, that there may be an authorial intent of conveying the broader "unquoted surrounding context" of the OT passage as part of their NT message.[16]

For example, Karen Jobes demonstrates the value of recognizing a broad reference approach in 1 Pet 1.[17] After it is observed that 1 Pet 1:24

---

12. For the assessment that "his word" refers to Paul's gospel message, Knight, *Pastoral Epistles*, 285; Towner, *Timothy and Titus*, 672; Guthrie, *Pastoral Epistles*, 203; Hendriksen and Kistemaker, *Matthew*, 342; Mounce, *Pastoral*, 381.

13. Also compare John 10:16.

14. I use here the terminology of Ian Turner. Turner, "Going Beyond," 577–78.

15. Turner, "Going Beyond," 578.

16. Turner, "Going Beyond," 578.

17. Jobes, *1 Peter*, 125–30; Beale and Carson, *Commentary on New Testament Use*, 1019–22.

quotes from Isa 40:6–8 (LXX), Jobes highlights how "Peter echoes Isaiah's thought elsewhere," by referencing other concepts expressed in Isa 40.[18] For example, it is significant that "the verses quoted [by Peter], . . . declaring that God's word stands forever, are the focal point of Isaiah's prologue to the revelation of God's . . . redemption of his people," as found in Isa 40–66.[19]

There are many additional parallels between Isa 40 and 1 Pet 1. Starting from the top of Isa 40, the careful reader will note that the famous "Comfort, O comfort my people, says God" declaration (Isa 40:1 LXX), which is directed towards Israel as they are about to go into exile, also aligns well with the exile motif employed in 1 Pet 1:1 (and 2:11).[20] Isaiah 40:2 anticipates redemption and pardon, which has affinity with Peter's declaration—of God's foreknowledge, the Spirit's sanctification, and the Son's sacrifice (1 Pet 1:2). Isaiah 40:3–5, with its promise of a messenger who proclaims the anticipated return of the king, has bearing on Peter's confidence in the promise of a second advent (1 Pet 1:3–5).[21] Isaiah 40:10, with its anticipated return of the LORD in judgment and reward, finds a parallel in Peter's reminder that believers are to conduct themselves with fear, for the Father will judge each one's deeds (1 Pet 1:17). Isaiah 40:12–26 emphasizes the power and transcendence of God, as encouragements to Israel, while 1 Peter speaks of those who are being guarded by God's power (1 Pet 1:5).

Additional parallels to Isa 40 could also be elaborated, such as in the encouragement offered to the Christians of Asia Minor, who are facing the trials of Roman might and culture (1 Pet 1:6).[22] When Peter follows his citation of Isa 40:6–8 by saying that "this word is the good news that was preached to you" (1 Pet 1:25), it should be apparent that Peter is not merely expressing his confidence in the enduring nature of the word of the Lord, but his confidence in the demonstrated trustworthiness of God to preserve, redeem, return, etc. as exhibited in Isa 40. Again, the value with this exegetical approach is that once it is recognized that Peter might be making a broad reference based on but a single explicit quote, one can then gain deeper insight into the "unquoted surrounding context" by identifying other allusions which connect the passages. The point of this digression

---

18. Jobes, *1 Peter*, 125.
19. Jobes, *1 Peter*, 126.
20. Jobes, *1 Peter*, 129.
21. Jobes, *1 Peter*, 127.
22. Jobes, *1 Peter*, 129–30.

The Impacts of an Early Matthew on NT Exegesis

into Peter's epistle has been to introduce the broad reference technique to those unfamiliar with such.

This technique can likewise be observed in how Paul refers to the Gospels, per our premise that one or more Gospels were written before Paul's epistles. In both examples below, an initial link is established via a short quotation. The link is then strengthened via secondary associations between the passages.[23] These links and associations are taken to suggest that Paul might have had a particular Gospel passage in view, which should then encourage one to assess whether the broader context of the Gospel passage may be applied to illuminate the Pastoral passage. The critical aspect of this technique is that the author (e.g., Paul) must assume that his readers are familiar with not only the quoted passage, but also the surrounding context, the fixed layout and content of the passage: "in order for readers to detect a biblical allusion, they must be able to recognize the words, themes, or structural similarities between the two texts."[24] This is a realistic assumption with an early Gospels presupposition.

In 1 Timothy, Paul refers to the trustworthy saying (*pistos ho logos*), that "Jesus came into the world to save sinners" (1 Tim 1:15). If the modern reader recognizes that Paul is paraphrasing Matt 9:13, when Jesus was eating in Matthew's house and was being condemned by the Pharisees, then Paul's subsequent self-condemnation, "of whom I am the foremost," is understood (per Matt 9:11) to be with reference to his previous life as a Pharisee. Both passages also speak of mercy. Thus, two secondary associations have been established between these passages. The illumination then comes in recognizing that in this context Paul is reflecting on his calling (1 Tim 1:12) and thus appears to be drawing parallels with Matthew's calling (Matt 9:9).

Additionally, in 1 Timothy, Paul applauds Jesus, "who gave himself as a ransom for all" (1 Tim 2:6), an apparent reference to the event in Matthew, where Jesus responds to the mother of James and John in Matt 20:28: "even as the Son of Man came . . . to give his life as a ransom for many." Given this connection with the pericope in Matt 20, the similar interest in kings and rulers becomes noteworthy—whereas Paul urges "prayers . . . for kings" (1 Tim 2:1–2), Jesus is contrasting the expected behavior

---

23. Turner offers a four-step process. "1. Identify the allusion. 2. Explore the precursor OT text. 3. Explore the broader context of the precursor text . . . with NT context in mind. 4. Shed light on NT meaning." Turner, "Going Beyond," 589. Also refer to Beale, *Handbook on the New Testament Use*, 33.

24. Kimble and Spellman, *Invitation to Biblical Theology*, 70.

of Christian leaders with the "rulers of the Gentiles" (Matt 20:25). Thus, we have a secondary correlation between these passages, which should encourage the reader to begin watching for any implications of the "unquoted surrounding context." The exegetical illumination comes when we recognize that Matthew's concern about servant leadership (Matt 20:26–27) provides background and insight into Paul's stated desire that men should not quarrel and that women should be submissive (1 Tim 2:8–12). Again, relative to both of these broad reference examples in 1 Timothy, familiarity with a physical copy of Matthew's Gospel would be required in order to fully understand Paul's implied message.[25]

OTHER IMPACTS ON NT EXEGESIS

Acts

Given the inference that terms such as *Scripture* and *the Word* are to be understood as inclusive of the written Gospels, as the context permits, and that written Gospels may be in view where preaching and teaching are discussed, certain passages in the book of Acts acquire new meaning. Three passages are evaluated below.

During Paul's second missionary journey, it is recorded that:

> They came to Thessalonica, where there was a synagogue of the Jews. And Paul went in, as was his custom, and on three Sabbath days he reasoned with them from the Scriptures, explaining and proving that it was necessary for the Christ to suffer and to rise from the dead, and saying, "This Jesus, whom I proclaim to you, is the Christ." (Acts 17:1–3)

Given the presupposition that Matthew and Mark were published before Paul's second missionary journey and the inference that *Scriptures* are elsewhere inclusive of the Gospels, it is therefore inferred that it was Paul's practice to reason from both the Hebrew scriptures and the Gospels—presumably leveraging Matthews's Old Testament citations, when speaking in the synagogues.[26]

---

25. Another powerful instance of broad reference is in 2 Tim 4:16, where "may it not be charged against them" connects to Stephen's stoning in Acts 7:60. Multiple secondary associations tie the broader passages together, as Paul reflects back on his first recorded interaction with a faithful Christian.

26. Likewise, in Berea (Acts 17:10–11).

Shortly thereafter, Acts reports that Apollos came to Ephesus and that he was "competent in the Scriptures," but that he "knew only the baptism of John" (Acts 18:25). By this, I infer that it was Matthew's Gospel which Apollos knew, as Matthew lacks any reference of the baptism of the Holy Spirit. Presumably, Apollos became familiar with the Gospel while he was in Alexandria and thus lacked knowledge of the events, revelations and teachings which are reflected in Acts 1–17:

> Now a Jew named Apollos, a native of Alexandria, came to Ephesus. He was an eloquent man, competent in the Scriptures. He had been instructed in the way of the Lord. And being fervent in spirit, he spoke and taught accurately the things concerning Jesus, though he knew only the baptism of John. He began to speak boldly in the synagogue, but when Priscilla and Aquila heard him, they took him aside and explained to him the way of God more accurately . . . for he powerfully refuted the Jews in public, showing by the Scriptures that the Christ was Jesus. (Acts 18:24–26, 28)

Then, after Paul arrived in Ephesus, he spent an extended period reasoning in the hall of Tyrannus. Following a series of miracles and exorcisms, many believed and "those who had practiced magic arts brought their books together and burned them in the sight of all" (19:8–19). The passage concludes with the triumphant assessment, "so the word of the Lord continued to increase and prevail mightily" (19:20).[27] Given the context, it may be inferred that this passage is actually contrasting the demise of the books of magic with the triumph of the written Word of the Lord.

Other Pauline Epistles

Beyond the Pastorals, most of Paul's references to *Scripture* are clearly with respect to the Old Testament.[28] And most of Paul's other *the Word* statements are ambiguous, as to whether he is referring to the spoken or written Word.

---

27. This is a unique variation of "the word of the Lord increased" statements, as also found in Acts 6:7; 12:24; 13:49.

28. In most of Paul's references to scripture it is clear that he is referring to the Hebrew scriptures, as he specifically refers to the *holy* scriptures (Rom 1:2) or the law (Gal 3:21–22), or as he quotes individuals or from a passage (Rom 4:3; 9:17; 10:11; 11:2; 15:3–4; Gal 3:8; 4:30; etc.).

However, another instance of broad reference is to be found in Rom 12; but, in this instance it is the quantity of common terms (e.g., bless, persecute, rejoice, weep, peaceably, hungry) which serve to connect the passages. In Matt 5, Jesus speaks of the blessings which come to the righteous sons of God, who are destined to receive the kingdom of heaven.[29] In contrast, in Rom 12:14–20, Paul recasts many of Jesus's blessings (from Matt 5) by turning them outward. These adjustments should be carefully noted as Paul transforms Jesus's proverbial statements into commands. For example, whereas Matthew states that those who mourn are blessed (Matt 5:4), Romans states that brothers are to "weep with those who weep" (Rom 12:15). Whereas Matthew states that those who are hungry are blessed (Matt 5:6), Romans declares that believers should feed their hungry enemies (Rom 12:20). Overall, Paul's goal in Rom 12 is to remind the audience that they are to present themselves as living sacrifices who are united in the body of Christ (12:1, 4). But the broad reference illumination comes as the reader recognizes that it is their status as fellow children of God, destined to receive the kingdom together per Matt 5, which empowers them to live transformed lives for each other.[30]

Other broad reference connections between the Pauline epistles and Matthew may yet be awaiting discovery, as we consistently approach the writings from an early Matthew perspective. For example, some scholars have identified apparent dependencies between the Thessalonian letters and Matthew.[31] This is particularly significant for those who claim that 1 Thessalonians was Paul's first epistle.

---

29. Lanier also sees "telltale signs of intracanonical awareness of the Gospels" between Rom 12–14 and the "phrasing from Jesus's Sermon on the Mount." Lanier, "Four-Fold Gospel Collection," 234.

30. Instead of recognizing a direct literary connection between Romans and Matthew, Moo instead postulates that Paul is quoting here from "a pre-Synoptic form of one of Jesus' best-known and most startling kingdom demands." Moo, *Romans*, 781.

31. For example, Michael Canham has noted connections between 1 Thess 2:14–16 and Matt 23 in the Olivet Discourse, where four keywords (forms of ἀποκτείνω, προφήτας, διώκω, πληρόω) "appear together in the same context only here in Thessalonians and its parallel passage in Matthew . . . especially since it is highly unusual for Paul to speak of Jesus' being killed." Likewise, Canham has noted several parallels between 2 Thess 2:1–8 and Matt 24 in the Olivet Discourse, and particularly the use of similar terms (forms of φάνεια and παρουσία) in 2 Thess 2:8 and Matt 24:27. Canham, "Overlooked Evidence for Matthean Priority?," app. A. Similarly, Orchard, "Thessalonians and the Synoptic Gospels."

CONCLUSION

The Pastoral Epistles, Acts, and Paul's other epistles have been reviewed to a limited extent, based on a presupposition that the Gospel of Matthew was published prior to Paul's missionary journeys. On this basis it has been inferred that references to *Scripture* and *the Word* can often be understood to be inclusive of Matthew and other previously published Gospels. This understanding then led to insights regarding Paul's practice of preaching in the synagogues, his expectations of Timothy, and the contrast which Acts makes between magic books and the triumphant written Words of Jesus. An exploration of Paul's use of broad reference to refer to the "unquoted surrounding context" of various Gospel passages demonstrated that the technique can also provide additional illumination into Paul's writings.[32]

Consequently, this study has shown that an early Gospel proposition does result in a coherent understanding of other portions of the New Testament and actually provides a more insightful understanding of Paul's writings, particularly in the observation that Paul used broad reference techniques to connect his writings and his train of thought to select passages within the Gospels. Contrary to some perspectives, this study has shown that there was a substantive dependent connection between Paul and the Gospels.[33] Based on the success of this study, it is recommended that additional NT passages be similarly evaluated.[34]

---

32. As referenced earlier, per Turner, "Going Beyond," 578.

33. Foster, working from the premise that Matthew's Gospel is later than the Pauline epistles, draws the conclusion that, "from the available evidence one could not even infer that Matthew had significant awareness of Paul." Foster, "Paul and Matthew," 114.

34. For example, Lanier has identified the potential relationship between the "thief in the night" metaphor in 1 Thess 5:2 and the Olivet Discourse in Matthew. Lanier allows that some of the "telltale signs of intracanonical awareness of the Gospels" may "have arisen via oral or pre-Gospel written traditions—but the possibility remains that some indicate a burgeoning literary access to written Gospels within the apostolic circle." Lanier, "Four-Fold Gospel Collection," 234.

9

Matthew as the Messiah's Royal Chronicler

IN THIS CHAPTER, I want to present a new paradigm for how we view Matthew. Assuming that it was indeed the disciple Matthew who wrote the Gospel which bears his name, should we view Matthew as an after-the-fact biographer of Jesus, who decided decades after the resurrection that an account of Jesus's life and teachings might be helpful? Or was Matthew committed from his earliest days as a disciple of Jesus to publishing a chronicle of the long-anticipated Messiah, who would ultimately assume the throne of David? If the present reader will indulge me, let us consider a scenario in which Matthew was intent on recording and publishing the account of the Messiah from his earliest days as a disciple, perhaps even before his calling to be part of the inner circle of twelve.

I will begin by arguing that Matthew was a disciple of Jesus even before his formal calling, then affirm that Jesus intended from the start to provide scribes to write new Scriptures, and then conclude by postulating that Matthew understood his role as being the royal chronicler of the Messiah with every intention of promptly publishing his account, even before understanding what kind of Messiah he was serving.

MATTHEW AS AN EARLY DISCIPLE OF JESUS

In each of the Synoptic Gospels there is an account of the calling of the tax collector Matthew (also named Levi), which follows the healing of the paralytic in Capernaum.[1] It is one of the briefest encounter narratives in the Gospels, as Jesus simply sees Matthew in the tax booth and commands him to "follow me," whereupon Matthew promptly leaves his post to follow Jesus (Matt 9:9). Some commentators find Matthew's immediate compliance to Jesus's demand to be "startling," given that "we know of no prior contact between them."[2] However, given that Matthew's tax station was evidently located on the lake shore in or near Capernaum (Mark 2:1, 13–14), it is quite likely that he was well aware of Jesus's preaching and healing ministry and had perhaps even interacted with Jesus as part of his official duties. In this context, other commentators see Matthew's quick response to Jesus as reflecting an informed conversion experience.[3] Yet, even this presupposes that Matthew had not already become a disciple of Jesus.

Certain elements within the broader narrative suggest that Matthew may already have been a follower of Jesus, even before being called to become one of the twelve. First, it is significant that the four fishermen who were the earliest disciples called to "follow me" were apparently already disciples, while also still maintaining their fishing businesses (Matt 4:18–22). In John's Gospel, we are told that Andrew and another disciple of John the Baptist, presumably John the brother of James, had gone to follow Jesus after the Baptist identified Jesus as "the lamb of God, who takes away the sin of the world!" (John 1:27–40).[4] After discovering where Jesus was staying, Andrew fetched his brother Simon Peter, announcing that "we have found the Messiah," and brought him to Jesus (John 1:41–42). According to John's Gospel, these would then be with Jesus as he performed a miracle in Cana (John 2:11), cleared the temple (2:17), baptized on the Jordan (3:22), met with the woman at the well (4:27), etc. Yet later we find these men up in Galilee back at work in their fishing business, as Jesus strolls by and issues his "follow me" to them, whereupon they leave everything behind

---

1. Bauckham rejects the correlation of Matthew with Levi. Bauckham, *Jesus and the Eyewitnesses*, 108.

2. Osborne, *Matthew*, 335.

3. Doriani, *Matthew*, 1:380.

4. The "traditional identification" is that the "unnamed disciple" is the somewhat anonymous "beloved disciple," who is commonly recognized as John, the brother of James. Carson, *John*, 154.

and follow Jesus (Matt 4:18–22). Therefore, with respect to Matthew, it is reasonable to suppose that Matthew's quick response to Jesus was likewise "the culmination of a prior relationship, similar to the call of the two sets of brothers . . . [whose] prior relationship with Jesus . . . lasted perhaps a year before their call to become fishers of men."[5] Indeed, the "follow me" charge to Matthew, expressed as a present imperative in Greek, "commands the action as an ongoing process."[6] This suggests not merely a call to a "lifetime of discipleship," as Osborne contends, but the continuation of an existing relationship.[7] Consequently, in this present encounter Jesus appears to be calling Matthew to now join his core team of disciples (Matt 10:1–4) and leave behind his present livelihood, even as the four fishermen had recently been called to leave behind their nets.

Secondly, it should be observed that the call of Matthew (Matt 9:9) follows, in short order, the Sermon on the Mount (Matt 5–7). This three-chapter monologue is the first of Matthew's five extended discourses, recounting the teachings of Jesus. If we accept that Matthew was indeed the author of the Gospel which bears his name, and that he primarily composed his Gospel based on his own recollections and notes of the events which he himself had witnessed, less the nativity, baptism, temptation, and other activities prior to Jesus's settling in Capernaum (Matt 4:13), along with select events later where the narrative makes clear that Matthew was not present, then the inclusion of the Sermon on the Mount in Matthew's Gospel suggests that Matthew himself was a first-hand witness of such, and thus one of the disciples or at least part of the crowd who followed Jesus up the mountain (5:1).

Ergo, we can envision Matthew as becoming a follower of Jesus around the time that Jesus settled in Capernaum (Matt 4:13), and thus a witness to Jesus's ministry throughout Galilee, as Jesus taught in the synagogues, proclaimed the gospel of the kingdom, and healed every kind of disease and sickness (Matt 4:23).

MATTHEW AS SCRIBE AND MAKER OF WINESKINS

In Matt 23, just before the Olivet Discourse, Jesus condemns the scribes and Pharisees as hypocrites, blind guides, white-washed tombs, and broods

---

5. Wilkins, "Apologetics Commentary on the Gospel of Matthew," 72.
6. Wallace, *Grammar*, 485.
7. Osborne, *Matthew*, 335.

of vipers. These leaders and teachers of the people, these self-appointed representatives of Moses, were obligated to faithfully shepherd the people according to the law and not prey on them (Ezek 34). Given their failure, Jesus declared that he was sending his own "prophets and wise men and scribes" (Matt 23:34), thereby indicating even before the crucifixion that the divine plan included the delivery of new Scriptures. Not only would there be prophets who could "authoritatively . . . pass on to the people . . . the authentic message of God," and wise men who understood the sacred writings, but also "learned men, men who write, men who teach."[8] Matthew would be one of those scribes.

Further, Matt 13 anticipates a new kind of scribe, one "who has been trained for the kingdom of heaven" (Matt 13:52), that kingdom which Jesus preached. This new kind of scribe would bring "out of his treasure [both] what is new and what is old" (13:52). Patrick Schreiner draws from this passage in characterizing Matthew as "the discipled scribe who narrates Jesus's life through the alternation of the new and the old."[9] This scribe of the kingdom would be disciplined by Jesus himself, who "trains his own scribes in the true interpretation of the Scriptures."[10] Reflecting such, Matthew's Gospel frames the teachings of Jesus (the new) within the context of the Hebrew scriptures (the old), in such a way that "he does not discard the past and simply cling to the new, but [rather] he employs the new to interpret the old."[11] This care in preserving both the old and the new leads us to a third passage, which I suspect also speaks to Matthew's role as scribe.

After Matthew's recruitment and the subsequent event at his house, Jesus is challenged for the failure of his disciples to fast (Matt 9:14). Jesus responds by speaking of the celebration which must occur while the bridegroom is present, as the fasting will occur when the "bridegroom is taken away from them" (9:15). Of interest for our purposes are the subsequent allegories, which Luke groups together as a parable (Luke 5:36). In the first allegory, it is said that a patch of unshrunk cloth is not to be added to an old garment, lest a worse tear occur (Matt 9:16). In the second allegory, new wine is not to be put in old wineskins; rather new wine is to be put into fresh wineskins so that both the old and the new may be preserved (9:17).

---

8. Morris, *Matthew*, 588.

9. Schreiner, *Matthew, Disciple and Scribe*, 9–10.

10. Schreiner presents Jesus as the ultimate "teacher of wisdom." Schreiner, *Matthew, Disciple and Scribe*, 16.

11. Schreiner, *Matthew, Disciple and Scribe*, 29.

One scholar interprets these allegories as making the "point that Jesus is not trying to patch up a worn-out Judaism."¹² Other commentators find the allegories to be making the point that "the new situation introduced by Jesus could not simply be patched onto old Judaism or poured into the old wineskins of Judaism. New forms would have to accompany the kingdom Jesus was now inaugurating."¹³

I contend that there is more to these allegories than granted by the above interpretive approaches. First, it must be recognized that even with these interpretive approaches, the parable does more than simply reinforce the didactic statement concerning the wedding party not fasting, which Jesus articulates before the parable. Though Jesus has evidently broken with local tradition by not requiring that his disciples participate in the unspecified fast, his stated reason doesn't go so far as to suggest that he will be disavowing participation in Judaism at large or its common forms or practices, as the allegories are commonly understood to suggest. Yet, if the intent is to declare that there will be new teachings, forms, and practices, then what are we to make of the desire to preserve both wine and wineskins, both old and new?

It is helpful to recall that Jesus will soon speak again to that which is old and new. In Matt 13:52, following a series of parables, a contrast is made between the teachings in the Hebrew scriptures and Jesus's own teachings concerning the kingdom. Hence, it is appropriate to suspect that the same distinction is in view here in chapter 9, immediately after Matthew is recruited. While Jesus is proclaiming new truths, the old truths are still to be preserved, for Jesus did not "come to abolish the Law or the Prophets" (Matt 5:17). If the wine represents Jesus's new teachings, such as those delivered in the Sermon on the Mount, then the wineskins represent the Scriptures which contain the divine teachings, whether old or new. Consequently, we can understand the new wineskins in the allegory as anticipating the delivery of new Scriptures, written by scribes, which would contain the new teachings.

Collectively then, there are three passages (Matt 9:16–17; 13:52; 23:34) which present Jesus as anticipating scribes who would be trained for the kingdom and who would author new scriptures which would stand alongside of and interpret the Hebrew scriptures. Given the context surrounding

---

12. Morris, *Matthew*, 226.

13. Carson, "Matthew," 227. France believes that this speaks to "new religious structures." France, *Gospel of Matthew*, 357.

Matthew's calling and dinner party, there is an implication that Matthew would play a scribal role in the publishing of these new scriptures.

MATTHEW AS CHRONICLER

In the era of the monarchy, the royal scribes or secretaries (Hebrew: *sôpēr*) were responsible for chronicling the reigns of the kings of Judah and Israel.[14] The duties of these royal secretaries encompassed "record-keeping and the drafting of royal letters and decrees; [and] in some cases, the secretary also served as a counselor in matters of state," leveraging their education and expertise (e.g., 1 Chr 27:32).[15] Besides recording significant events of the dynasty, some of the scribes are also said to have had responsibility for overseeing aspects of the royal treasury (e.g., 2 Kgs 12:10; 22:9; 2 Chr 24:11), which is perhaps the imagery which Jesus was alluding to, when speaking of a new kind of scribe, one who would bring "out of his treasure [both] what is new and what is old" (Matt 13:52). The names of several of these scribes are preserved, including those who served under David (2 Sam 8:17), Solomon (1 Kgs 4:3), Hezekiah (2 Kgs 18:18), Josiah (2 Kgs 22), and others.[16] And, the historical books of the OT repeatedly refer to the chronicles of the kings, presumably produced by these court scribes—the "Book of the Chronicles of the Kings of Judah" (e.g., 1 Kgs 14:29; 2 Kgs 12:19) and the "Book of the Chronicles of the Kings of Israel" (e.g., 1 Kgs 14:19; 2 Kgs 15:31; 1 Chr 9:1). In addition, the historical books speak of writings such as the "Book of the Acts of Solomon" (1 Kgs 11:41), which stood alongside histories written by various prophets (2 Chr 9:29). The bottom line here is that the great kings had royal scribes who chronicled their reigns.

And so now the day of the long awaited Messiah had arrived. He was the righteous branch of David, the king who would execute justice and righteousness in the land, in whose days Judah would be saved and Israel would dwell securely in the land (Jer 23:5–6). Can we not envision Matthew as an eager scribe, ready to chronicle the emergence of this one whom the prophets had anticipated?

John the Baptist had borne witness that Jesus was the supreme one, who would baptize with the Spirit and with fire (Matt 3:11). He would

---

14. Schreiner, *Matthew, Disciple and Scribe*, 21.
15. Gamble, "Amanuensis," 172.
16. Schreiner, *Matthew, Disciple and Scribe*, 21.

gather the faithful as wheat and condemn the unfaithful to be burned as chaff (Matt 3:12; Mal 4:1). He was "my beloved Son," the voice from heaven had said (Matt 3:17). He was the "Lamb of God, who takes away the sin of the world" (John 1:29). He was the one who healed, cast out demons, and taught with authority throughout Galilee (Matt 4:23–24; 7:29). Surely, Matthew had a sufficient basis for believing that this was the Messiah. And Matthew had the skills to serve this messianic king.

Let us therefore consider a scenario in which Matthew resolved to serve in the role of royal scribe, as chronicler of the Messiah, making his decision sometime after Jesus began his ministry in and around Capernaum (Matt 4:13). The Sermon on the Mount, therefore, is Matthew's first major foray into this endeavor, as he sat before the heir apparent and captured his words. Matthew then takes note of a series of miracles as Jesus heals a leper, a centurion's servant, Peter's mother-in-law, and others (Matt 8). Matthew is perhaps even there to record Jesus's calming of the storm, casting out of demons, and healing of a paralytic (Matt 8:1—9:8). Then, perhaps during a brief lull in Jesus's ministry, Matthew returns to work. And hitherto comes Jesus to call Matthew to be one of the twelve (9:9).

Jesus made two declarations in this context which may have cemented Matthew's loyalty. In the healing of the paralytic, Jesus had claimed the authority to forgive sins (Matt 9:1–8).[17] Then, following the meal at Matthew's house, Jesus responded to the Pharisees by speaking of the special need which tax collectors and sinners had for a physician. Situated between these two declarations is the calling of Matthew, one who was a tax collector and, therefore, a sinner. Thus, Matthew's calling is bracketed by Jesus's declaration of his authority to forgive sin and his readiness to do so, even for those who are ostracized by the religious elites of the day. If we recognize that Matthew's recruitment stands at the center of these events, then the subsequent metaphors, and particularly that of the wineskins, take on a more personal meaning for Matthew.[18] He would be that one who would provide the new wineskin, who would chronicle and publish the new teachings of

---

17. Note that it is the claim that "the Son of Man has authority on earth to forgive sins" which most distinguishes this paralytic healing from prior paralytic healings (Matt 4:24). Hence, the close proximity of this claim to the subsequent reference to sinners brings extra emphasis to this theme.

18. Also note that in the earlier story of the paralytic, it is the scribes who reject Jesus's claim to be able to forgive sins as blasphemy (Matt 9:3). "The scribes considered themselves the official interpreters of Torah." Osborne, *Matthew*, 327. Jesus needs a new kind of scribe, who will properly interpret the Torah.

Jesus, which would stand alongside of the ancient Scriptures, "so that both are preserved" (Matt 9:17).

CONCLUSION

This chapter has offered a new paradigm for how we can view Matthew. Rather than accepting the premise that Matthew waited for decades before stepping up to the task of writing a *Christobiography*, as Craig Keener has characterized the Gospels, perhaps we can instead view Matthew as the royal chronicler of the long-awaited Messiah.[19] Indeed, there are elements within Matthew's Gospel which suggest that he became a follower of Jesus around the time that Jesus settled in Capernaum, even before Jesus called Matthew to leave his tax booth and join the twelve. The meticulous care evident in the text of the Sermon on the Mount itself, "Jesus's *magnum opus*," is one of these key elements.[20] Further, several passages within the Gospel indicate that Jesus was intent on sending scribes who would capture and publish his teachings. Therefore, we may postulate, though certainly not prove, that Matthew saw himself in this role, akin to the chroniclers of the kings of Judah and Israel, who would record the proclamations and achievements of the messianic king, and eventually publish such.

Can we embrace this view of Matthew, as intentionally recording—in written form for future publication—the key events of Jesus's travels and healing ministry, his lengthy discourses, his conflicts with the religious authorities, his triumphal entry, crucifixion, resurrection, and commissioning of the eleven disciples? Ultimately, you and I must judge whether this paradigm coheres with the testimony and character of Scripture, the needs of the early church, the testimony of the church fathers, and our own apologetic need for an authentic and authoritative Gospel. However, is this not a better paradigm to affirm than the supposition that Matthew and the other disciples waited for decades before publishing, and that their primary source material for such was the aging memories of those who heard and witnessed the teachings and life of the Messiah?

---

19. Keener, *Christobiography*, 1–2.

20. "One of the best-known and loved passages in Scripture, the Sermon on the Mount, has been considered Jesus' *magnum opus*." Osborne, *Matthew*, 159.

10

Conclusion
A Trustworthy Gospel

THERE ARE MANY METHODS by which we know that the Gospels are trustworthy.[1] I find two to be particularly significant. Foremost is the conviction that the Gospel authors were moved and inspired by the Holy Spirit (2 Tim 3:16; 2 Pet 1:20–21) in such a way that everything they wrote is "truthful and trustworthy" (ref. John 17:17).[2] For, "scripture is . . . a special and divine revelation from God to men (Heb 1:1)."[3] God providentially worked through and influenced each human author—"his immediate family, his cultural context . . . his educational training, and all of his various life experiences . . . to prepare his chosen vessels to communicate his Word in precisely the way he intended."[4] Regardless of what we may think or know about who the authors were or when they wrote, we can affirm the inerrancy and truthfulness of the Gospels on this basis.[5] In a similar vein, with regard to Hebrews, Robert Gromacki can say that "only God knows for sure who the author was. . . . [nevertheless] this fact does not detract from the authenticity or inspired authority of its contents." Thus, we may

---

1. Peter Williams presents a series of strong arguments for why the Gospels should be judged as reliable. Williams, *Can We Trust the Gospels?*
2. MacArthur and Mayhue, *Biblical Doctrine*, 390.
3. MacArthur and Mayhue, *Biblical Doctrine*, 74.
4. Waymeyer, "Words of God and Words of Man," 295.
5. Gromacki, *Survey*, 321.

Conclusion

acknowledge that the New Testament declares a supernatural basis for affirming that the Gospels are trustworthy.

Yet the apostles frequently made an additional assertion. Namely, that the Gospels should be judged as trustworthy because they are grounded in the eyewitness testimony of those who traveled with Jesus, who observed the events described in the Gospels, and who sat under his teaching. Jesus told his disciples, "You also will bear witness, because you have been with me from the beginning" (John 15:27; Luke 24:48). And this privileged status was repeatedly voiced by the apostles. Before the Sanhedrin, Peter and the apostles defended their sanction to preach and teach concerning Jesus, for "we are eyewitnesses" (Acts 5:32; similarly, 10:39). In Peter's letters, Peter claimed both moral and doctrinal authority based on his status as an eyewitness (1 Pet 5:1; 2 Pet 1:16).[6] John likewise leveraged his status as a witness to give credibility to his testimony and to his expectations of the church (John 20:30; 1 John 1:1–3; 4:14). Luke attributes his source material to "those who from the beginning were eyewitnesses," with the goal that he might give Theophilus "certainty concerning the things you have been taught" (Luke 1:2–4). Clearly, the apostles deferred to their witness credentials because they expected their audiences to value such and thereby judge their testimony and teachings to be more trustworthy and authoritative.

Within the writings of the apostles (e.g., 1 Pet 5:1; John 20:30), their witness credentials were generally presented without reference to any claims of supernatural inspiration.[7] Yes, the Spirit empowered the witnesses in their mission (Acts 1:8), but their stature as witnesses leveraged a different type of authority. Hence, the New Testament presents both a supernatural and a non-supernatural basis for affirming that the Gospels are trustworthy. Whether a Gospel audience consists of believers or non-believers, both claims to authority have a role in establishing the trustworthiness of the Gospels.

My concern in this book has been to offer a defense relative to the non-supernatural testimony of the eyewitnesses. Of course, defending the integrity of this testimony can be challenging, given that the Gospels make at best only indirect claims concerning authorship, dating, setting, etc. This

---

6. "Often ancient historians of the Greco-Roman tradition were prone to invent tales or myths about a person's life," but in 2 Pet 1:16, "Peter firmly distanced himself from such ancient practices in the writing of his accounts." Farnell, "Are the Gospel Accounts Reliable?," 132.

7. Refer to chapter 2 for my treatment of the limits of Spirit empowered remembrance, as anticipated per John 14:26.

ambiguity has fostered modern Gospel origin theories which claim late publications, and this supposition has then led some scholars, in my opinion, to either distort the nature of eyewitness testimony by making claims that Gospel authors retained perfect memory over decades, or to instead defer to the supernatural claim too quickly, as the basis for trustworthiness, while other scholars simply dispute the reliability of the Gospels given their perception of the limitations of oral traditions.[8] However, let us not forget that the New Testament advances both claims—supernatural and natural. Andreas Köstenberger expresses well the importance of defending the testimony of those who were witnesses, with regard to defending John as the author of the fourth Gospel:

> But what does it matter? Is it not possible to accept John's gospel regardless of who wrote it and to benefit from its lofty portrayal of Christ and its manifold lessons on what it means to follow him? Clearly, this is possible. And it must be acknowledged that affirming John the son of Zebedee as the author of John's gospel is not an issue of biblical inerrancy or inspiration, since the Fourth Evangelist falls short of making such identification explicit. Nevertheless, affirming John the son of Zebedee as the author of John's gospel matters a great deal. For Johannine authorship safeguards this gospel's character as apostolic eyewitness testimony (which, as has been shown, is clearly suggested by the gospel's internal evidence).
>
> This, in turn, is highly significant in light of the unique, foundational, and authoritative function awarded apostolic teaching in the early church (cf. Acts 2:42; Eph 2:20; cf. also John 14:26; 15:27; 16:13). Therefore, it does matter whether the author of John's gospel was an apostolic eyewitness or an anonymous member of a late-first-century sect (as is proposed by the Johannine community hypothesis), whether John's gospel is a mainstream apostolic writing or a sectarian fringe document. Therefore, it was necessary to present a thorough account of the gospel's internal evidence, which turned out to be decidedly in favor of apostolic authorship.[9]

---

8. In Sproul's commentary regarding the Chicago Statement of Biblical Inerrancy, allowance is made for academic inquiry into issues of authorship "to discover the unstated authorship of books in sacred Scripture, such as the epistle to the Hebrews." Sproul, *Can I Trust the Bible?*, 63. By extension, investigation into the dating appears appropriate; however, we must be cautious when proposals are made which reduce the effectiveness of witness testimony contained within the Scriptures.

9. Köstenberger, *Encountering John*, 6–7.

Conclusion

Along these same lines, I have expressed the view that the trustworthiness of Matthew's Gospel, in so far as it depends on witness testimony, is inherently related to the dating of the Gospel. Therefore, a series of arguments have been advanced for a publication date within a decade of the resurrection. These arguments include a reasonableness argument, a patristic testimony argument, an exegetical argument, an apologetic-motivational argument, a historical (original audience) argument, and an explanatory power argument. And as a final chapter, the reader was invited to adopt a new paradigm concerning Matthew's role. Each of these arguments are summarized below.

First, I aspired to show that it was reasonable to propose that one or more Gospels could have been published within the earliest years of the church, while the disciples were still resident in Jerusalem. I have shown that the means, motive, and opportunity was present. Perhaps most consequential was the claim that because of the collaboration within the early church and the availability of the Roman trade network, it is reasonable to assume that Gospel authors had access to previously published Gospels. This realization serves to discount Gospel origin theories which assume that the authors wrote in relative isolation.

Second, arguments from the early church fathers, that Matthew published first, were affirmed and solutions were presented for resolving perceived conflicts between the church fathers. Most significant was the realization that *Rome* was not merely the city but could also be understood as referring to the empire; in particular, for one to preach in a Roman bastion such as Caesarea Maritima or in the regions outside of Palestine was to preach in Rome. On this basis, Irenaeus can be understood as affirming an early publication of Matthew "among the Hebrews," as Peter and Paul were preaching "in Rome," whether to Cornelius in Caesarea Maritima or to those in Antioch. Other apparent difficulties in the testimonies of the church fathers were also addressed, such that there is scant reason for not accepting the patristic testimony regarding Matthew as being both first and published very early in the history of the church.

Third, exegetical arguments were articulated, primarily based on Paul's letter to the Galatians. In this perhaps earliest of Paul's letters, we find him presenting his own biographical history and core teachings. The argument for an early Gospel was thereupon extrapolated from the observation that if Paul found it essential to write a circular letter so soon after his visit to the region, then he would likewise have found it essential to have in his possession a similar writing concerning Jesus, to support his evangelistic endeavors. This was further supported by Paul's expectation that others should follow the example of his ministry through the issuance of written materials; surely, he would have expected the apostles to write an account of their Lord and Savior. In addition, it was shown that the "publicly portrayed" language in Gal 3:1 is better translated as "previously written," as though referring to a Gospel, which had been previously presented "before your eyes."

Next, apologetic arguments from scholars of the post-Reformation era were explored to show that they considered a publication of Matthew's Gospel within a few years or perhaps a decade after the ascension to be defensible based on the needs of the early church. Twelve motivational arguments for the necessity of an early Gospel publication were elaborated, including the need to secure the church against the spread of falsehoods, to facilitate training in Christian belief and practice, to resolve concerns that oral traditions are liable to uncertainty and resistance, etc. But further, these authors believed that the defense of an early Gospel was necessary to maintain the integrity and authority of the Gospels against then contemporary secular and Christian skeptics. I contend that we would do well to incorporate these same motivational arguments into our modern Gospel origins dialogue, given the existence of skeptical challenges yet in our modern age.

The subsequent historical argument was intent on demonstrating that the *original audiences* of the gospel message, those contemporaries of the apostles, were concerned over the frailty and reliability of aging memories. Further, it was shown that the great Greco-Roman orators of the era expected that orators would be active writers, drafting out their messages in writing and then publishing their teachings. To illustrate this, the concerns and expectations of Cicero, Livy, Philo, Quintilian, Plutarch, and other ancient writers and orators were cited. Therefore, on the premise that contemporary society embraced these concerns and expectations, it was surmised that there would be skepticism over the accuracy of Jesus traditions which were primarily preserved by a reliance on the long-term memory of witnesses. On this basis, I asserted that Richard Bauckham, in his *Jesus and the Eyewitnesses*, has not adequately recognized the environment within which the apostles ministered when he claimed that the eyewitnesses accurately preserved the Jesus traditions, primarily based on their personal memories, over thirty to fifty years before publishing. The key assertion of

Conclusion

this chapter is that those who were proclaiming Jesus's life and teachings would themselves be aware of and sensitive to these audience expectations. Namely, that a primary reliance by witnesses on aging memories would have reduced the credibility of the gospel message, when preached, and of the Gospels themselves, once ultimately published.

The following chapter made a similar argument that the ancients valued written materials, such as biographies and written testimony, and therefore Gospel origin theories which deprecate the value of these materials, in favor of oral traditions, do not reflect the situation of the first century.

It was then argued that there is valuable explanatory power for understanding other portions of the New Testament if one accepts that there was an early publication of Matthew's Gospel. For example, some of the references to *Scripture* and *the Word*, particularly in the Pastorals, can now be clarified as inclusive of earlier Gospels. These include: "devote yourself to the public reading of Scripture" (1 Tim 4:13), "all Scripture is . . . profitable . . . that the [Christian] man of God may be complete" (2 Tim 3:16–17), "preach the word" (2 Tim 4:2), and "hold firm to the trustworthy word as taught" (Titus 1:9). More significantly, *broad reference* connections between Paul's epistles and the Gospels can be identified, such as connections between 1 Tim 1 and Matt 9, 1 Tim 2 and Matt 20, etc. Other examples were also offered, illustrating the explanatory power inherent in the acceptance of an early Gospel publication. Overall, this suggests an area of exegetical and theological study which begs for additional research.

And finally, if the present reader perhaps found the arguments of this book to be persuasive and even preferable over competing Gospel origin theories, then the reader was encouraged to consider adopting a new paradigm when visualizing Matthew. Let us recognize that Matthew became a disciple of Jesus and began chronicling his life and teachings shortly after the Messiah began his residency in Capernaum, that Matthew diligently recorded the Sermon on the Mount while sitting at the feet of the King, and that from his earliest involvement, he was intent on publishing a chronicle of the long-awaited Messiah.

To say it once again, I contend that the contemporary needs and expectations of the early church and of the Greco-Roman audiences would have motivated the apostles to publish a Gospel within the first decade after the resurrection and ascension of Jesus Christ, in order to maximize the trustworthiness of the gospel message. But further, I contend that the same need for trustworthiness exists today and is intimately linked to the publication dates of the Gospels, and particularly of the first Gospel published.

You, dear reader, have a variety of theories to choose between relative to the origin of the Gospels—their authors, their dates, their interrelationships, their acceptance and use by the early Christian communities, and their authority. None of these theories are provable, and so you will naturally form an opinion based on the available data, on what seems reasonable. You may choose to concede to "the scholarly consensus" that the early church did not see value in having a written testimony concerning Jesus, and therefore did not bother to publish a Gospel until decades had transpired. Or you may choose to not vest yourself in a specific theory or in the debate itself. I hope instead that this polemic has adequately conveyed why an early publication of the first Gospel makes the most sense, in terms of what we know of the sentiments and needs of the early church and of the contemporary audience, to whom the gospel of Jesus Christ was preached both orally and in writing.

Let us therefore recognize the situation of the early church, embrace the testimony of the church fathers, preserve a rational approach to the limitations of long-term memory, and accept the evidence presented within the Scriptures themselves. The proposition that Matthew was published within a decade of the resurrection is reasonable, defensible, and even preferable, over the popular belief that the church instead waited for decades before publishing the life and teachings of Jesus in written form. May we also affirm that God's primary means for speaking to his people over the ages has indeed been his written word, and that this was even true during the earliest years of the church. Let us recognize that the very words which Matthew chronicled on behalf of the messianic King were the words which Paul laid before the Galatians, as he presented the crucified Christ; and that these are the same trustworthy words which we can employ, as we now present this Christ to our world.

Bibliography

Alexander, Loveday. "Ancient Book Production and the Circulation of the Gospels." In *The Gospel for All Christians: Rethinking the Gospel Audiences*, edited by Richard Bauckham, 71–105. Grand Rapids, MI: Eerdmans, 1998.

———. "The Living Voice: Skepticism toward the Written Word in Early Christian and in Greco-Roman Texts." In *The Bible in Three Dimensions: Essays in Celebration of Forty Years of Biblical Studies in the University of Sheffield*, edited by David J. A. Clines et al., 221–46. Journal for the Study of the Old Testament 87. Sheffield, UK: Sheffield Academic, 1990.

Alikin, Valeriy A. *The Earliest History of the Christian Gathering*. Boston, MA: Brill, 2010.

Allison, Dale C. "The Pauline Epistles and the Synoptic Gospels: The Pattern of the Parallels." *New Testament Studies* 28.1 (Jan 1982) 1–32.

Allison, Dale C., and W. D. Davies. *The Gospel according to Saint Matthew: Introduction and Commentary on Matthew I–VIII*. Vol. 1. 3 vols. A Critical and Exegetical Commentary. London: T. & T. Clark, 2004.

Angus, Joseph. *The Bible Handbook: An Introduction to the Study of the Sacred Scripture*. Revised. Philadelphia: James S. Claxton, 1866.

Arichea, Daniel C., and Eugene A. Nida. *Paul's Letter to the Galatians*. UBS Handbook Series. New York: United Bible Societies, 1976.

Aune, David E. "Jesus Tradition and the Pauline Letters." In *Jesus in Memory: Tradition in Oral and Scribal Perspectives*, edited by Werner H. Kelber and Samuel Byrskog, 63–86. Waco, TX: Baylor University Press, 2009.

Bagnall, Roger S. *Everyday Writing in the Graeco-Roman East*. Berkeley: University of California Press, 2011.

Bailey, Kenneth E. "Informal Controlled Oral Tradition and the Synoptic Gospels." *Themelios* 20.2 (Jan 1995) 4–11.

Balz, Horst Robert. "Προγράφω." In *Exegetical Dictionary of the New Testament*, edited by Horst Robert Balz and Gerhard Schneider, 3:154. Grand Rapids, MI: Eerdmans, 1990.

Bauckham, Richard. *2 Peter, Jude*. Word Biblical Commentary. Dallas, TX: Word, 1983.

———. "Eyewitnesses and Critical History: A Response to Jens Schröter and Craig Evans." *Journal for the Study of the New Testament* 31.2 (Dec 2008) 221–35.

———. "The General and the Particular in Memory: A Critique of Dale Allison's Approach to the Historical Jesus." *Journal for the Study of the Historical Jesus* 14.1 (Jan 2016) 28–51.

Bibliography

———. "Gospel Traditions: Anonymous Community Traditions or Eyewitness Testimony?" In *Jesus Research: New Methodologies and Perceptions—The Second Princeton-Prague Symposium on Jesus Research*, edited by James H. Charlesworth et al., 483–99. Grand Rapids, MI: Eerdmans, 2014.

———. *Jesus and the Eyewitnesses: The Gospels as Eyewitness Testimony.* 2nd ed. Grand Rapids: Eerdmans, 2017.

———. "The Psychology of Memory and the Study of the Gospels." *Journal for the Study of the Historical Jesus* 16.2–3 (2018) 136–55.

———. "Response to the Respondents." *Nova et Vetera*, English Edition 6.3 (Summer 2008) 529–42.

Bauer, Walter, et al. *A Greek-English Lexicon of the New Testament and Other Early Christian Literature.* 3rd ed. Chicago: University of Chicago Press, 2000.

Beale, G. K. *Handbook on the New Testament Use of the Old Testament: Exegesis and Interpretation.* Grand Rapids, MI: Baker Academic, 2012.

Beale, G. K., and D. A. Carson, eds. *Commentary on the New Testament Use of the Old Testament.* Grand Rapids: Baker Academic, 2007.

Bernier, Jonathan. *Rethinking the Dates of the New Testament: The Evidence for Early Composition.* Grand Rapids, MI: Baker Academic, 2022.

Best, Ernest. *The First and Second Epistles to the Thessalonians.* Black's New Testament Commentaries. Peabody, MA: Hendrickson, 2003.

Bird, Michael F. "The Formation of the Gospels in the Setting of Early Christianity: The Jesus Tradition as Corporate Memory." *Westminster Theological Journal* 67.1 (Spring 2005) 113–34.

———. *The Gospel of the Lord: How the Early Church Wrote the Story of Jesus.* Grand Rapids, MI: Eerdmans, 2014.

Birks, Thomas R. *Horae Evangelicae: The Internal Evidence of the Gospel History.* London: George Bell, 1852.

Black, David Alan. *Why Four Gospels? The Historical Origins of the Gospels.* 2nd ed. Gonzalez, FL: Energion, 2010.

Black, David Alan, and David R. Beck. *Rethinking the Synoptic Problem.* Grand Rapids, MI: Baker Academic, 2001.

Blass, Friedrich, and Albert DeBrunner. *A Greek Grammar of the New Testament and Other Early Christian Literature.* Translated by Robert W. Funk. Chicago: University of Chicago Press, 1961.

Blomberg, Craig L. *The Historical Reliability of the Gospels.* 2nd ed. Downers Grove, IL: IVP Academic, 2007.

———. *The Historical Reliability of the New Testament: Countering the Challenges to Evangelical Christian Beliefs.* Nashville: B&H Academic, 2016.

———. *Jesus and the Gospels: New Testament: Introduction and Survey.* 2nd ed. Vol. 1. Nottingham: Apollos, 2009.

———. "Matthew." In *Commentary on the New Testament Use of the Old Testament*, edited by G. K. Beale and D. A. Carson, 1–109. Grand Rapids, MI: Baker Academic, 2007.

———. "Memory, Jesus, and the Synoptic Gospels." *Themelios* 37.2 (Jul 2012) 325–26.

———. "Quotations, Allusions, and Echoes of Jesus in Paul." In *Studies in the Pauline Epistles: Essays in Honor of Douglas J. Moo*, edited by Matthew S. Harmon and Jay E. Smith, 129–43. Grand Rapids, MI: Zondervan, 2014.

Bibliography

Blomberg, Craig L., and Darlene M. Seal. "The Historical Jesus in Recent Evangelical Scholarship." In *Jesus, Skepticism, and the Problem of History*, edited by Darrell L. Bock and J. Ed Komoszewski, 43–66. Grand Rapids, MI: Zondervan, 2019.

Bock, Darrell L. "Questions about Q." In *Rethinking the Synoptic Problem*, edited by David Alan Black and David R. Beck, 41–64. Grand Rapids, MI: Baker Academic, 2001.

Bock, Darrell L., and Buist M. Fanning, eds. *Interpreting the New Testament Text: Introduction to the Art and Science of Exegesis*. Wheaton, IL: Crossway, 2006.

Boice, James Montgomery. *Foundations of the Christian Faith: A Comprehensive and Readable Theology*. Downers Grove, IL: InterVarsity, 1986.

Botha, Pieter J. J. "Greco-Roman Literacy as Setting for New Testament Writings." *Neotestamentica* 26.1 (1992) 195–215.

———. *Orality and Literacy in Early Christianity*. Performance Biblical Criticism 5. Eugene, OR: Wipf & Stock, 2012.

Brenton, Lancelot C. L. *The Septuagint with Apocrypha: Greek and English*. London: Samuel Bagster and Sons, 1851.

Bretscher, Paul G. "Light from Galatians 3:1 on Pauline Theology." *Concordia Theological Monthly* 34.2 (Feb 1963) 77–97.

Brewer, Burton Keith. "Models for the Oral Transmission of the Gospel Traditions and the Problem of Continuity: An Analysis and Evaluation." PhD diss., Drew University, Madison, NJ, 2005.

Bruce, F. F. *The Epistle to the Galatians: A Commentary on the Greek Text*. New International Greek Testament Commentary. Grand Rapids, MI: Eerdmans, 1982.

Burdick, Donald W. "James." In *Hebrews through Revelation*, edited by Frank E. Gaebelein, 159–205. The Expositor's Bible Commentary. Grand Rapids, MI: Zondervan, 1981.

Byrskog, Samuel. "Introduction." In *Jesus in Memory: Traditions in Oral and Scribal Perspectives*, edited by Werner H. Kelber and Samuel Byrskog, 1–20. Waco, TX: Baylor University Press, 2009.

———. *Story as History, History as Story: The Gospel Tradition in the Context of Ancient Oral History*. Tübingen: Mohr Siebeck, 2000.

———. "A 'Truer' History: Reflections on Richard Bauckham, Jesus and the Eyewitnesses: The Gospels as Eyewitness Testimony." *Nova et Vetera, English Edition* 6.3 (2008) 483–90.

Canfield, George L. "The Roman Lawyer: A Sketch." *Michigan Law Review* 7.7 (May 1909) 557–69.

Canham, Michael M. "Thessalonians and Matthew: Overlooked Evidence for Matthean Priority?" Paper presented at the 64th annual meeting of the Evangelical Theological Society, Milwaukee, WI, 2012.

Carson, D. A. *Exegetical Fallacies*. 2nd ed. Grand Rapids, MI: Baker Academic, 1996.

———. *The Gospel according to John*. Pillar New Testament Commentary. Grand Rapids, MI: Eerdmans, 1991.

———. "Matthew." In *Matthew, Mark, Luke*, edited by Frank E. Gaebelein, 1–599. The Expositor's Bible Commentary. Grand Rapids, MI: Zondervan, 1984.

Carson, D. A., and Douglas J. Moo. *An Introduction to the New Testament*. 2nd ed. Grand Rapids, MI: Zondervan, 2005.

Cave, William. *Antiquitates Apostolicae: Or, The History of the Lives, Acts and Martyrdoms of the Holy Apostles of Our Saviour, and the Two Evangelists SS. Mark and Luke*. London: R. Royston, 1676.

Bibliography

Chapman, John. "St. Irenaeus on the Dates of the Gospels." *Journal of Theological Studies* 6.24 (Jul 1905) 563–69.

Christian, Adam J. "Restoring the Unique Voices of the Synoptic Gospels: An Application of Oral Theory to the Synoptic Problem." ThM thesis, Western Seminary, Portland, OR, 2016.

———. *Synoptic Composition: The Use of Oral and Written Sources in the Synoptic Gospels.* Eugene, OR: Wipf & Stock, 2023.

Cicero, M. Tullius. *Cicero, with an English Translation.* Translated by William Armistead Falconer. Loeb Classical Library. Cambridge, MA: Harvard University Press, 1923.

———. *De Oratore.* Translated by H. Rackham and E. W. Sutton. Revised. Vols. 1–2. Loeb Classical Library. Cambridge, MA: Harvard University Press, 1948.

———. *The Letters of Cicero.* Translated by Evelyn Shuckburgh. Vol. 3. 4 vols. London: George Bell and Sons, 1908.

———. *The Orations of Marcus Tullius Cicero.* Edited and translated by C. D. Yonge. New York: Henry G. Bohn, 1856.

Cockburne, Robert. *An Historical Dissertation on the Books of the New Testament; or, An Enquiry into Their Authority and Particular Character.* Vol. 1. Edinburgh: 1755.

Cole, R. Alan. *Galatians: An Introduction and Commentary.* Tyndale New Testament Commentaries. Downers Grove, IL: InterVarsity, 1989.

Cribiore, Raffaella. *Gymnastics of the Mind: Greek Education in Hellenistic and Roman Egypt.* Princeton, NJ: Princeton University Press, 2001.

Crossan, John Dominic. *The Birth of Christianity: Discovering What Happened in the Years Immediately after the Execution of Jesus.* San Francisco: HarperCollins, 1998.

Cruttwell, Clement, ed. *The Holy Bible; Containing the Books of the Old and New Testaments.* Vol. 3. 3 vols. Bath: R. Cruttwell, 1785.

Curran, John L. "St. Irenaeus and the Dates of the Synoptics—Part 3." *Catholic Biblical Quarterly* 5.3 (Jul 1943) 301–10.

———. "St. Irenaeus and the Dates of the Synoptics—Part 4." *Catholic Biblical Quarterly* 5.4 (Oct 1943) 445–57.

Curran, John T., and John L. Curran. "St. Irenaeus and the Dates of the Synoptics—Part 1." *Catholic Biblical Quarterly* 5.1 (Jan 1943) 34–46.

Cyril. "The Catechetical Lectures." In *S. Cyril of Jerusalem, S. Gregory Nazianzen*, edited by Philip Schaff and Henry Wace, translated by Edwin H. Gifford, 7:144–57. Nicene and Post-Nicene Fathers 2. New York: Christian Literature, 1894.

Davids, Peter H. "James." In *New Bible Commentary: 21st Century Edition*, edited by G. J. Wenham et al., 1354–68. 4th ed. Downers Grove, IL: InterVarsity, 1994.

de Boer, Martinus C. *Galatians: A Commentary.* The New Testament Library. Louisville, KY: Westminster John Knox, 2011.

deSilva, David A. *An Introduction to the New Testament: Contexts, Methods and Ministry Formation.* Downers Grove, IL: InterVarsity, 2004.

Donne, Anthony Le. *The Historiographical Jesus: Memory, Typology, and the Son of David.* Waco, TX: Baylor University Press, 2009.

Doriani, Daniel M. *Matthew.* Vol. 1. 2 vols. Reformed Expository Commentary. Phillipsburg, NJ: P&R, 2008.

Du Pin, Louis Ellies. *A Compleat History of the Canon and Writers of the Books of the Old and New Testament: By Way of Dissertation with Useful Remarks on That Subject.* Vol. 1. 2 vols. London: H. Rhodes, 1699.

Bibliography

———. *A Compleat History of the Canon and Writers of the Books of the Old and New Testament: By Way of Dissertation with Useful Remarks on That Subject*. Vol. 2. 2 vols. London: H. Rhodes, 1699.

———. *A New History of Ecclesiastical Writers*. 2nd ed. Vol. 1. 2 vols. London: Abel Swall and Tim Childe, 1693.

Dunn, James D. G. *The Epistle to the Galatians*. Black's New Testament Commentary. London: Continuum, 1993.

———. *Jesus, Paul, and the Gospels*. Grand Rapids, MI: Eerdmans, 2011.

Eddy, Paul Rhodes, and Gregory A. Boyd. *The Jesus Legend: A Case for the Historical Reliability of the Synoptic Jesus Tradition*. Grand Rapids, MI: Baker Academic, 2007.

Edwards, James R. *The Gospel according to Mark*. Grand Rapids, MI: Eerdmans, 2002.

Edwards, John. *A Discourse concerning the Authority, Stile, and Perfection of the Books of the Old and New Testament*. Vol. 3. 3 vols. London: J. D., 1695.

Ehrman, Bart D. *The New Testament: A Historical Introduction to the Early Christian Writings*. 2nd ed. New York: Oxford University Press, 2000.

English, E. Schuyler. "Was St. Peter Ever in Rome?" *Bibliotheca Sacra* 124.496 (Oct 1967) 314–20.

Epictetus. *The Discourses of Epictetus, with the Encheridion and Fragments*. Translated by George Long. London: George Bell and Sons, 1890.

Epiphanius. *The Panarion of Epiphanius of Salamis: Books II and III, De Fide*. Translated by Frank Williams. 2nd ed. Nag Hammadi and Manichaean Studies 79. Leiden: Brill, 2012.

Erickson, Millard J. *Christian Theology*. 2nd ed. Grand Rapids, MI: Baker Academic, 1998.

Etheridge, Samuel, ed. *The Holy Bible, Containing the Old and New Testaments*. Charlestown, MA: Samuel Etheridge, 1803.

Eusebius. *Eusebius: Church History, Life of Constantine the Great, and Oration in Praise of Constantine*. In vol. 1 of *Nicene and Post-Nicene Fathers* series 2, edited by Philip Schaff and Henry Wace. Translated by Arthur Cushman McGiffert. New York: Christian Literature, 1890.

———. *The Ecclesiastical History*. Translated by Kirsopp Lake et al. Vol. 1. 2 vols. Loeb Classical Library. London: William Heinemann, 1932.

———. *The Ecclesiastical History*. Translated by Kirsopp Lake et al. Vol. 2. 2 vols. Loeb Classical Library. London: William Heinemann, 1932.

Evans, Craig A. *Ancient Texts for New Testament Studies*. Peabody, MA: Hendrickson, 2005.

———. "Two Source Hypothesis Response." In *The Synoptic Problem: Four Views*, edited by Stanley N. Porter and Bryan R. Dyer, 113–25. Grand Rapids, MI: Baker Academic, 2016.

Eve, Eric. *Behind the Gospels: Understanding the Oral Tradition*. Minneapolis: Fortress, 2014.

Ewing, Todd William. "An Inquiry into the Preference for Oral Tradition over Literary Solutions to the Synoptic Problem through an Analysis of the Verbal Agreements in Matthew and Mark." PhD diss., Southwest Baptist Theological Seminary, Fort Worth, TX, 1997.

Farmer, William R. "The Case for the Two-Gospel Hypothesis." In *Rethinking the Synoptic Problem*, edited by David Alan Black and David R. Beck, 97–135. Grand Rapids, MI: Baker Academic, 2001.

Bibliography

Farnell, F. David. "Are the Gospel Accounts Reliable?" In *The Harvest Handbook of Apologetics*, edited by Joseph M. Holden, 129–33. Eugene, OR: Harvest, 2018.

———. "The Case for the Independence View of Gospel Origins." In *Three Views on the Origins of the Synoptic Gospels*, edited by Robert L. Thomas, 226–309. Grand Rapids, MI: Kregel, 2002.

———. *How Reliable Are the Gospels? The Synoptic Gospels in the Ancient Church: The Testimony to the Priority of Matthew's Gospel*. Cambridge, OH: Christian Publishing House, 2018.

———. "How Views of Inspiration Have Impacted Synoptic Problem Discussions." *The Master's Seminary Journal* 13.1 (Spring 2002) 33–64.

———. "The Synoptic Gospels in the Ancient Church: The Testimony to the Priority of Matthew's Gospel." *The Master's Seminary Journal* 10.1 (Spring 1999) 53–86.

Fernandes, Phil. "Redating the Gospels." In *Vital Issues in the Inerrancy Debate*, edited by F. David Farnell et al., 466–88. Eugene, OR: Wipf & Stock, 2015.

Fernandes, Phil, and Kyle Larson. *Hijacking the Historical Jesus: A Christian Response to Recent Attacks on the Historical Jesus*. Bremerton, WA: IBD, 2012.

Finley, M. I. "The Elderly in Classical Antiquity." *Greece & Rome* 28.2 (Oct 1981) 156–71.

Foster, Paul. "Paul and Matthew: Two Strands of the Early Jesus Movement with Little Sign of Connection." In *Paul and the Gospels: Christologies, Conflicts, and Convergences*, edited by Michael F. Bird and Joel Willitts, 86–114. London: Bloomsbury T. & T. Clark, 2011.

France, R. T. *The Gospel of Matthew*. New International Commentary on the New Testament. Grand Rapids, MI: Eerdmans, 2007.

———. "Matthew." In *New Bible Commentary: 21st Century Edition*, edited by G. J. Wenham et al., 904–45. 4th ed. Downers Grove, IL: InterVarsity, 1994.

———. "Reading the Gospels." In *New Bible Commentary: 21st Century Edition*, edited by G. J. Wenham et al., 896–903. 4th ed. Downers Grove, IL: InterVarsity, 1994.

Fung, Ronald Y. K. *The Epistle to the Galatians*. New International Commentary on the New Testament. Grand Rapids, MI: Eerdmans, 1988.

Gamble, Harry Y. "Amanuensis." In *Anchor Yale Bible Dictionary*, edited by David Noel Freedman, 1:172. New York: Doubleday, 1992.

Geisler, Norman. *Christian Apologetics*. 2nd ed. Grand Rapids, MI: Baker, 2013.

Gerhardsson, Birger. *Memory and Manuscript: Oral Tradition and Written Transmission in Rabbinic Judaism and Early Christianity and Tradition and Transmission in Early Christianity*. Biblical Resource Series. Grand Rapids, MI: Eerdmans, 1998.

Goodacre, Mark S. *The Case against Q: Studies in Markan Priority and the Synoptic Problem*. Harrisburg, PA: Trinity, 2002.

———. "The Farrer Hypothesis." In *The Synoptic Problem: Four Views*, edited by Stanley E. Porter and Bryan R. Dyer, 47–66. Grand Rapids, MI: Baker Academic, 2016.

Goodspeed, Edgar J. *Matthew, Apostle and Evangelist*. Philadelphia: John C. Winston, 1959.

Greswell, Edward. *Dissertations upon the Principles and Arrangement of an Harmony of the Gospels*. Vol. 1. 4 vols. 2nd ed. Oxford: Oxford University Press, 1837.

Gromacki, Robert G. *New Testament Survey*. Grand Rapids, MI: Baker Academic, 1974.

Groothuis, Douglas. *Christian Apologetics: A Comprehensive Case for Biblical Faith*. Downers Grove, IL: InterVarsity, 2011.

Grudem, Wayne A. *Systematic Theology*. Grand Rapids, MI: Zondervan, 1994.

Bibliography

Gruen, Erich S. "Hellenistic Judaism." In *The Construct of Identity in Hellenistic Judaism*, edited by Erich S. Gruen, 21–76. Essays on Early Jewish Literature and History. Berlin: De Gruyter, 2016.

Guthrie, Donald. *Pastoral Epistles: An Introduction and Commentary*. Tyndale New Testament Commentaries. Downers Grove, IL: InterVarsity, 1990.

Hagner, Donald A. "Determining the Date of Matthew." In *Jesus, Matthew's Gospel and Early Christianity: Studies in Memory of Graham N. Stanton*, edited by Daniel M. Gurtner et al., 76–92. Library of New Testament Studies 435. London: T. & T. Clark, 2011.

Hansen, G. Walter. *The Letter to the Philippians*. Pillar New Testament Commentary. Grand Rapids, MI: Eerdmans, 2009.

Harris, William V. *Ancient Literacy*. Cambridge, MA: Harvard University Press, 1989.

Heiss, M. *The Four Gospels: Examined and Vindicated on Catholic Principles*. Milwaukee, WI: Hoffman, 1863.

Hendriksen, William. *Exposition of the Gospel according to Matthew*. New Testament Commentary. Grand Rapids, MI: Baker, 1973.

Hendriksen, William, and Simon J. Kistemaker. *Exposition of the Gospel according to Matthew*. New Testament Commentary. Grand Rapids, MI: Baker, 2002.

Herodian. *History of the Empire: Books V-VIII*. Translated by C. R. Whittaker. Loeb Classical Library. Cambridge, MA: Harvard University Press, 1970.

Hezser, Catherine. *Jewish Literacy in Roman Palestine*. Edited by Martin Hengel and Peter Schäfer. Texts and Studies in Ancient Judaism 81. Tübingen: Mohr Siebeck, 2001.

Hills, Margaret T., ed. *The English Bible in America: A Bibliography of Editions of the Bible and the New Testament Published in America 1777–1957*. New York: New York American Bible Society and New York Public Library, 1961.

Holmes, Michael W., ed. *The Greek New Testament: SBL Edition*. Bellingham, WA: Lexham, 2011.

The Holy Bible, Containing the Old and New Testaments. Boston, MA: Greenough and Stebbins, 1810.

Horne, Thomas Hartwell. *Introduction to the Critical Study and Knowledge of the Holy Scriptures*. Vol. 4. 4th ed. Philadelphia: E. Littell, 1825.

Howard, Jeremy Royal, ed. "Introduction." In *Holman Apologetics Commentary on the Bible: The Gospels and Acts*, 1–6. Nashville: B&H, 2013.

Hurtado, Larry W. *Destroyer of the Gods: Early Christian Distinctiveness in the Roman World*. Waco, TX: Baylor University Press, 2016.

Hyppolytus. *The Refutation of All Heresies*. In vol. 5 of *The Ante-Nicene Fathers*. Edited by Alexander Roberts et al. Translated by John H. MacMahon. Buffalo, NY: Christian Literature, 1886.

Irenaeus. "Irenæus against Heresies." In vol. 1 of *The Apostolic Fathers with Justin Martyr and Irenaeus*, edited by Alexander Roberts et al., 307–567. Translated by Alexander Roberts and James Donaldson. Buffalo, NY: Christian Literature, 1885.

———. *Sancti Irenæi*. Edited by W. Wigan Harvey. Vol. 2. Cambridge: Typis Academicis, 1857.

Ito, Akio. "The Written Torah and the Oral Gospel: Romans 10:5–13 in the Dynamic Tension between Orality and Literacy." *Novum Testamentum* 48.3 (Jul 2006) 234–60.

Iverson, Kelly R. "Orality and the Gospels: A Survey of Recent Research." *Currents in Biblical Research* 8.1 (Oct 2009) 71–106.

Bibliography

Jerome. "Prefaces to the Commentaries." In vol. 6 of *The Nicene and Post-Nicene Fathers* series 2, edited by Philip Schaff and Henry Wace, 483–502. Translated by W. H. Fremantle. New York: Christian Literature, 1893.

Jobes, Karen H. *1 Peter*. Baker Exegetical Commentary of the New Testament. Grand Rapids, MI: Baker Academic, 2013.

Jones, Jeremiah. *A New and Full Method of Settling the Canonical Authority of the New Testament*. Vol. 3. 3 vols. Oxford: Clarendon, 1798.

Josephus, Flavius. *Flavii Josephi Opera*. Edited by Benedictus Niese. Vol. 3. Berlin: Weidmann, 1892.

———. *The Jewish War: Books 1–7*. Translated by Henry St. J. Thackeray. Loeb Classical Library. Cambridge, MA: Harvard University Press, 1927.

———. *The Life against Apion*. Translated by Henry St. J. Thackeray. Loeb Classical Library. Cambridge, MA: Harvard University Press, 1966.

———. *The Works of Josephus: Complete and Unabridged*. Translated by William Whiston. Peabody, MA: Hendrickson, 1987.

Keating, Karl. *What Catholics Really Believe: Setting the Record Straight: 52 Answers to Common Misconceptions about the Catholic Faith*. Ann Arbor, MI: Servant, 1992.

Keefer, Tracy. "Livy." In *Ancient Greek and Roman Writers*, 172–82. Concise Dictionary of World Literary Biography. Farmington Hills, MI: Gale, 1999.

Keener, Craig S. *Christobiography: Memory, History, and the Reliability of the Gospels*. Grand Rapids, MI: Eerdmans, 2019.

———. *A Commentary on the Gospel of Matthew*. Grand Rapids, MI: Eerdmans, 1999.

———. *Galatians: A Commentary*. Grand Rapids, MI: Baker Academic, 2019.

———. *The IVP Bible Background Commentary*. Downers Grove, IL: InterVarsity, 2014.

Kelber, Werner H. "Rethinking the Oral-Scribal Transmission/Performance of the Jesus Tradition." In *Jesus Research: New Methodologies and Perceptions—The Second Princeton-Prague Symposium on Jesus Research*, edited by James H. Charlesworth et al., 500–530. Grand Rapids, MI: Eerdmans, 2014.

Kessler, David, and Peter Temin. "The Organization of the Grain Trade in the Early Roman Empire." *Economic History Review* 60.2 (May 2007) 313–32.

Kimble, Jeremy M., and Ched Spellman. *Invitation to Biblical Theology: Exploring the Shape, Storyline, and Themes of Scripture*. Grand Rapids, MI: Kregel Academic, 2020.

Kirk, Alan. "Memory." In *Jesus in Memory: Tradition in Oral and Scribal Perspectives*, edited by Werner H. Kelber and Samuel Byrskog, 155–72. Waco, TX: Baylor University Press, 2009.

Kittel, Gerhard, and Gerhard Friedrich, eds. *Theological Dictionary of the New Testament: Abridged in One Volume*. Translated by Geoffrey W. Bromiley. Grand Rapids, MI: Eerdmans, 1976.

Kloppenborg, John S., et al. *The Critical Edition of Q: Synopsis including the Gospels of Matthew and Luke, Mark and Thomas*. Minneapolis: Fortress, 2000.

Knight, George W. *The Pastoral Epistles: A Commentary on the Greek Text*. New International Greek Testament Commentary. Grand Rapids, MI: Eerdmans, 1992.

Köstenberger, Andreas J. *Encountering John: The Gospel in Historical, Literary, and Theological Perspective*. Edited by Walter Elwell. 2nd ed. Grand Rapids, MI: Baker Academic, 2013.

Köstenberger, Andreas J., and Michael J Kruger. *The Heresy of Orthodoxy: How Contemporary Culture's Fascination with Diversity Has Reshaped Our Understanding of Early Christianity*. Wheaton, IL: Crossway, 2010.

Bibliography

Köstenberger, Andreas J., and Richard D. Patterson. *Invitation to Biblical Interpretation: Exploring the Hermeneutical Triad of History, Literature, and Theology*. Grand Rapids, MI: Kregel, 2011.

Kruger, Michael J. *The Question of Canon: Challenging the Status Quo in the New Testament Debate*. Downers Grove, IL: InterVarsity, 2013.

Kruse, Colin G. *Paul's Letter to the Romans*. Edited by D. A. Carson. Pillar New Testament Commentary. Grand Rapids, MI: Eerdmans, 2012.

Laertius, Diogenes. *Lives of Eminent Philosophers*. Translated by R. D. Hicks. Vol 2. Loeb Classical Library. Cambridge, MA: Harvard University Press, 2005.

Lanier, Gregory R. "The Four-Fold Gospel Collection." In *Canon Formation: Tracing the Role of Sub-Collections in the Biblical Canon*, edited by W. Edward Glenny and Darian R. Lockett, 229–50. London: T. & T. Clark, 2023.

Lardner, Nathaniel. "A History of the Apostles and Evangelists, Writers of the New Testament." In *A Collection of Theological Tracts, in Six Volumes*, by Richard Watson, 1–533. 2nd ed. London: 1791.

Liddell, Henry George, et al. *A Greek-English Lexicon: With a Revised Supplement*. 9th ed. Oxford: Clarendon, 1996.

Lincoln, Andrew T. "Matthew—A Story for Teachers?" In *The Bible in Three Dimensions: Essays in Celebration of Forty Years of Biblical Studies in the University of Sheffield*, edited by David J. A. Clines et al., 103–25. Journal for the Study of the Old Testament 87. Sheffield, UK: Sheffield Academic, 1990.

Livy. *Ab Urbe Condita*. Translated by Benjamin Oliver Foster. Vols. 5–7. Medford, MA: Harvard University Press, 1924.

———. *Ab Urbe Condita*. Translated by Evan T. Sage. Vols. 38–39. Medford, MA: Harvard University Press, 1936.

Longenecker, Richard N. *Galatians*. Word Biblical Commentary. Dallas, TX: Word, 1990.

Lowrie, Michèle. "Rome: City and Empire." *Classical World* 97.1 (Autumn 2003) 57–68.

Luther, Martin. *A Commentary on St. Paul's Epistle to the Galatians*. Translated by Theodore Conrad Graebner. 3rd ed. Grand Rapids, MI: Zondervan, 1940.

MacArthur, John. *1 Timothy*. MacArthur New Testament Commentary. Chicago: Moody Press, 1995.

———. *2 Timothy*. MacArthur New Testament Commentary. Chicago: Moody Press, 1995.

———. *The Inerrant Word: Biblical, Historical, Theological, and Pastoral Perspectives*. Wheaton, IL: Crossway, 2010.

MacArthur, John, and Richard Mayhue. *Biblical Doctrine: A Systematic Summary of Bible Truth*. Wheaton, IL: Crossway, 2017.

Martin, Ralph P. *Philippians: An Introduction and Commentary*. Tyndale New Testament Commentaries. Downers Grove, IL: InterVarsity, 1987.

May, James M. "Cicero." In *Ancient Greek and Roman Writers*, 68–81. Concise Dictionary of World Literary Biography. Farmington Hills, MI: Gale, 1999.

McDowell, Sean. *Evidence That Demands a Verdict*. Revised. Vol. 1. San Bernardino, CA: Here's Life, 1979.

McIver, Robert K. "Collective Memory and the Reliability of the Gospel Traditions." In *Jesus, Skepticism, and the Problem of History*, edited by Darrell L. Bock and J. Ed Komoszewski, 125–44. Grand Rapids, MI: Zondervan, 2019.

———. *Memory, Jesus, and the Synoptic Gospels*. Atlanta: Society of Biblical Literature, 2011.

Bibliography

Michaelis, John David. *Introductory Lectures to the Sacred Books of the New Testament.* London: J. and R. Tonson, 1761.

Miller, Charles D. T. "The 'Write' Stuff: The Plausible Capability of Jesus' Followers to Author the Gospels." *Eleutheria* 6.2 (Fall 2022) 83–93.

Montefusco, Lucia Calboli. "Quintilian and the Function of the Oratorical Exercitatio." *Latomus* 55.3 (Summer 1996) 615–25.

Moo, Douglas J. "'Gospel Origins': A Reply to J. W. Wenham." *Trinity Journal* 2.1 (Spring 1981) 24–36.

———. *The Epistle to the Romans.* New International Commentary on the New Testament. Grand Rapids, MI: Eerdmans, 1996.

Moreschini, Claudio, and Enrico Norelli. *Early Christian Greek and Latin Literature: A Literary History.* Peabody, MA: Hendrickson, 2005.

Morris, Leon. *The Gospel according to Matthew.* Pillar New Testament Commentary. Grand Rapids, MI: Eerdmans, 1992.

Moulton, J. H., and G. Milligan. *Vocabulary of the Greek Testament.* London: Hodder and Stoughton, 1930.

Mounce, William D. *Pastoral Epistles.* Word Biblical Commentary. Nashville: Thomas Nelson, 2000.

Mournet, Terence C. "The Jesus Tradition as Oral Tradition." In *Jesus in Memory: Tradition in Oral and Scribal Perspectives*, edited by Werner H. Kelber and Samuel Byrskog, 39–61. Waco, TX: Baylor University Press, 2009.

Murphy, Todd J. "Tradent." In *Pocket Dictionary for the Study of Biblical Hebrew*, 170. Downers Grove, IL: InterVarsity, 2003.

Newcome, William, trans. *The New Testament, in an Improved Version.* London: The London Society, 1808.

Niemelä, John H. "The Case for the Two-Gospel View of Gospel Origins." In *Three Views on the Origins of the Synoptic Gospels*, edited by Robert L. Thomas, 126–97. Grand Rapids, MI: Kregel, 2002.

Nolland, John. *The Gospel of Matthew: A Commentary on the Greek Text.* New International Greek Testament Commentary. Grand Rapids, MI: Eerdmans, 2005.

Nourse, James, ed. *The Holy Bible, Containing the Old and New Testaments.* New York: American and Foreign Bible Society, 1847.

Orchard, Bernard. *Matthew, Luke, and Mark.* Manchester, Engl.: Koinonia, 1976.

———. "Thessalonians and the Synoptic Gospels." *Biblica* 19.1 (Jan 1938) 19–42.

———. "Why Three Synoptic Gospels? A Statement of the Two-Gospel Hypothesis." *Irish Theological Quarterly* 46.4 (Dec 1979) 240–55.

Orchard, Bernard, and Harold Riley. *The Order of the Synoptics: Why Three Synoptic Gospels?* Macon, GA: Mercer University Press, 1987.

Osborne, Grant R. *Matthew.* Grand Rapids, MI: Zondervan, 2010.

Osborne, Grant R., and Matthew C. Williams. "The Case for the Markan Priority View of the Gospel Origins." In *Three Views on the Origins of the Synoptic Gospels*, edited by Robert L. Thomas, 19–96. Grand Rapids, MI: Kregel, 2002.

Ovid. *Fasti.* Edited by George Patrick Goold. Translated by James George Frazer. Revised. Vol. 5. Loeb Classical Library. Cambridge, MA: Harvard University Press, 1996.

Owen, Henry. *Observations on the Four Gospels: Tending Chiefly, to Ascertain the Times of Their Publication; and to Illustrate the Form and Manner of Their Composition.* London: T. Payne, 1764.

Bibliography

Parkin, Tim G. *Old Age in the Roman World: A Cultural and Social History*. Baltimore, MD: Johns Hopkins University Press, 2004.

Parsons, Mikeal C., and Martin Culy. *Acts: Baylor Handbook on the Greek New Testament*. Baylor Handbook on the Greek New Testament. Waco, TX: Baylor University Press, 2003.

Peabody, David Barrett. "The Two Gospel Hypothesis." In *The Synoptic Problem: Four Views*, edited by Stanley E. Porter and Bryan R. Dyer, 67–88. Grand Rapids, MI: Baker Academic, 2016.

Pernot, Laurent. "The Rhetoric of Religion." *Rhetorica: A Journal of the History of Rhetoric* 24.3 (Summer 2006) 235–54.

Philo. *Philo: Volumes I-X*. Translated by F. H. Colson et al. Vol. 2. Loeb Classical Library. Cambridge, MA: Harvard University Press, 1929.

———. *Philo: Volumes I-X*. Translated by F. H. Colson et al. Vol. 3. Loeb Classical Library. Cambridge, MA: Harvard University Press, 1930.

———. *Philo: Volumes I-X*. Translated by F. H. Colson et al. Vol. 6. Loeb Classical Library. Cambridge, MA: Harvard University Press, 1935.

———. *The Works of Philo: New Updated Edition*. Translated by C. D. Yonge. Peabody, MA: Hendrickson, 1993.

Pliny the Elder. *The Natural History*. Edited by John Bostock. Translated by John Bostock and H. T. Riley. Vol. 2. London: Henry G. Bohn, 1855.

Plummer, Robert L. "Imitation of Paul and the Church's Missionary Role in 1 Corinthians." *Journal of the Evangelical Theological Society* 44.2 (Jun 2001) 219.

Plutarch. *Plutarch's Lives*. Translated by Bernadotte Perrin. Medford, MA: Harvard University Press, 1914.

———. *Plutarch's Morals*. Edited by William W. Goodwin. Boston: Little, Brown, 1878.

Porter, Stanley E., and Bryan R. Dyer, eds. *The Synoptic Problem: Four Views*. Grand Rapids, MI: Baker Academic, 2016.

Potter, David S. *Literary Texts and the Roman Historian*. New York: Routledge, 1999.

Powelson, Mark, and Ray Riegert, eds. *The Lost Gospel Q: The Original Sayings of Jesus*. Berkeley, CA: Ulysses, 1999.

Quintilian. *Quintilian, with an English Translation*. Edited by Harold Edgeworth Butler. Loeb Classical Library. Medford, MA: Harvard University Press, 1920.

Reinhartz, Adele. "On the Meaning of the Pauline Exhortation: 'Mimētai Mou Ginesthe—Become Imitators of Me.'" *Studies in Religion* 16.4 (Fall 1987) 393–403.

Richards, E. Randolph. *Paul and First-Century Letter Writing: Secretaries, Composition and Collection*. Downers Grove, IL: InterVarsity, 2004.

Richardson, James H. "The Complications of Quellenforschung: The Case of Livy and Fabius Pictor." In *A Companion to Livy*, edited by Bernard Mineo, 178–89. Blackwell Companions to the Ancient World 154. Chichester, UK: Wiley-Blackwell, 2015.

Rickman, G. E. "The Grain Trade under the Roman Empire." In *Memoirs of the American Academy in Rome*, 36:261–75. Seaborne Commerce of Ancient Rome: Studies in Archaeology and History. Ann Arbor: University of Michigan Press, 1980.

Robinson, John A. T. *Redating the New Testament*. Philadelphia: Westminster, 1976.

Rubin, David C. "Introduction." In *Remembering Our Past: Studies in Autobiographical Memory*, edited by David C. Rubin, 1–15. Cambridge: Cambridge University Press, 1996.

BIBLIOGRAPHY

Schellenberg, Ryan S. "Τὸ Ἐν Λόγῳ Ἰδιωτικὸν Τοῦ Ἀποστόλου [The Private Word of the Apostle]: Revisiting Patristic Testimony on Paul's Rhetorical Education." *Novum Testamentum* 54.4 (Oct 2012) 354–68.

Schreiner, Patrick. *Matthew, Disciple and Scribe: The First Gospel and Its Portrait of Jesus*. Grand Rapids, MI: Baker Academic, 2019.

Schreiner, Thomas R. *Galatians*. Grand Rapids, MI: Zondervan, 2010.

Scofield, C. I., and E. Schuyler, eds. *The New Scofield Reference Bible*. New York: Oxford University Press, 1967.

Shepherd, Massey H., Jr. "The Epistle of James and the Gospel of Matthew." *Journal of Biblical Literature* 75.1 (Mar 1956) 40–51.

Silva, Moisés. "Galatians." In *Commentary on the New Testament Use of the Old Testament*, 785–810. Grand Rapids, MI: Baker Academic, 2007.

Sproul, R. C. *Can I Trust the Bible?* Lake Mary, FL: Reformation Trust, 2009.

Spurr, John. "'A Special Kindness for Dead Bishops': The Church, History, and Testimony in Seventeenth-Century Protestantism." *Huntington Library Quarterly* 68.1-2 (Mar 2005) 313–34.

Stambaugh, John E. "Cities: Greco-Roman Cities." In *Anchor Yale Bible Dictionary*, edited by David Noel Freedman, 1:1031. New York: Doubleday, 1992.

Stambaugh, John E., and David L. Balch. *The New Testament in Its Social Environment*. Edited by Wayne A. Meeks. Philadelphia: Westminster, 1986.

Stein, Robert H. *Studying the Synoptic Gospels: Origin and Interpretation*. 2nd ed. Grand Rapids, MI: Baker Academic, 2001.

Stott, John R. W. *The Message of Galatians: Only One Way*. Downers Grove, IL: InterVarsity, 1986.

Strauss, Mark L. *Mark*. Zondervan Exegetical Commentary on the New Testament. Grand Rapids, MI: Zondervan, 2014.

Swinson, L. Timothy. *What Is Scripture? Paul's Use of Graphe in the Letters to Timothy*. Eugene, OR: Wipf & Stock, 2014.

Tacitus. *Tacitus: Dialogus, Agricola, Germania*. Edited by T. E. Page and H. D. Rouse. Translated by Maurice Hutton and William Peterson. Loeb Classical Library. New York: Macmillan, 1914.

Thomas, Robert L., ed. *Three Views on the Origins of the Synoptic Gospels*. Grand Rapids, MI: Kregel, 2002.

Thomas, Robert L., and F. David Farnell. "Preface." In *The Jesus Crisis: The Inroads of Historical Criticism into Evangelical Scholarship*, 11. Grand Rapids, MI: Kregel, 1998.

Thompson, Michael B. "The Holy Internet: Communication between Churches in the First Christian Generation." In *The Gospel for All Christians: Rethinking the Gospel Audiences*, edited by Richard Bauckham, 49–70. Grand Rapids, MI: Eerdmans, 1998.

Tomline, George. *An Introduction to the Study of the Bible: Elements of Christian Theology*. Vol. 1. 14th ed. London: T. Cadell, 1822.

Torrey, Charles Cutler. *The Four Gospels*. 2nd ed. New York: Harper, 1947.

Towner, Philip H. *The Letters to Timothy and Titus*. New International Commentary on the New Testament. Grand Rapids, MI: Eerdmans, 2006.

Townson, Thomas. *Discourses on the Four Gospels, Chiefly with Regard to the Peculiar Design of Each, and the Order and Places in Which They Were Written*. 1st ed. Oxford: Clarendon, 1778.

———. *The Works of the Reverend Thomas Townson*. Vol. 1. London: John Nichols and Son, 1810.

Bibliography

"Translator's Preface." In *A Compleat History of the Canon and Writers of the Books of the Old and New Testament: By Way of Dissertation with Useful Remarks on That Subject*, 1:i-vi. London: H. Rhodes, 1699.

Turner, Ian. "Going beyond What Is Written or Learning to Read? Discovering OT/NT Broad Reference." *Journal of the Evangelical Theological Society* 61.3 (Sep 2018) 577–94.

Ulery, Robert W., Jr. "De Senectute Studiorum: On Old Age And Antiquity." *Classical Journal* 106.2 (Winter 2011) 229–36.

———. "Sallust." In *Ancient Greek and Roman Writers*, 300–309. Concise Dictionary of World Literary Biography. Farmington Hills, MI: Gale, 1999.

Upham, Francis W. *Thoughts on the Holy Gospels: How They Came to Be in Manner and Form as They Are*. New York: Phillips & Hunt, 1881.

Vansina, Jan. *Oral Tradition as History*. Madison: University of Wisconsin Press, 1985.

Verbrugge, Verlyn D. "Γραφή." In *New International Dictionary of New Testament Theology, Abridged Edition*, 113–16. Grand Rapids, MI: Zondervan, 2000.

Wallace, Daniel B. *Greek Grammar beyond the Basics: An Exegetical Syntax of the New Testament*. Grand Rapids, MI: Zondervan, 1996.

Wallace, J. Warner. *Cold-Case Christianity: A Homicide Detective Investigates the Claims of the Gospels*. Colorado Springs: David C. Cook, 2013.

Wall, William. *Critical Notes, Especially on the Various Readings of the New Testament Books*. London: William Innys, 1730.

Ward, Richard. *Theological Questions, Dogmatical Observations, and Evangelical Essays, upon the Gospel of Jesus Christ according to St. Matthew*. London: 1646.

Watson, Francis. *Gospel Writing: A Canonical Perspective*. Grand Rapids, MI: Eerdmans, 2013.

Watson, Richard. *An Exposition of the Gospels of St. Matthew and St. Mark and of Some Other Detached Parts of Holy Scripture*. New York: G. Lane and P. P. Sandford, 1844.

Waymeyer, Matt. "Words of God and Words of Man: Inerrancy and Dual Authorship." In *The Inerrant Word: Biblical, Historical, Theological, and Pastoral Perspectives*, edited by John MacArthur, 288–303. Wheaton, IL: Crossway, 2010.

Wendt, Heidi. "Galatians 3:1 as an Allusion to Textual Prophecy." *Journal of Biblical Literature* 135.2 (Summer 2016) 369–89.

Wenham, David. *Paul: Follower of Jesus or Founder of Christianity?* Grand Rapids, MI: Eerdmans, 1995.

Wenham, John. *Redating Matthew, Mark and Luke: A Fresh Assault on the Synoptic Problem*. Sevenoaks, Kent: Hodder and Stoughton, 1991.

Wessel, Walter W. "Mark." In *Matthew, Mark, Luke*, edited by Frank E. Gaebelein, 601–793. Expositor's Bible Commentary. Grand Rapids, MI: Zondervan, 1984.

Wilkins, Michael. "Apologetics Commentary on the Gospel of Matthew." In *Holman Apologetics Commentary on the Bible: The Gospels and Acts*, edited by Jeremy Royal Howard, 7–198. Nashville: B&H, 2013.

Williams, Peter J. *Can We Trust the Gospels?* Wheaton, IL: Crossway, 2018.

Willitts, Joel. "Paul and Matthew: A Descriptive Approach from a Post-New Perspective Interpretive Framework." In *Paul and the Gospels: Christologies, Conflicts, and Convergences*, edited by Michael F. Bird and Joel Willitts, 62–85. London: T. & T. Clark, 2011.

Winsbury, Rex. *The Roman Book*. London: Bloomsbury, 2011.

Ancient Documents Index

OLD TESTAMENT
Genesis
1	xii

Exodus
34:27	110

Leviticus
10:11	106

Deuteronomy
17:18–20	106
17:18–19	52
25:4	16
30	106
30:10	106
30:14	106
31:9–13	106

2 Samuel
8:6	28
8:17	143

1 Kings
4:3	143
11:41	143
13:32	28
14:19	143
14:29	143

2 Kings
12:10	143
12:19	143
15:31	143
18:18	143
20:14	29
22	143
22:9	143

1 Chronicles
9:1	143
27:32	143

2 Chronicles
9:29	143
24:11	143

Isaiah
40–66	132
40	131–132
40:1 (LXX)	132
40:2–5	132
40:3–5	132
40:6–8 (LXX)	131
40:10	132
40:12–26	132

Jeremiah

23:5-6	143
35:10 (LXX)	59
36:2	110
50:9 (LXX)	59

Ezekiel

34	141

Malachi

4:1	144

APOCRYPHA

1 Maccabees

8:20	57
10:22-35	56
10:36	57
13:40	57

2 Maccabees

5:5	33

3 Maccabees

2:29	57
4:14	57

NEW TESTAMENT

Matthew

1:1	45
1:3	44
1:5	44
1:18	46
1:21	44
1:22-23	45
2:1	70
2:5-6	45
2:15	45
2:17-18	45
3:1-2	45
3:5	46
3:11	143
3:12	144
3:16	46
3:17	45, 144
4:13	140, 144
4:18-22	139-40
4:23-24	144
4:23	140
4:24	45, 144
5-7	49, 140
5	136
5:1	140
5:4	136
5:6	136
5:17-18	46
5:17	142
5:29	11
5:48	45
6:1-6	46
7:12	46
7:29	144
8	144
8:1—9:8	144
8:13	45
8:16	45
8:27	45
8:29	45
9	151
9:1-8	144
9:2	45
9:3	144
9:9	133, 139-40, 144
9:11	133
9:13	133
9:14-15	141
9:16-17	141-42
9:17	145
9:22	45
9:28-29	45
10:1-4	140
10:10	130
10:20	46
11:16-24	46
11:26	45
13	49, 141
13:52	141-43
14:33	45
15:2-9	76

15:7	46	18:31	31
17:5	45	19:2	11
18	49	24:48	147
18:27	44		
20	133, 151		

John

20:13–15	44		
20:25	134	1:27–40	139
20:26–27	134	1:29	144
20:28	45	1:41–42	139
21:14	45	2:11	139
21:38	52	2:17	16, 139
21:42	46	2:22	16
22:29	46	3:22	139
22:40	46	4:27	139
23	136, 140	5:39	116
23:8–9	47	10:16	131
23:13–29	46	12:16	16
23:23	46	13:19	16
23:34	11, 141–42	14:26	15, 76, 109, 147–48
24	136	15:27	147–48
24:27	136	16:4	16
25:32	47	16:13	148
26:28	45	17:17	16, 146
26:63–64	45	19:35–36	116
27:54	45	19:35	91
28:16–20	78	20:9	16
28:19	46–47	20:30–31	84
		20:30	147
		21:24–25	116

Mark

21:24	91
2:1	139
2:13–14	139

Acts

6:4	29
1–17	135

Luke

		1–12	39
		1:8	91, 147
1:2–4	147	1:19	32
1:2	91	1:26	36
1:5	70	2:42	148
2:1	57	2:47	11, 148
2:34	29	5:32	147
4:16–21	7	6:7	7, 11, 135
4:17	123	7:38	116
5:36	141	7:60	134
8:15	52	8	37
10:1	92	8:1–4	110
10:7	16, 130	8:1	7, 11
16:37–38	28	8:27–29	88

Acts (continued)

9:2	7
9:31	11
10–11	19, 22
10	30, 47
10:1	88
10:24	88
10:39	147
11	30, 36
11:19–20	110
12	39
12:12–13	11
12:17	37
12:24	135
13–14	41
13	49
13:7	88
13:15	105
13:22	116
13:49	135
15:6	41
15:21	7, 105
15:23	7
16:1	89
17:1–3	134
17:2	43, 61, 72, 105
17:10–11	134
17:11–12	88
17:11	43, 61, 72, 105
17:18	88
18	49
18:24–26	135
18:25	135
18:28	135
19:8–19	135
19:9–10	88
19:20	135
22:1	32
23:25	7
24:1	105
26:14	32

Romans

1:2	105, 135
1:9–15	106
2:16	131
3:2	68, 116
3:20	46
3:21	116
3:28	45
4:3	135
7:7	46
9:17	135
10	106
10:4–6	106
10:5–11	106
10:6–21	106
10:8–9	106
10:11	135
10:14–17	105
11:2	135
12–14	136
12	136
12:1	136
12:4	136
12:14–20	136
12:15	136
12:20	136
15:3–4	135
15:4	46, 51, 56, 58, 105
15:15–16	106
16:3–16	27
16:16	52
16:25	131

1 Corinthians

4:14–17	50–51
7:30	51
10:11	51
10:33	51
11:1–2	51
11:2	52–53, 84
11:23	84
15:1–4	105
16:20	52

2 Corinthians

4:13	105
13:12	52

Galatians

1:1–2	41
1:3–5	44
1:6	46
1:7	60
1:10	46, 51
1:11–16	41
1:11–13	48
1:11–12	47
1:11	48
1:13—2:14	51
1:13	48
1:15–16	50
2:2	60
2:4	46
2:15—4:11	51
2:15—3:14	49
2:16	45, 50
2:18	60
2:20	60
2:21	60
3:1–3	55
3:1–2	41
3:1	40, 46, 50, 55–61, 150
3:2–5	46
3:6–29	60
3:6	50
3:8	46, 50, 135
3:10–13	50
3:14	46
3:16–17	50
3:19	46
3:21–22	135
3:24–25	46
4:12	50
4:14	50
4:21–31	49
4:22	50
4:27	50
4:30	50, 135
5:1–2	51
5:1	46
5:10	46
5:12	46
5:13	46
5:14	50
5:16–25	46
5:25–6:10	49

Ephesians

2:20	148
3:1–6	47
3:3	46, 56, 58
3:6	131
6:21	104

Philippians

1:5	52
1:12	52
1:27—2:4	52
3:1	52
3:17–18	52
3:17	52
4:9	53
4:15	52
4:21–22	52

Colossians

4:7	104
4:15	53
4:16	90, 129

1 Thessalonians

1:8	53
2:13	43
2:14–16	136
5:2	137
5:26	52
5:27	90, 129

2 Thessalonians

2:1–8	136
2:1–5	107
2:8	136
2:15	52–53, 107
3:6–14	53
3:6–7	53
3:8	53
3:14	129

1 Timothy

1	151
1:12	133
1:15	133
2	151
2:1–2	133
2:6	133
2:7	58
2:8–12	134
4:13	12, 74, 90, 105, 123, 129, 151
5:17	130
5:18	16, 130
6:14	53
6:20	53, 105

2 Timothy

1:14	105
2:2	53, 127
2:15	129
3:10	127
3:14–16	74
3:14	129
3:15–17	12, 129
3:16–17	151
3:16	16, 146
4:2	129–130, 151
4:13	34
4:16	134

Titus

1:2–3	131
1:9	129–130, 151
2:1	53

Philemon

1:1	89

Hebrews

1:1	146
3:6	52
7:17	116

1 Peter

1	131–32
1:1	132
1:2	132
1:3–5	132
1:5	132
1:6	132
1:17	132
1:24	131
1:25	132
2:11	132
5:1	91, 147

2 Peter

1:16	147
1:20–21	16, 146
1:20	130
3:15–16	16
3:16	129

1 John

1:1–3	147
1:1	91
4:14	147

3 John

1:12	116

Jude

4	46, 56, 58
5–19	58

Revelation

3:14	116

GRECO-ROMAN WRITINGS

Aeschines

False Embassy

60	46, 56

Ancient Documents Index

Aristophenes

Frogs

626	59

Aristotle

Economics

1352a.1	46, 56

Cicero

De Amicitia

1	101
3	101
96	100

De Officiis

2.3	101

De oratore

1.21	100
1.3	100
1.32–33	100
2.84	100
3.14	100
3.44	100

De senectute

13	100
21–23	95
22–23	122
35–36	95

Epistulae ad Atticum

1.16	100
2.20	100
12.1	96
13.44	101
14.20	100

Epistulae ad familiares

5.4	100
15.6	100

In Catalinum

3.5	101
3.6	101

Pro Archia

4.8	101, 122

Pro Flacco

16.39	101

Demosthenes

Against Evergus and Mnesibulus

47.42	46, 56

Diogenes Laertius

Lives of Eminent Philosophers

6.1.3	124
6.1.5	123

Epictetus

Diatribai

2.16	104

Herodian

History of the Empire

7.3.1	28

Horace

Carmina

11–12	27–28
54–56	28

Ancient Documents Index

Josephus

Against Apion
2.252	57
2.289	115

Jewish Antiquities
11.283	46, 56
12.144	115
12.32–33	57
14.137	28
15.330–341	29
20.266	113

Jewish War
1.2–3	122
1.14–15	110

The Life
359–66	113

Juvenal

Satires
10.232–236	99

Livy

Ab urbe condita
2.4.4–6	122
5.18.4–5	97
6.1.1–2	104
39.8.3–8	122
39.40.7	97

Ovid

Fasti
2.684	27

Philo

Allegorical Interpretation
3.142	115
3.4	115

On Giants
49	101

On Planting
137–138	101
173	115

On the Cherubim
65–68	97
65	98
69	97
84	98
116	98
118	98
124	101, 115

On the Decalogue
138–140	122

On the Life of Abraham
258	115

On the Life of Moses
2.188	101

On the Rewards and Punishments
1	101
79	115

Prelim. Studies
39–42	97

That Every Good Person Is Free
82	123

Ancient Documents Index

That God is Unchangeable

43	83

That the Worse Attacks the Better

63–66	102
65–68	102

Who is the Heir?

249	97

Plato

Phaedrus

274c–275c	100
275a	100, 114
275d–276d	100
276d	100, 114

Pliny the Elder

Naturalis historia

7.24	98
8.3	116
22.43	116
33.36	116

Plutarch

Adversus Colotem

1	104

Aemilius Paulus

38.4	56

Agesilaus

20.3	104

Antonius

20.2	104

Caesar

2.2	104

Camillus

39.3	46, 56

Cato the Younger

2.1	28

Cicero

24.2	104
27.3	46, 56
46.2	46, 56

Comparatio Demosthenis et Ciceronis

2.2	104

De communibus notitiis contra stoicos

7	98

De Garrulltate

5	104

Demosthenes

8.4	104
15.1–2	104

De Pythiae oraculis

27	99

Galba

14.4	104

Lysander

25.1	104

Mulierum virtutes

0   104

Pompeius

64.4   104
79.2   104

Quaestionum convivalum

3.3.1   98

Quomodo adolescens poetas audire debeat

1   104

Solon

11.1   116

Vitae decem oratorum

1   56
4   104

Quintilian

Institutio oratoria

1 Pr 7–8	73, 120
1.0.1	102
1.0.27	102
1.1.1	102
1.1.15–19	102
1.1.27–37	102
2.11.7	73, 120
3.3.1	102
3.5.2	103
4.0.25	103
4.1.1–3	102
5.7.1–2	122–123
5.7.1–3	102
5.7.25	102
5.7.32–34	123
6.3.42–44	103
6.5.9	103
7.2.24	103, 120
9.5.4	103
10.1.1–2	103
10.1.8–9	103
10.1.19	103
10.2.106	102
10.3.3	103
10.3.5–6	102
10.7.30–33	103
11.4.73	103
11.6.32	103

Sallust

Bellum catalinae

16   122

Bellum jugurthinum

1   96
9   96
11   96

Strabo

Geography

12.4.8   116
15.1.30   116

Tacitus

Dialoges de oratoribus

32   116
36   122

Historiae

1.41.3   113

EARLY CHRISTIAN WRITINGS

Eusebius

Historia ecclesiastica

2.1–12   36
2.1.11–12   37

2.13–14	66	**Hippolytus**	
2.13.1–3	37		
2.13.3	37	*Refutation of all Heresies*	
2.14	66	6.15	37
2.14.4–6	37		
2.15	66	**Irenaeus**	
2.15.1–2	23, 37		
2.15.2—2.16.1	23	*Adversus haereses*	
3.24.5–7	23, 36, 65–66	1.23	37
3.24.5–6	67	1.27.3	38
3.39.1	68	3.1.1	19, 20, 24–26, 29–30, 32–34, 65–67
3.39.4	119		
3.39.14–16	22	3.11.8	22
3.39.16	30, 32, 34, 67, 69	4.33.3	38
5.8.1–4	20, 22	5.33.4	30
5.8.1–2	31, 65		
5.8.2	25–26, 29, 30, 32, 69	**Jerome**	
5.8.3	32		
5.10.2–3	67	*Commentary on Matthew*	
6.14.5–7	23, 33, 35	Preface	65
6.25.3–6	65		
6.25.3–4	23, 36, 67	*Lives of Illustrious Men*	
		36	67
Epiphanius			
Panarion		**Justin**	
51.4.12–51.5.1	65	*First Apology*	
		26	37

www.ingramcontent.com/pod-product-compliance
Lightning Source LLC
Chambersburg PA
CBHW071449150426
43191CB00008B/1288